AIRBORNE

UNITED
STATES

BERMUDA

MIAMI

LEE BUCKLEY

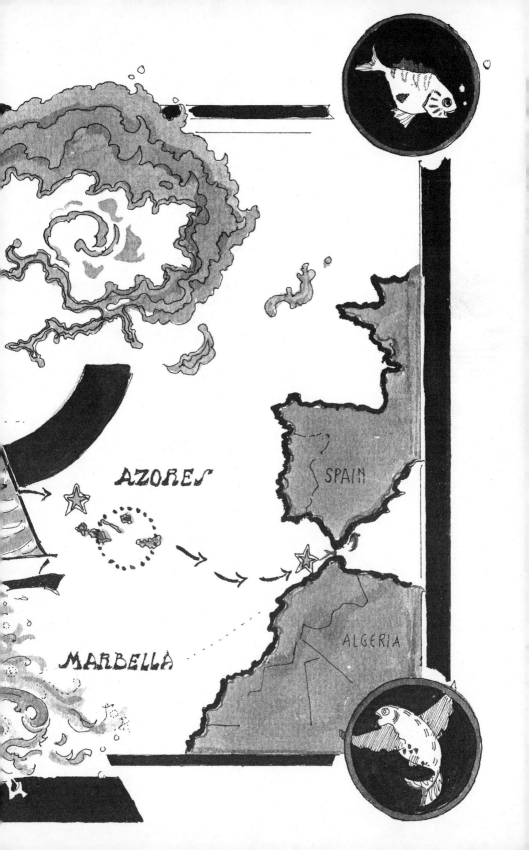

By the Same Author

GOD AND MAN AT YALE

McCARTHY AND HIS ENEMIES (with L. Brent Bozell)

UP FROM LIBERALISM

RUMBLES LEFT AND RIGHT

THE UNMAKING OF A MAYOR

THE JEWELER'S EYE

THE GOVERNOR LISTETH

CRUISING SPEED

INVEIGHING WE WILL GO

FOUR REFORMS

UNITED NATIONS JOURNAL: A Delegate's Odyssey

EXECUTION EVE

SAVING THE QUEEN

STAINED GLASS

A HYMNAL: The Controversial Arts

WHO'S ON FIRST

MARCO POLO, IF YOU CAN

ATLANTIC HIGH

OVERDRIVE

THE ADVENTURES OF HENRI TODD

Editor

THE COMMITTEE AND ITS CRITICS

ODYSSEY OF A FRIEND: Whittaker Chambers' Letters to
William F. Buckley, Jr.

W.F.B.: An Appreciation

DID YOU EVER SEE A DREAM WALKING?:
American Conservative Thought in the
Twentieth Century

Contributor

THE INTELLECTUAL

OCEAN RACING

WHAT IS CONSERVATISM?

SPECTRUM OF CATHOLIC ATTITUDES

ESSAYS ON HAYEK

AIRBORNE

A Sentimental Journey

WILLIAM F. BUCKLEY, JR.

LITTLE, BROWN AND COMPANY · BOSTON · TORONTO

A

A portion of this book appeared originally in *The New Yorker*.

BP

Published simultaneously in Canada
by Little, Brown & Company (Canada) Limited

PRINTED IN THE UNITED STATES OF AMERICA

For

Kathleen ("Bill") Taylor Finucane

ACKNOWLEDGMENTS

I am grateful to Daniel Merritt, Evan Galbraith, and Christopher Buckley, portions of whose journals I reproduce, and again to Christopher Buckley for the photographs. He took all of them except those in which he appears. The other exceptions are the photograph on page 73, which is from Morris Rosenfeld & Sons, Inc., and the technical photographs of Jan Lukas. I have integrated into the text parts of two articles originally published in *Rudder* and *Yachting*. Portions of this book were published in *The New Yorker*. My compliments to Barbara Scholey for her free-hand sketches. And my thanks to Mr. Ray Roberts of Macmillan for his encouragement and editorial suggestions; as also to Mrs. Lorraine Steurer for her editorial management; and, as ever, to Frances Bronson for all manner of editorial aid; and to Tony Savage for his patient typing of the drafts. Finally, my thanks once again to Joseph Isola for his fine proofreading. And to Sophie Wilkins for her unique help.

Stamford, Connecticut   W.F.B.
June 1, 1976

Cyrano's bowsprit, reflected in Danny's Elton John superreflecting red, white, and blue sunglasses.

PROLOGUE

It is one twenty-five in the morning. Moreover, it is one twenty-five *because I say it is one twenty-five.* I *could* have announced, after taking my noon sight, that we would all advance our watches by one hour; and so would it be, like an act of Congress establishing daylight saving time. Or—that we would put back our watches by one hour. I'd have said something slightly esoteric about the advantage just here, a few hundred miles from the Azores, of slipping back from daylight time. Naked Power. To be sure, in less than three days I had to produce the Azores. Bermuda had materialized just about when I said it would. And every day save one of the eight days since slipping out of Bermuda into a rough northwesterly, there had been sun. The fine-tuning in navigation comes when you are *very* near to land, which is not yet. Then you need more frequent sights, including star sights, and electronic help. We have no electronic help, except an anaemic old radio direction finder. Oh, sure, we have the equipment. But the two-year-old radar isn't working. The one-week-old loran isn't working. I am not in the least concerned.

Something else concerns me. I spoke sharply to my son when he and Danny relieved my watch. It is pitchy tonight, we are close-hauled, and the rule is that in such circumstances you reach for your lifebelt immediately on coming on deck. His wasn't on. I told him to fetch it, and he replied in his relax-dad-old-shoe-all-in-due-course tone of voice.

I let him have it. In the presence of Danny. I think back, try to remember. He is twenty-two. Have I spoken to him sharply three times in his life, or was it only twice? My father raised his voice with me twice (his hand, never), and he might as well have loosed a bolt of lightning into my soul. Had I done that just now to Christopher? I wondered, anxious. I reach for my plastic glass of grapefruit juice and vodka, nestling securely in the chrome ring bracket adjacent to the wash basin, level with my head, which is propped up on two pillows. I sip, letting my hardback notebook lie on my stomach, and turn my head and look out through what I used to call a porthole, until learning that the little rectangular kind that do not open are called nose ports. I had six installed throughout the boat when I bought her seven years ago, to the dismay of the hovering naval architect who kept lecturing me about the integrity of the hull until, finally, I unleashed Reggie on him; Reggie, soft-spoken, imperturbable Reggie, who will let anyone get away with any asseveration in his presence, only provided (a) that no blot is left on his friends, and (b) that there is no inexactitude committed in respect of plastics, about which they taught him twenty-five years ago at MIT at the infancy of a science which he has made his own. Reggie prescribed a formula for a nose port you cannot drive an acetylene torch through—perhaps he used a more modest metaphor; and when on a run to Bermuda, after seven years' satisfaction, I bolted out of my cabin in the middle of the night and summoned him from his sleep, in the cockpit section above, to show him the jigger of water that had accumulated in the well between my nose and the nose port, wondering whether the whole plate might be insecure, ready to flap loose and out and sink the craft, he calmly applied a little putty—a 30-second round trip to the engine room—and the leak stopped. I complained while I was at it that the glass was getting a little milky, and asked had MIT come up with a solvent that would repristinate my nose port, so that I might gaze right through the waves to the moon and stars without any sense of looking through a veil? Reggie said that such a solvent exists and was on board: tooth paste. "Any tooth paste?" I struggled to regain my composure.

It worked, of course, and now I can see the moon's light skittering like those honor-guard dolphins that see you into port, along the extended waves, feisty, here and there responding to the fitful wind from the northeast. Our sails are strapped tight, but we can't make course. Danny and Christopher have put on a little power (that is the

rule: at night, when the speed under sail drops below seven knots),
and the boat has steadied down on a light heel and only about a third
of my nose port is under water at the moments of maximum heel,
once or twice per minute.

The reading light above my head is lit—it sits over a (narrow)
double bed, all mine on this trip. I keep my reading glasses in the well,
and my paperback; I'll read a bit before going to sleep, after finishing
with the notebook. This is my long-sleep—I am not on duty again until
eight. I stretch out in the fresh sheets Augustino the Argentinian
steward laid on this morning. If I raise my head more than four
inches, I come up against the porcelain-smooth white underside of
the deck. If I move my toes up six inches, I come up against a large
ledge that stretches right across the bunk, from the hull on my left
to the hanging locker: I have there more books on the sea and on
navigation than I'll read. It is hard to see, past the glare of my reading light, more than the outlines of the deep ledge that runs from the
hull across the top of the hanging locker to the bulkhead that, with
its sliding venetian door, gives me my privacy. But I know exactly
what is on it: the sweater and pants for instant action, the cap for
when it is very windy or stormy, the dark glasses, extra books, my
sextant, my HP-65 computer and its paraphernalia, my wallet, an
extra blanket. In the locker, a single blazer and grey-flannel city-
pants (for use in Bermuda and, perhaps, the Azores—Pat, with her
reliable ingenuity, will bring me an onshore wardrobe when we
meet in Marbella); a terry-cloth dressing gown, for after swimming
or showering; a half dozen Bermuda shorts and khaki pants; one
corduroy, in case it gets cold; and a laundry bag for dirty clothes.
Van Galbraith's city clothes are here too—the hanging locker in his
forward cabin was already full with Christopher's, Danny's, and
Reggie's gear when he boarded, and, good-natured as ever, he did
not plead seniority, though he got off a nice crack or two about how
Cyrano treats people who fly all the way from London. Under my
bunk are two deep drawers—for underwear, shorts, socks, and the
extensive medicine and toilet kit Pat has equipped me with—not, as
she has several times told me, that she ever expects to see me again.
("If he comes through this thing alive," she told a friend, "I'll kill
him.") Much of the contents of the kit, twenty days out from Miami,

are permanently strewn on the ledge, with its rounded corners, above the wash basin; protected, like everything else movable in the cabin, from slipping out or springing out, at the caprice of the seas, by a resolute wooden lip, an inch high, that fences them in. And in one of the drawers what, on reading the early pages of Christopher's journal, I ever after referred to as "WFB's eighteen blue Lacoste sports shirts." Reduced now in number to five, not because I have consumed thirteen since leaving Bermuda, but because I have given Christopher two during the last two days, Christopher electing the mortification of drawing on a supply he had originally disdained as self-indulgent, over against the alternative of wearing dirty shirts, even if soaked in (prickly-itchy) salt water.

I emptied the glass, closed my notebook, and stared out into the silent running seas. There is practically no noise, the motor barely audible at 1200 rpm, the sails doing most of the work, pushing sixty thousand pounds of schooner and nine of us—the two youngest on watch, the rest asleep—almost noiselessly through the water, five miles up from the ocean floor: higher than the highest mountain. I look at my little pocket compass in the well. The boys (they do not like to be referred to as such, and the designation is no longer used within their earshot—Reggie, Pat's sister Bill Finucane, Van, and I quietly signed the protocol) are holding nicely, just south of east; at least the wind is not heading us—which is to say forcing us away from our objective, which lies north of east. I decide to skip the reading; I keep thinking about Christopher. Perhaps I'll make an excuse. Slide open the door, step into the saloon, lit at this time of night only by the picture lights that diffuse the oil colors of those splendid sea scenes by Richard Grosvenor; climb up the companionway, into the dark, canvas-covered cockpit section—a huge part of Cyrano; out the side door, down the deck walk to the steering section, where the boys would be. Christopher sitting on top of the steering box, cross-legged, handling the wheel; Danny in one of the two deck chairs on either side, one leg perched against a locker or, if he is sitting to windward, up against the binnacle post in that posture of complete relaxation from which he can spring into action as nimbly as Nureyev. He has so arranged himself in every situation I have seen him in since Christopher brought him to the house at Stamford as a playmate as a very little boy. Danny would look perfectly relaxed in an iron lung during the countdown before lurching down a ski chute. He is a year older than Christopher, just out of college, just married. Danny is the enthusiast, the quintessential American boy with red-blond straw hair, the quick smile, the high cheek, and just the hint of the Yankee trader. Christopher is introspective, but there are trip wires everywhere, which bring on the most infectious laughter in the house. Their common weapon against their elders has for years been a gentle sarcasm. Just enough sandpaper in it to keep the nerves tingling, and their victims alert. I take a modest pride in the years of tutoring in the art I have spent on both of them (Christopher once told me I have the faculty for "sometimes driving me crazy-mad at you"). Danny no doubt feels the same way, but although he has worked for me for seven summers and lived at our (rented) house in Switzerland (while going to school) for as long as two months, he has never expressed this exasperation—he is too resilient. On the other hand, I don't remember ever having talked sharply to him. Not even the night he called me at two in the morning in New York. He was eighteen, and his high-pitched voice was shaky. Something terrible has happened, he said. I asked in a whisper, not wanting to wake Pat, Was anybody hurt?

No, he said.

Tell me, I said in normal tones—Pat was now awake, so there was no point in whispering; or in leaving the room to talk over another telephone.

He had been standing in for the skipper, who had the week off. After I and a dozen friends left the boat at midnight, after a dinner cruise up the Hudson, Danny consulted the cook and steward and asked whether they were willing to head back home to Stamford, a three-hour trip, rather than lay out at anchor off the 23rd Street pier and make the trip early in the morning. Sure, they said; so Danny took the wheel, fired up the engine, and started up the East River.

There is a critical fork in that river, up around 50th Street. Both the river channels corseting Welfare Island end you up at the same point, where the river turns east and slides under the Triboro Bridge. Danny took the right fork, not having read the chart closely. And halfway up the channel he suddenly realized that the stolid bridge toward which he was heading was clearly lower than Cyrano's foremast, let alone mainmast. The current was carrying him toward that critical mass at four knots. He jammed the gear into reverse—stripping it into immobility (it had been misbehaving). In desperation he swung the wheel to the left, hoping to effect a U-turn in time— only to discern a tug in the darkness a few dozen yards away, into which, pursuing his turn, he would crash. By then there was no time left over to maneuver. With a roar, the two masts, the radar, the fourteen shrouds, crashed over the deck, making driftwood of the taffrail and cockpit, the thousand-pound wooden masts falling fifty feet, missing Danny and the cook by inches. The tug threw out a line, and now they were secured to a wharf in the Bronx, and Danny had trudged to the pay phone, a very frightened little boy. I told him never mind, these things happen, try to get some sleep, I'd be around in the morning. He would receive punishment enough. Even now, six years later, some of his friends call him Captain Crunch.

They would be talking—Danny loves to talk, is interested in everything and delights in recalling jointly shared experiences, pleasant and harrowing. Christopher is alternately laconic and talkative, but Danny doesn't mind; he will do all the talking, if necessary. Christopher will probably be drinking a Coca-Cola, Danny the same, though he might have a beer. They will be wearing dungarees and sweaters—and lifebelts around the waist. (They would know that the purpose of my visit was not to spy on them.) Danny would be splashing a flashlight's beam every now and then on the Kenyon to check the speed, and then up at the telltale on the shroud to spot any change in the wind direction. The heading is highly visible from the steering post and from the deck chairs. It shines out in red from the compass on the binnacle mount. If you are seated to one side, looking crosswise at the compass, you quickly get used to adding, or subtracting, 90° in order to calculate the heading. Every hour or two, one of them will check the bilges, read the taffrail log we stream out, which is the equivalent of a milometer on an automobile—except that you must not rely too heavily on it, because it is insensitive to the vicissitudes of current and overly sensitive to the vicissitudes of floating seaweed and the like, which distort the registrations. Every two hours they will record their estimated progress in the logbook and make such other entries as they deem appropriate. At five in the morning they will wake the relief watch . . .

I decide, restlessly, that I must go up. I reach for the flashlight, wresting it from the bracket at the side of the door, and walk silently up the companionway, maintaining my balance easily after so many days at sea. Before walking aft and evaluating the necessity for diplomatic therapy, I think to check the logbook.

I had actually forgotten what I wrote in it after the episode with Christopher, only an hour and a half ago. I leaned over the navigating table, ran my flashlight over the open page. "0100 (I had written). DR plotted: Lat 37-55, Long 37-50. Shifty winds from front-line squall area. Took in Genoa and vanged main staysail and mainsail. Attempting course of 115 degrees with difficulty—averaged 125°, plotted same. Using 1200 rpm except when wind puffs up. Checked bilges. Relieved by Capt. Merritt and Lt. Buckley, whose lifebelts were, in due course, located."

I read on to the next line.

My heart leapt up with pleasure. I turned off the flashlight, peeked outside the canvas, and studied their silhouettes against the wind and stars, exactly as I had imagined, complete with Coca-Colas and animated gestures. I ducked noiselessly back, down the companionway, into my bunk, drawing the door silently shut, suppressing my impulse to wake Bill and Van and Reggie to share my delight with them.

Emerging from the cabin.

Everything was all right. The boys had evidently seen my entry. Their indignation was furious, but not internalized. They had made their own entry, using my pen for the purpose:

"*My ass, Buckley*—DTM." And from my son, "*Screw you*—CTB." Nowhere in the vast Atlantic that night was any skipper better pleased with the junior members of his crew, and just think of it, one of them my own flesh and blood.

AIRBORNE

"Peter," I said, late on a white summer afternoon about fifteen years ago to Peter Starr, who had sailed with me since he was thirteen when he began looking after my boat during the summers, "let's face it. Some day we'll have to sail across the Atlantic." We were walking gingerly about the mossy rocks that surround York Harbor, in Maine, getting some exercise after a long day's sail from Gloucester, before returning to *The Panic*, moored in the Hansel-and-Gretel harbor, for dinner. The first three days of our cruise we—my wife, Peter, and our friends—raced with the New York Yacht Club, then we struck out to cruise in Maine.

Peter agreed.

I first acknowledged my unalterable affection for Peter on meditating that in the five years I had known him, he had never said No to any request I made ("Please repaint the hull black by next weekend"), never betrayed by any inflection the implausibility of any proposal I made ("Can you get a week off from school and sail to Bermuda with us in October?"), never betrayed any lack of enthusiasm for any suggestion made anytime, anywhere. I would think nothing of calling him at his home in Stamford, Connecticut, a mile from my own, at eleven or twelve at night on a Friday, late in the season. "Peter, let's sail." "Sure!" "I'll pick you up in ten minutes"—Peter wasn't old enough for a driving license in those days— and in twenty minutes we would be powering out of Stamford Harbor; in another ten minutes the sails would be up. In an hour or so, depending on the wind, we would make out the little flashing red light signaling the entrance to the tortuous channel—rocks on either side —winding into the little harbor off what we called Treasure Island (actually, Eaton's Neck Point), because it was there that we took Christopher in midsummer when he was six, with his little friend Danny, and the pirate's map that Reggie, who could draft the inside of an HP-65 computer, had so painstakingly contrived the day before, marking where a chest of treasure was said to have been buried during the seventeenth century. I have a movie of Christopher, dressed in short pants and solemn mien, counting out the steps— stretching out his little legs to approximate the distance Long John Silver would have intended to suggest when writing, "Count 20 paces NNW,"—treasure chart in hand, with Reggie, head bent over the hand compass, pointing the way.

"I figure it ought to be about here," Reggie said finally, reflectively, and Christopher and Danny went down on their knees and began with bare hands to shovel out the sand—two inches, four inches, eight inches . . .

"Try a little deeper, Christopher. After all, if it's still here, it's been here three hundred years." And then the yelps of joy as they spotted wood and, after furious application, hauled out, reverently, a small old chest. The padlock was conveniently rusted, and Reggie pried it open for them. They were aghast. A crock of jewels. Pearl necklaces, gold brooches, huge amethyst rings, diamond bracelets: It had taken Pat an hour at Woolworth's the morning before to accumulate the stuff, and she complained of having had to spend well over ten dollars. Christopher and Danny, though they had exchanged vows of eternal fidelity, clearly did not trust each other to exclusive dominion, however temporary, over their precious burden. So, although it did not weigh five pounds, they walked off in tandem, in elated silence; four arms around the little chest.

What happened in the fall is a subject we didn't bring up lightly for a while, not until Pat's sense of humor caught up with her, which it always does. Christopher, through the balance of the summer, couldn't get over the fixation that there might be yet more treasure on "Treasure Island," and pestered Reggie on the point until, unguardedly, Reggie divulged that indeed he had heard that someone in New York—a great great great great great great great (Reggie furrowed his brows, as though counting carefully down the generations from the middle of the seventeenth century to 1959) grand-

Christopher and his mother set out for *Suzy Wong*, which will sail them to where the treasure is buried.

daughter of a famous pirate indeed survived, who had a chart of another buried treasure. When we couldn't put it off any longer, Reggie busied himself creating the new chart—ten times as ornamental as its predecessor—and Pat, fearing that another assortment from Woolworth might arouse suspicions, collected four or five superb Georgian silver pieces of various design that her mother had given her and that had just arrived in a wooden crate, the contents as yet unseen by Christopher. When Christopher discovered them on Treasure Island, Pat would "buy" them from him. Besides, the silver was safer for other reasons. In a characteristic access of generosity, two days after the original discovery at Treasure Island, Christopher asked his nurse for some wrapping paper and ribbon, and then mysteriously disappeared. When Pat and I went to bed, a bulky package lay under her pillow. It contained Christopher's half of the ancient treasure, with a six-year-old's love note. This, of course, required Pat during that long summer to wear, whenever Christopher was anywhere in sight—which was most of the time—a full suit of Woolworth's jewelry, which was bad enough when just Christopher was around, but positively arresting when there were a lot of other people

5

around who clearly wondered what on earth had happened to the taste in jewelry of the chic and stunning Mrs. Buckley. Exhibiting her son's pirate collection of Georgian silver she could contemplate doing with serenity.

On Friday, Peter, Reggie, and I sailed over and planted the box, leaving a telltale stick to guide us the next day, even as we would affect to be guided by the compass markings on the chart.

Unhappily, the following Saturday we got, not our happy little picnic sail across the Sound, but Hurricane Hilda. By the time Hilda had allowed the seas to settle down, three days had passed. Instantly we set out, and Christopher and Danny went through their paces, using the new chart. Two hours and six excavations later, Pat's sobering expression having graduated to fixed stares of stupefaction and loathing aimed alternately at Reggie and me when the boys were not looking, we gave up. Back on board, after the boys were asleep in the forward section, she demanded in no uncertain terms that we find her beautiful Georgian silver. "There there," we said, "of course we'll find it." Reggie and I conferred privately and wondered what we would have to do to lease a mine detector from the Corps of Engineers. We tried a half dozen times over the next months to find the buried casket. It is still there, somewhere.

"Of course, we must cross the Atlantic," Peter said, without looking up from the mossy stones he glided over. "Is there anything *else* we haven't done on *The Panic*?"

That was my first ocean boat. I loved her dearly and raced her three times to Bermuda, cruised her to Nova Scotia and up the St. John's River, and a dozen times throughout the Maine coast. One day in November of 1961 I called from Washington to the harbor master at the Stamford Yacht Club and asked him to check the mooring lines of *The Panic*, as a hurricane was predicted. Two days later he called the house and asked me to come down. The storm had subsided, but one of the boats had come loose and was piled on the jetty at the harbor entrance. "I think it's *The Panic*." He took me, in the club launch, as close as we could get—the winds were still at gale force. I looked at her grinding into the rocks with every onset of waves and estimated that her steel hull must be punctured in a

The Panic, racing to Bermuda, June 1958.

hundred different places. Only her single rugged mast—she was a cutter—was clearly visible in the high tide. At low tide, her broken body was fully, immodestly exposed; like lowering the bedsheet on the ravaged corpse.

There is a curious superstition at sea, as illegitimate as the apocryphal law that permits you to kill your cuckolder if you catch him with his pants down. It is that a boat loosed from its mooring is deemed to have been abandoned and is therefore public property. Even in that wind, in those waves, the vultures ventured out at night and stripped *The Panic*—taking even such useless objects as her companionway, which would not fit any other boat afloat.

That night Peter called, enthusiastic as always, from Georgetown University, where he was a sophomore, to tell me the new spinnaker for next year's Bermuda race was ready and he would pick it up at Annapolis at the sailmaker's and bring it up to Stamford, as he was coming home for the weekend in any case. I gave him the news. He had to put down the telephone. That reaction was not only the teenager's who had grown up with *The Panic*. I gave the same news to the critic Hugh Kenner. He reacted in a letter. "She had done much for her friends, in the summers before her side was stove in. She had taken them all around the Sound, and along the New England coast,

Peter Starr on *The Panic*, 1958.

and even to Bermuda (thrice), and shown them Wood's Hole, and the Great Fish that eats taffrail logs, and the Kraken, and the strange men of Onset with their long faces, and perfect Edgartown; and lapped them at night gently to rest; and given them the wind and sun and often more rain than they knew how to be comfortable in; and made for them a place of adventure and refreshment and peace; and taught them this, that beyond illusion it is possible to be for hours and days on end perfectly and inexpressibly happy."

It is because you remember this kind of thing about cruising that you go back to sailing in the ocean. *This* was what Hugh remembered about that trip! Mercifully his memories of that initial cruise were less distinct; or perhaps, on the occasion, they were merely . . . transcended. He and his first wife (Mary Jo, RIP) and I flew to Portland, Maine. Peter was waiting for us, having just unloaded a charter party. Though it was very late in the afternoon, Peter had been working since six in the morning, and Hugh was exhausted from a round of lectures and meetings with publishers, we decided exuberantly to set out across a one hundred-mile track of ocean to Provincetown, Massachusetts. Peter and Mary Jo took the watch from eight to midnight. It had begun to storm at eleven, and Mary Jo was blue with fear and *mal de mer*, while Peter was very nearly faint from having to cope, virtually alone, with the sail-shortening. But they stuck it out till twelve (an iron protocol aboard ship, except in case of emergency). He came forward, woke me, and I, grabbing every fixed object en route to keep my balance, went aft and nudged Hugh. He sat up in the bunk stark white, put on his glasses with great, silent dignity, looked at me as if I were a perfect stranger, rose, walked uncertainly forward to the head, clutched two handy pipes, leaned over, vomited a day's food into the toilet, groped his way somnambulistically back to his bunk, got in, pulled the covers over him, and passed out. Mary Jo, wrestling with the strange tiller, wasn't good for another ten minutes. Peter looked up at me—he looked as young as the day, four years earlier, when he had bicycled to my house to apply for a job he hoped to find more interesting than his paper route. "I'll stay awake with you, Mr. Buckley."

"Go to bed," I told him. "I'll call you if I need you." I put on foul-weather gear, relieved Mary Jo at the wheel, felt the boat surging at hull speed with a No. 3 jib and main, and wondered (this happens at sea as often as people who write about the sea tell you it does)—facing four hours alone, already soaked, beginning to feel the cold, the boat's erratic needs exacting every nerve of concentration, arm and back muscles taxed like a galley slave's, facing God knows what ahead, the human reserves aboard comprising one seasick poet, his incapacitated wife, and an exhausted sixteen-year-old—what madness finds me here, in these conditions, at this time. The hoariest line in the literature, which even so never ceases to amuse me, is: "Ocean racing is like standing under an ice cold shower, tearing up thousand-dollar bills."

There was a lot to think about during that long and hectic night, but Walt Disney was in his heaven, and by the time the sun rose, the storm had abated; and I even managed to hoist the spinnaker utterly alone—sad, in the radiant early sun, the wind steady off the port quarter, only that no one was witness to this feat of virtuosity. Finally I woke the ship's company and they were all, miraculously, quite cured and ravenously hungry. As we chatted, picking up now a land-speck on the horizon, the tower at the tip of Cape Cod Canal, validating a night of navigation by dead reckoning, spirits soared, and I mentioned to Hugh that one day Peter and I would cross the Atlantic. But even though, fifteen years later, the voyage was set, and even though the date of departure was fixed fifteen months ahead, when we set out from Miami, on May 30, 1975, Peter was not aboard. He was thirty-four now and had discovered the well-known American phenomenon called the Business Crisis; and three days before our departure, he called to blurt out in a voice that took me back to the phone call from Georgetown, news I had known for three weeks was coming. Not intuition. Peter was president and chief executive officer of a company of which I was board chairman, and I knew something about the crisis in which, as it happened, our common sailing experience figured tangentially. I wondered, when Peter called, whether I could imagine any crisis such as would cause me to cancel the B.O., as we had come to refer to it—the Big One. I refused to let my imagination travel across that stygian frontier.

10

Having undertaken, however irresolutely, to set out one unspecified day to sail across the Atlantic, I found myself focusing haphazardly on the trials of such a passage. These questions would accost me with special force during the longer sea voyages; when racing to Bermuda, for instance. When becalmed, I would think very hard about them. I thought about them while heading south from Bermuda to the Virgin Islands, as I did once on a crazy impulse. During four days of heaving, pursued by following winds and seas that roller-coastered us a thousand miles; during an overnight sail from Cuttyhunk back to Stamford, lost, drenched, blinded by fog, I wondered about crossing the ocean. The negative factors accumulated. For one thing, though I and my sailing friends are devotees of the sea, we are that in a qualified sense. We never fancied ourselves as "the everlasting children of the mysterious sea." Rather their "successors," accurately anticipated by Conrad as "the grown-up children of a discontented earth." We were "less naughty, but [also] less innocent; less profane, but perhaps also less believing." And indeed, if we have learned how to speak, we have "also learned how to whine."

Really, it came down to two basic questions. The first was, How much protracted physical discomfort can you put up with before discomfort overwhelms the memory of an ocean passage? Hugh Kenner and I sailed a half dozen times together on *The Panic*. But only once—on that first run—in circumstances distractingly, even preemptively, uncomfortable. Almost anything is made tolerable at sea, if it is guaranteed to end *that very day*—at, say, cocktail time, at a quiet anchorage. A young, tough, phlegmatic friend who raced twice across the Atlantic told me that on the second passage (Newport to

Sweden), beginning on the tenth day out he had been so cold, so bitterly, awfully, gnawingly cold, day in day out, night after endless night, that he solemnly pledged to himself—days before arriving finally in Scandinavia—never, *ever* again, to sail across the North Atlantic.

I engaged once in a polemic with a veteran seaman who teaches English to fortunate students of St. George's School. He took public issue with me over a complaint I had published against the creeping professionalization of the sport. In pointing out the mysterious inexactitude of specialized knowledge about a boat and its accessories, I gave as only one of many examples the demonstrated inadequacy of foul-weather gear advertised as competent to keep a man dry at sea. With great huff Mr. Hoyt (who, disappointedly, I subsequently discovered to be a most engaging and undogmatic man) replied, in a published article, that he had made eight transatlantic crossings, and that he had not once—not o-n-c-e—been either cold or wet.

Now you must understand the gravity of this kind of boast in the amateur community I write of. It is—simply—*unbelievable.* I wrote once about an erstwhile friend who, at age seventeen, resolved never again to make a typing mistake. Forty years later, he has yet to make one.

Why should he? he asked. If Horowitz can play at hurricane speed horribly intricate pieces of music, using ten fingers simultaneously without making a mistake, why should he—Revilo Oliver—a full professor in the classics, master of seventeen tongues—make a mistake, typing at his own speed, and using, at *whatever* speed he typed, what comes down to *only one finger at a time?*

Still they don't believe me about Revilo; even as, still, I don't really believe it about my friend at St. George's. But I must report that in his article he gave a step-by-step account of just how he handles the problem of dressing in a sailboat at sea for the cold and the wet. I have traveled in the Antarctic, and before doing so, submitted to a technician's lecture on how to keep warm, and walked away with a trunkload of clothes supplied by the United States Navy which, when I donned them, left me entirely comfortable in temperatures that brushed up against 50° below zero. But I must add that it could not have taken the Queen of England as long to dress for her Coronation as it took me to put on my costume in the mornings I was in the Antarctic; and it is a wonder that Mr. Hoyt had time left over to devote to watch duty, after preparing himself for it. But let us leave the point moot and agree to say modestly: You *can* keep warm on a boat, but the preparations necessary for doing so vitiate, substantially, the pleasure of the day's sail.

On the matter of keeping dry, I remain, perforce, a skeptic. My brother-in-law Firpo, who believes in attacking problems head on, designed his own foul-weather gear for our first race to Bermuda. It was the grandest and most elaborate piece of gear I ever saw, not less imposing for its responsibility to keep dry 250 pounds of human flesh. It had rubber gloves with shock-cord belts, all-directional zippers, seamless balaclavas; everything except perhaps a catheter tube.

The first hard wave that tore into *The Panic*'s cockpit left Firpo totally drenched, and, on top of that, facing twenty minutes of disassembly before he could dry his bare skin. Van, who had observed with awe the design and engineering of the ultimate foul-weather suit, comforted Firpo with a practical suggestion for the next trip. "You must go to a garage, strip, and have yourself vulcanized." It was in any case a fact that my ocean-racing friend remembered about his North Atlantic passage *only* the cold. Like C. S. Lewis recalling, about his first year at boarding school, primarily that he was painfully, achingly *tired*; *all* day, *every* day, *through* the semester.

Now it is much closer to Europe from America via the North Atlantic and, accordingly, I hadn't ever thought of going by any other route. But that is the compulsion of *genus Americanus*: to focus automatically, and unthinkingly, on the shortest distance between two points. It was humiliating to remind myself that electing sail as a means of transportation is itself the major commitment, to which the corollaries should naturally suggest themselves. If speed is the only objective, then *sailing* across the Atlantic is, well, perverse. This much one can accept without difficulty. But even having grandly rejected the shortest route, consistent adjustments are difficult—particularly if, on boarding a sailboat, you are incapable of leaving ashore a nervous system that pushes you on and on, impatient, disdainful, insensible of delays. "Pup has it figured out," Christopher

13

—out of a lifetime's knowledge of his father's inclination to hecticity would write, amused and annoyed, in his journal—"how we can see *all* the Azores in five hours." It is one thing to decide *not* to take the Northern passage, even if it means adding fifteen hundred miles to the trip. It is something else to calm down your metabolism to accept an *unhurried* trip. It is something else to tarry four days—instead of, say, two—in Bermuda; or two weeks, rather than three days, in the Azores. Or to sail on in a light wind for four hours rather than turn on your engines and help out the wind.

Racing a boat is, in this unique sense, as satisfying as army life. The rules are explicit: Under no circumstances do you turn on your engine, except to save a drowning man, preferably a member of the Race Committee. So that when a calm attacks you, as a notable one did in the 1960 Bermuda Race, when the sails flopped, the sun excreted its heat upon us, and we moved not one hundred yards in thirty-six agonizing hours, it was all strangely tolerable *only* because there was no alternative—save abandoning a race the preparations for which had taken hundreds of hours, dissipated thousands of dollars, and required major adjustments in the schedules of eight busy men. Where there are no alternatives, the wise man has said, there are no problems. There was, of course, a major alternative in our crossing. It was exercised when we elected to take the long southerly route. The next question was whether to race across the Atlantic, or cruise across. Here again thought must be given to pleasure-pain factors.

There are other forms of discomfort aboard a boat than physical cold. When William Snaith (whose enthralling account of the transatlantic race from Bermuda to Sweden in 1960 is given in *On the Wind's Way*) gave the exhortation to his crew just before starting out, he pledged that they would "race the boat to the point of discomfort." No one who has written about modern racing has recited more vividly what these discomforts can add up to, and although his journal shows the fierce pride the author and his crew took in winning the race, sometimes, on reading him, one has the same sensation one had on reading Amundsen's account—also triumphant—of his passage to the South Pole. I wrote a brief account, in 1958, of my second race to Bermuda, recalling my first, in 1956: Yes, "My first trip and

14

—the thought crossed my mind as I bit at a salt-soaked sandwich while tugging at the helm, heeled over 35°; or as I grappled in the claustrophobic reaches of the forepeak with yet another sail to drag up and hang on the base of a headstay which, like a submarine's periscope, slid in and out of the water; or as I lay sleepless in my tossing bunk, lusting after the comforts of a Carthusian cell, jets of water streaming in from a leaky deck, the waves pounding two inches from my ear upon the arching bow—surely, I thought, my last." That was my first long ocean trip with Van, my classmate, and until lately, my landlocked friend. He was quite simply unbelieving. For one thing, he had been seasick. Not once, or ten times, but more or less continuously. Several times he announced himself as over the hump; and a few hours later he would arch over the rails in a movement as dexterous by now as the golf stroke of the professional. What was more phenomenal than his extraordinarily unmanageable stomach was his good humor. He lived on bouillon and Bonamine and promised to contribute a testimonial to the antimotion-sickness company on arrival: "Bonamines I Have Barfed, Starring Van Galbraith." On landing finally at St. George's in Bermuda he told me he intended to write an article which would consist quite simply of a minute-by-minute log of the typical hour aboard our boat during the race. The effect of the piece, he confidently predicted, would be to certify the insanity of all participants in the "sport"; and very possibly, by its exposure of the real, awful nature of the ordeal, extirpate ocean racing from the civilized world. I was utterly convinced. I *am* utterly convinced. We talked about it every time we raced together to Bermuda thereafter.

I have done a lot of racing: on a lake as a boy; at sea on *The Panic* (and its successor *Suzy Wong*), beginning in 1955. I am not absolutely sure whether I wouldn't be out there yet, had I, with *Suzy*, developed into a highly successful racing combination. Though the estrangement came gradually, I think I can trace the seeds of it to 1965. I disappeared surreptitiously from the race for Mayor of New York in order to participate in the race from Marblehead, Massachusetts, to Halifax, Nova Scotia, which I had roughly the same chance of winning. Though it was a rough ride, I and Reggie, and Peter, and Van, and two other friends with whom now we raced

15

more or less regularly, managed the boat well. We made no significant errors in seamanship or navigation or strategy; but when finally we slipped across the finish line, there was only a single boat that hadn't yet come in (it was Lee Bailey's. He told me later that on learning I had come in ahead of him, he deserted ocean racing and bought a jet airliner. I comforted him that at least he had effected an economy). By contrast, in the very first race to Bermuda on *The Panic*, we had done quite creditably, halfway in our class. But never on *Suzy*, beautiful, all-teak *Suzy*, built in Hong Kong and sailed from there by four GI's (discharged, by their choice, in Tokyo) across the Indian Ocean, up the Red Sea, through the Suez Canal, across the Mediterranean, down to the Canary Islands, over to Antigua, and finally Miami, where the young owners, following their design, sold her in order to launch their professional careers, get married, and muse for the rest of time on their great adventure. They turned a small profit on the sale, given the difference in construction costs in Hong Kong and the United States, and calculated, working back, that their year's vacation at sea had cost them each about two dollars per day. But *Suzy*, although designed by Sparkman & Stephens, which is like saying about a violin that it was designed by Stradivarius, could not live up to her theoretical rating. This is something called The Rule. It is as romantic an adventure in Procrusteanism as has ever been engaged in by otherwise serious men. It is designed to make all vessels that compete in an ocean race theoretically equal in speed by imposing graduated handicaps. These are calculated by such compounded anfractuosities that nowadays only a half dozen men even affect to understand The Rule, and no one can give you your rating without feeding all the relevant factors into a computer. Not just any computer, but a monster-type bunkered somewhere in Long Island for the purpose of guiding missiles to Mars, and giving yachtsmen their ratings.

The original idea of The Rule was to keep ocean racing from being only a rich man's sport. It is still that, substantially, but certainly not so much so as it would have been in the absence of The Rule. It began by discouraging the idea that every yachtsman had to own two boats —one to race in, the other to be comfortable in. Fifty years ago it was assumed that a very narrow-hulled boat would easily beat a boat

16

with a beamy hull. Since narrow hulls make for uncomfortable living quarters, the very rich had begun the practice of racing in their sleek, thin boats, after which ordeal their second boat, tubby and comfortable, would rescue them from asceticism.

Other factors crept in as The Rule grew in complexity. For instance, the desirable balance between safety and speed. In order to support a mast on which you have run up a huge stretch of canvas whose purpose is to trap the wind and convert its force into forward motion, you must relieve it of unbearable strain. The cables that reach from the top of the mast fore and aft (they are called, respectively, the headstay and the backstay) present no problem. The angle going up from the bow and stern will be sufficiently acute to give the mast fore and aft stability. But the cables that go to the beam ends of a boat (they are called shrouds) are something else.

Exaggerate the problem. Suppose your responsibility is to secure a thousand-foot-high radio tower. If you ran a wire from the top of the tower to a point not more than six feet away from the base of the tower, you would have a shroud that ran very nearly parallel to the tower itself, providing practically no additional support. Accordingly, the closer to the base of the tower the shroud is fastened, the heavier the cable has to be.

At the other extreme, if you were permitted, say, to go out five hundred feet from the base of the tower to rivet down the shroud, you would end with an equilateral triangle of sorts, and the two shrouds would head up from the ground to the top at a comfortable angle of about 60°, permitting relatively light cable. So it is on a boat: the wider the beam, the easier it is to provide stability for the mast, with the lightest cable. The slimmer the beam—conversely—the more difficult the matter of stability; the greater the need for heavy cable; and ultimately—since something has to give if you keep narrowing the beam—you will have to shorten the mast. The Rule penalizes masts according to their length.

When a vessel almost the sister ship of *Suzy* disappeared on a New Year's Eve trip (the owner-skipper was a teetotaler) from Key West to Miami in 1958, one of the greatest manhunts in nautical history was mounted. To begin with, the elements of an awful personal tragedy were there. On board was an entire family: husband, wife, son,

17

daughter-in-law. Besides, Harvey Conover had been Commodore of the Cruising Club of America, perhaps the most prestigious post in the American ocean-going fleet. And he was greatly beloved.

After a week's search, all they came up with was a fragment of the transom (the back end) of the boat's dinghy (you could discern *Revonoc, Jr.* painted on it). It was unofficially concluded that the sleek little racing yawl had run into a tempestuous sea brewed that evening from a hard extemporaneous northerly (that is, a wind that comes from the north) battering against a hard northerly current (that is, a current that flows out of the south—I know; I know). In such a sea, a large merchant vessel proceeding with careless concern for little sailboats crazy enough to be out on such a night could have pulverized the unsuspecting craft without anybody's noticing so much as a tremor. A hollow wooden boat displacing fifteen tons is, after all, less substantial than the hundred-ton waves the merchant ships regularly pound down their bows on.

That was one explanation. I heard another, from an experienced yachtsman of very great experience who privately concluded that the *Revonoc's* centerboard, pushed and pulled by the writhing seas, had wedged apart the very bottom of the boat, opening up the bilges into which the oceans poured, giving the sailors perhaps less than five seconds' time to maneuver. Presumably, coping with the storm, they had latched themselves, with their lifebelts, to the heaving hull, attaching the snap hook at the end of the four-foot line secured to the belt on handy cleats, or lifelines. If so, they would not have been wearing life preservers, and their total disappearance is accounted for.

But why should a centerboard capable of doing that to a boat be tolerated by first-rate designers? The Rule. A proper centerboard, whose purpose is, basically, to lower or raise the bottom of your boat —raise it in shallow water to permit you to glide over the shoals, lower it in deeper water when you want to increase your lateral resistance, and diminish leeway: i.e., resist the tendency of the wind coming in from your side to push the boat to one side (you want to go forward)—is lowered into the water until the end that lay on your bilge is now perpendicular to it. From the bottom point, your centerboard arcs up back to the hull, giving you, under the keel,

18

something shaped like the bottom half of a lemon wedge. A fin, or dagger-type centerboard, eliminates one half or so of the centerboard's area by simply doing away with the area that descends last into the water, the part that completes the curve. The elimination of this surface, for esoteric reasons, used to permit you an advantage in calculating The Rule. . . . In due course, after *Revonoc*, The Rule was discreetly changed. Every two years or so The Rule changes, mostly to frustrate the loopholer, the rule-beater. One inventive yachtsman discovered that *his* handicap was decreased much more than his speed by simply eliminating his mainsail. By a single modification in The Rule, a hundred million dollars' worth of racing boats can be anachronized.

Nowadays, a successful racing boat is a tangle of expensive mechanisms designed to beat The Rule. *Suzy*, with her noble teak, is probably too heavy to have profited even from such radical surgery. We raced her that fall, in the annual race from Stamford, to Martha's Vineyard and back. Once again, boat and crew were in nearly perfect sync; and once again we trailed the fleet. So in due course I retired her from regular campaigning, though I would still race her, if I got around to it, for the fun of it, which was mostly why I raced her and *The Panic* all those years, my point (elaborated once upon a time in a chapter of a book, *Racing at Sea*) being that an ocean race is really a test of yourself and your crew, that there are too many variables to permit one to conclude that this vessel, or that crew, is superior to that other vessel or crew. But no doubt the phasing out of *Suzy* as a racing boat led me to the conclusion that when I sailed to Europe, I would cruise there, rather than race there. There are considerable differences.

Normally, a cruise is conceived as a daytime sail from one harbor to another. You arrive late in the afternoon (say), drop anchor, swim, hike, have a drink, cook and eat dinner, then perhaps play cards, or simply talk, perhaps address yourself to a specially recalcitrant part of the boat's equipment neglected during the day. Everyone in due course turns in, sleeps soundly, wakes up rested. The whole of the ship's complement is up, and down, together.

So is it, of course, in the day-time race. It is when sailing over

19

Suzy Wong, on the Vineyard Race, 1964. The hull was black then; is now red.

distances that require shifts in crew that the nature of the experience radically changes. When you race, you need more men on watch: at least three (in boats up to fifty feet long), and if you need to perform intricate work such as jibing the spinnaker or reefing the mainsail, you generally rouse a fourth. When cruising, you don't, in serene circumstances, need more than two men on watch. This means, assuming you carry the full complement of crew, that in overnight cruising you are on duty less than half the time. To go on duty for four hours, then off duty for eight hours, is manifestly more relaxing than to go back on duty after only four hours off. Moreover, since under such arrangements you have roughly sixteen hours of leisure to deploy, there is more time than otherwise to be gregarious; more time to read; to attend to miscellaneous projects.

That is one difference between cruising and racing—important but not, really, the principal difference. When, during a race, the wind is very light, say two or three knots, you itch with frustration, tread carefully as you go back and forth on deck, lest you upset the delicately weighted list of the boat, calculated to expose the sails most seductively to the anaemic winds. At the other end, you struggle to keep hoisted the maximum serviceable canvas, driving the boat through discomfort as fast as you can make it go without blowing out the sails, or generating counter-productive nose dives into the sea, or heeling over so far on your side as to neutralize the top area of your sail and compose the boat at an incompatible angle. If you are working on the wind—that is, if you are zigzagging toward your objective because it lies ahead of you in the same direction whence blows the wind—you strap in the sails ("close-hauled") and, depending on the characteristics of the vessel and the strength of the wind and the nature of the seas, it will heel over, making its way over and under, breaking waves that roar down the deck and periodically inundate you, your sandwich, and, occasionally, your spirits. There is the single objective: to get there as fast as possible.

When you cruise and the wind roars, you reef, or even lower, a sail that is inimical to your special purposes. It does not matter to you that, during that night, you will travel seventy miles, instead of seventy-five. And anyway, over the long haul, over stretches of sea in which all conditions are met, you will get where you are going as

21

quickly as the racer because you will use engine power during the slack stretches. Although there is no reason, when cruising, to emasculate a sailing boat, and no way to assure comfort—in very heavy weather, a boat racing and a boat cruising will behave almost identically—there are times when little concessions, made at the sacrifice of speed, give you a margin of comfort you are denied in a race—dousing your Genoa (the largest forward sail) and putting up the No. 2 at midnight, if it is getting rough; leaving off the fisherman in a schooner or the mizzen staysail in a yawl; leaving the reef tucked in for an extra hour when the wind lightens, rather than shaking it out the moment you think the boat is capable of taking the extra strain.

I stress that even a long cruise cannot guarantee comfort. A few years ago I induced six classmates from Yale, only Van among them an experienced sailor, to share a trip with me from Bermuda to St. Thomas in the Virgin Islands. So the professional crew, Ned Killeen as captain, brought Cyrano to Bermuda with a first mate, cook, steward, and a couple of hired hands who then flew back to New York, and the rest of us flew in, and took off at midnight. Not because midnight is a melodramatic time to take off, but because the sixth friend came in from South America at eleven, and we all had to be home for Thanksgiving.

The strategy was to head south (St. Thomas is exactly south of Bermuda) as fast as possible for the two hundred miles necessary to get into the trades and out of the formal limits of the North Atlantic gale area. I decided we might as well baptize the passengers into discomfort beginning at midnight, inasmuch as we *had* to get to St. Thomas by the following Wednesday at the latest. So there we were, excited, tucked away, the shifts assigned (four hours on, eight hours off), headed out of the little cut at St. George's through which, coming the other way, I had passed so often before, exhausted, elated, at the end of a Bermuda race. We expected the worst, and were pleasantly surprised. Light winds from the northeast, quite moderate seas, and, darting in and out of the clouds, a moon that would be full in mid-passage.

A large storm front, unfortunately, was at that moment kicking up most monstrous waves north of Bermuda, and these rolled down on

22

us beginning on the second day, and pursued us through the whole of our passage, severely taxing the equanimity of the green passengers, who looked at me, as the days went by, as at an incubus, with intensifying hatred. I remember that on the fourth day it looked as if, finally, the whale-sized waves would dissipate, and the sun shining merrily, I decided at lunchtime, as my friends began to show a more than purely biological interest in their food, that the time had come to try a little R & R, to which end I brought up the big Zenith portable radio—we had heard no voice from the mainland for four days. I flicked on the switch and the cockpit was filled with a familiar voice engaging in some solemn didacticism or other. It was mine. The Voice of America, rebroadcasting a "Firing Line" exchange with someone or other. They all stopped eating, and for a few seconds I feared for my life; but, gentlemen songsters that they proved to be even under such duress, they caucused, and decided finally to accept my fevered assurance that the entire thing was an unholy coincidence.

During the worst of it we had up only a storm trysail and the forward staysail (that is to say, about 25 percent of our sail). I had set out to unfurl at least a part of the Genoa (which on Cyrano is rigged on a roller-reefing fitting that theoretically permits the exposure of any amount of it). But the main fitting on the halyard slipped overboard while I was making an adjustment, the smaller substitute swivel proved too weak, and the sail tumbled down after a few hours. I went theatrically up the masthead on the bo'sun's chair to bring down the halyard and put on yet another swivel. But this one too gave way after a few hours; and now it was too rough to go up again. The result was a heavy-weather helm which was unpleasant, and which put too great a strain on the automatic pilot, reducing us to the humility of having to steer our own boat—imagine, with only ten people aboard. It was especially galling to lose the extra knot or two from the rudder's brake action—like driving a sports car in low gear mile after mile, day after day. If it had been a race, of course we'd have figured some way to get the Genoa up. The wind and seas were relentless, and it wasn't until we got right into the harbor at St. Thomas, bruised and strained, my Cyrano rather weatherbeaten, that we got any relief. The twelve-year-old daughter of one of my friends wrote me a letter a week or so later on some vexing political question and added the P.S., "What *did* you do to my daddy?" The wife of another of my friends, who is a very nice man even though he did run for Congress against Shirley Temple, recounted a week or so later when we came upon them in California that three times, at three in the morning, her husband had suddenly risen stiffly out of bed, stared straight ahead, and declared somnambulistically but firmly, *"I have to go on deck!"*—whereupon he would walk straight ahead, into a closet, which sharply, but reassuringly, jolted him back into the knowledge that his nightmare cruise was over.

Even before I drifted away from racing, I inclined to the notion that a trip across the Atlantic should be done as a cruise rather than as a race. The aesthetic and human factors seemed to me more and more important. When I bought Cyrano, the question was automatically settled. Because Cyrano is not designed as a racing boat. And anybody who owns Cyrano and *Suzy Wong* and elects to cruise to Europe in *Suzy* is either crazy, or a Chichester-type. I speak not of personal safety—the argument could be made that *Suzy* is the safer boat in the ultimate situation. It is a question of comfort. The physical specifications don't adequately convey the point, but here is a profile. Cyrano's hull speed under sail is 10½ knots. *Suzy*'s is 8½. But *Suzy* will spring to life under light air, and Cyrano is a dog in winds of less than ten knots. When Columbus pulled away from San Salvador heading back to Spain, he faced an east wind (plus ça change). Accordingly, he had to tack. His journal records that two days after setting out, he was *still* within sight of the bloody island. What this means is that his boat performed poorly "on the wind": i.e., performed ineffectively in pursuing a zigzag course upwind. The sailors talk in terms of "splitting an angle." Suppose you are located at six o'clock on a round chart and desire to travel to a point at twelve o'clock on that chart; but the wind is blowing directly at you from twelve o'clock. If your boat, when tacking, can only "split an angle" of 180°, then you will end up spending all day traveling first due west (90°, one half of 180°), and then due east, back and forth—never getting any closer to your goal of twelve o'clock. If you split 90°, your first tack would take you at a 45°-

angle to nine o'clock; your second tack, again at a 45°-angle, right to twelve o'clock. *Suzy* will split about 100°; Cyrano, about 125°. So that when you work to windward with Cyrano, you are wise to provide a little engine power. By cutting down on the leeway (which causes the boat to slip sideways), you improve your bite on the wind and your windward progress.

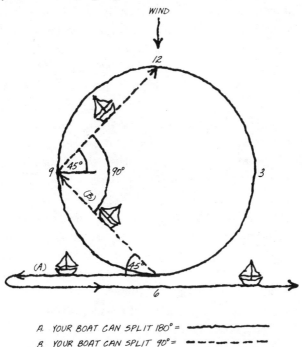

A. YOUR BOAT CAN SPLIT 180° = ▬▬▬▬▬▬

B. YOUR BOAT CAN SPLIT 90° = ▬ ▬ ▬ ▬ ▬ ▬

Cyrano is half again as long as *Suzy*, half again as wide. The difference in cubic space, believe it or not, is about two and one-quarter times. Racing *Suzy*, we carried eight persons on board. Cruising Cyrano, we planned to carry nine.

I mentioned one of two concerns about sailing the Atlantic, one being the tolerable measure of physical discomfort during a substantial part of the journey. I am attracted by adventure, repelled by marathons. I could be persuaded to jump out of an airplane and land in a well in Death Valley; I could never be persuaded to hike across Death Valley, or for that matter, up the Matterhorn. Evel Knievel makes more sense to me than the Long Distance Runner.

The fear of boredom is a cognate aversion. The same friend who told me about the bitter cold sailing to Sweden gave me heartening news on this point. After six days on board a sailing boat, he said, perceptions change radically. You come to do routinely those things you have to force yourself to do when first you come on board, wrenched from a life different in so many rhythms. After five or six days, he said, the hours fly by. The watches, once interminable, diminish in length; anxiety ebbs; on reaching your bunk you are instantly asleep; on being roused, you are instantly and eagerly awake. The ocean and the sky and the night are suddenly alive, your friends and your enemies, but not any longer just workaday abstractions. It is most surely another world and a world worth knowing.

I had never sailed longer than seven days—a stormy cruise to Bermuda, into the edge of a hurricane. It was an experience, except for the three perfect days at the outset, so uniformly unpleasant, dangerous, frightening, that it qualified not at all as a countdown toward that serenity I might have expected on the seventh day, which was spent tacking at a 30°-angle of heel for fourteen hours, the cockpit half submerged in water under relentless pounding from the seas. In prospect, assuming the southern run, we would face a thirteen- or fourteen-day cruise from Bermuda to the Azores. What if, after two days out, I thought suddenly to myself: I am trapped. What if the hours then lengthened and I grew listless with boredom— it is all very well to say, Hell, sit down and study the Pisan Cantos. When you are bored at sea, and I have been bored on much shorter trips, there are suddenly no efficacious distractions, neither Pound nor Agatha Christie; not even music over the radio or on the tape recorder. There is nothing in the ship's medicine cabinet for acedia. There is only industry, that "enemy of melancholy" isolated in his diaries by Sir Harold Nicholson. But what if, per impossibile, everything were in working order? The weather fine? The engine room and its paraphernalia in perfect condition? I'd take a sight at eight, another at noon, another at four, and star sights at seven. Fourteen days? And if my friends were similarly afflicted, and conversation slowly ground to a halt, and, by the seventh night out, human communication reduced to asking for the ketchup? Boredom is the deadliest poison, and it is a truism that it strikes hardest at the most

26

comfortable. Ivan Denisovich suffered everything—except boredom. In due course I would think about devising a few practical hedges, but it was not too soon to think about the right crew.

I have had the unusual background of sailing since I was thirteen, yet sailing other than as captain of the vessel I was on a total of only four times. Except for reading about it, I am very ignorant of how other captains and their crews behave. The first of the four exceptions was aboard my own boat, on my very first ocean race, from Stamford to the lightship off Martha's Vineyard and back (260 miles). My experience had been only in lakes, and, after buying *The Panic*, a couple of weeks of poking about in Long Island Sound before signing on for the race. I asked a friend of vast experience to serve as skipper, and he agreed. He had raced at sea all his life, and in the three days that weekend I learned great gobs of things about starting tactics, racing strategy, flag protocol, current and drift anticipation, weight distribution, and about the importance to me of the skipper's relentless, if tough-minded, good humor. The next spring, having resolved to make the glamorous race to Bermuda, I looked again for a skipper. I was still too inexperienced and had not yet taught myself celestial navigation. A young banker was recommended, but withdrew late in the spring after detecting an insuperable incompatibility between us—I enjoyed writing about this at the time, the article that activated Mr. Hoyt of St. George's. My friend of the Vineyard Race (he was himself committed to another vessel) recommended an old sailing partner from St. Louis, who was agreeable and competent; and I brought on the phlegmatic, genial, supercompetent Mike Mitchell, my insurance agent; and all went well, if that can be said about any ocean passage. From then on, I was on my own.

It was five years after that before I sailed under another skipper. It was at the invitation of Mike Mitchell, who was acting as first mate on a gorgeous gold-plater (i.e., a boat designed and maintained exclusively to win races) in an afternoon race on Long Island Sound. The owner-skipper, altogether civil on shore, became the legendary tyrant on board, and yelled out orders as though he were Ahab espying the whale at last. These orders came out in a complex, largely incoherent, tangle, omnidirectionally beamed to his eight subjects, including one sixteen-year-old whom he addressed only as "Boy!" All this commotion seemed especially incongruous in an afternoon of winds so lazy they nearly fell asleep in the sun. At one point I walked over to the windward side, to slacken a snagged Genoa sheet, and the skipper exploded with imprecations to the effect that I had fatally unbalanced the boat. I looked sideways at Mike Mitchell, who returned me a Yankee smile, part pain, part amusement, part cunning—Mike sold insurance to the old tyrant. It was worse in that every time he spoke, he proved he knew less about sailing than any of the eight of us. Less, even, than Boy! One leaves such people alone. Permanently.

Ten years after that, I was invited to sail on an overnight race with my hero. My hero was William Snaith, whose book *Across the Western Ocean* I had read with near idolatrous pleasure. We knew each other only slightly, and when, expansively, he asked me at a friend's house one night if I would like to navigate for him the following weekend, I accepted, with trepidation. It was as if Toscanini had invited me to play first violin at his concert the following weekend. I would be sailing, for the first time, on a boat every member of whose crew could be expected to be a finished ocean racer. I recognized, on being introduced to them, his two sons and a regular sailing companion, described in Snaith's first book (and again in the book he published a few years later on his race to Sweden). The mood struck at the outset was a kind of short, competent civility irradiating from the volatile, brilliant skipper. Before it was over, the rhetoric developed into a surrealistic, sustained hostility, mostly between the skipper and his older son, spokesman for the crew, which I still take to have been metaphorical in nature, but which once or twice flirted toward the border of a stridency that freezes my own blood; but which, I take it, is accepted as entirely routine aboard many happy vessels.

But I was already too old to adapt to that kind of thing. Besides which, even if I could succeed in breaking a lifetime habit and substituting billingsgate for my normal hearty commands—laced only with a little genial sarcasm when its absence would clearly disappoint, perhaps even confuse—I would so surprise my companions that they would either walk off or send in their resignations on reaching home. George Skakel once told me about crewing for his contemporary and lifelong friend John F. Kennedy in Cape Cod one afternoon, shortly before Kennedy's election as President. "I knew twice as much as Jack about every aspect of sailing," said Ethel Kennedy's urbane and adventurous older brother, killed in his private airplane a couple of years later; "so after about a half hour I said, 'Jack, goddammit, stop crapping with me, and let's race this boat or—' Jack said, 'Goddammit, George pull in on the f------ sheet.' So," said George, smiling with intense pleasure at the memory of it, "I got up, dove off the boat, and swam a mile to Hyannisport. I could hear Jack screaming with rage and could see him trying to handle the boat by himself a half mile away!"

Ocean-going crews do not have the practical alternative Skakel treated himself to, but the spirit of the Narodniki lives on. Bill Snaith's crew, in particular the younger members, showed, during the Swedish race, just the right blend of dutifulness and irreverence. In the endless hours on deck, when the skipper was below, they played at awarding themselves points as the helmsman succeeded in tilting the boat in just such a way as to cause a torrent of water to tear down the lee deck to serve sometimes a useful purpose such as washing dishes, but most often malevolent purposes. The highest score registered by midpassage was 50 points. The captain, after presiding over a body-and-spirit breaking watch in cold cold and tumultuous weather requiring untold changes in rig, hours of sail-patching, trips to the masthead, public séances on inscrutable meteorological developments, finally finished his watch, exhausted, and fell dead asleep. When

". . . by some freak of timing, *Figaro* rolled to leeward at the moment of meeting a wave, took on a boarding sea which came roaring up the waterway, hit the cabin house like a breaker hitting a cliff, broke high in the air, poured over the cabinhouse, and shot down the companionway. Most incredibly it found me in my *bunk*, some distance from the opening. It came over me like a firehose. The shock was indescribable. The gasp which normally comes with a sudden cold immersion was choked off by water in my nose and mouth. I coughed and sputtered. I could hardly grasp what had happened. But the cause of that spreading wet and cold was not long in making itself known. All peace and contentment gave way to rage. I crawled from the berth, mad as a wet captain, shouting my wrath, trying in some

29

way to release the outrage that flooded my being, only to hear my first-born, Cleody, my son, carrier of my name, the staff and rod to comfort me in my declining years, shouting, '*I get a thousand points! I get a thousand points!*' "

Your companions on board are a crucial specification. For me, there is one, no-further-questions-asked disqualifier: personal rudeness of any sort; rudeness, including any sign of impatience (the exception: the captain or the helmsman shouting out impatiently the need for a snatchblock, a flashlight, a scotch and soda). I know of a yacht that raced across the Atlantic—everyone aboard a perfect gentleman, but inexperienced in the absoluteness of the law of proper shipboard behavior. And so it happened that a few days out, the A-watch (at sea, the watches are divided "A" and "B"; the members of a watch usually staying with it throughout the passage) made a rather provocative entry in the log respecting the inferior achievements of B-watch during the antecedent tour of duty. B-watch fired back in its own entry four hours later. Twenty-two days later, arriving at Santander, the four members of A-watch and the four members of B-watch got off the boat with their gear, and from that moment on, no member of either watch ever addressed a single word to a member of the other, even when they were all cozily back in New York, or wherever.

I had a young captain on Cyrano a few years ago with whom I had sailed during the summer, and we had all but concluded arrangements for him to stay on as a professional skipper through the charter season, into the next summer and beyond, during which I had reason to suppose I'd have worked out a long-term arrangement with a prospective partner. He was thoroughly competent in all nonelectrical matters, and truly agreeable, though there was a tightness in the set of the lips that caused misgivings. Peter and I and friends were ferrying the boat back to Miami for the charter season, and at Norfolk, landing at the fuel dock at night, the captain raised his voice to Peter who had given out an instruction to someone on the dock concerning the bow line.

"Peter, *I* am giving the landing instructions."

Peter waited a moment, and shouted back: "If you had given the landing instructions without me, we'd have banged our bowsprit into the dock."

Later, the captain ostentatiously declined to say goodnight to Peter or, the following day, good morning. I let him go on reaching Miami. The resonance, aboard a yacht, of bad humor shatters everything the entire experience is designed to bring you—like an alarm clock going off in Carnegie Hall. I remember years ago resolving never again to invite to race with me one friend for the simple sin, on his day as breakfast cook, of responding to a request from the cockpit to pass the honey: "Can't you just wait a minute!" On board, the protocol is that anyone will do anything for anyone, the perfect crucible for the Golden Rule. "While you're below, would you bring me up some foul-weather gear? (my sunglasses) (my book) (an aspirin)" is the operative social convention aboard a sailing boat, and was pushed to its limit with great amusement by a famous yacht designer whose eighteen-year-old son slipped down the companionway to visit the head, leaving his father and six companions at the wheel. "John? While you're below, would you cook dinner?"

Peter, Christopher, Danny, Reggie, Van. Perfect. And destined, in the preambular formulation of our Constitution, to become even more perfect when Bill Finucane, who is a woman, only sister of my wife, who knows as much about sailing as I know about lacrosse, told me she wanted to come. Everyone knew her. The vote was unanimous, and elated. We had our crew.

31

When I first saw Cyrano I was undecided whether to let Pat aboard. Better to wait until after the renovations? . . . I knew that on examining it, she would pronounce it a lost cause, even as I might do on first seeing a room or a house before such transformations as she can visualize. But I did let her see the boat, and it was as I had thought: Cyrano would *never* do. I bought it anyway. Ned Killeen, the broker in the transaction, had himself once owned a shipbuilding yard, and volunteered to take a leave of absence and serve as my agent for the purpose of effecting the alchemy; later he became the boat's captain for three years. Our initial sail was memorable.

We would begin the little cruise by sailing the boat from the yard at Fort Lauderdale where it had been rebuilt, down to Miami—a four-hour sail. Pat brought along her matronly, endearing, spartan, humorous, arthritic mother, Babe Taylor. Christopher and Danny were about sixteen, and my sister Priscilla and Reggie were there— and off we went.

To reach the harbor of Fort Lauderdale from the boatyard one has to proceed along a canal about fifty feet wide for about one mile; then through the harbor, and out to sea. Mrs. Taylor was comfortably installed in a deep deck chair in the covered cockpit section, and I was at the wheel. About a quarter of a mile down the canal, suddenly the engine stopped. I roared out to Ned, and he tore down to the engine room. Two long minutes later he came up, his Douglas Fairbanks moustache twitching, and explained that the drive shaft had been frozen by the octopus action of electric wires that had wound 'round it. Why had the wires wound 'round it? Because they had not been properly tied down, said Ned, a little defensively—and the revolving motion of the drive shaft had caused one of those knobbly protuberances on the shaft to snag a wire and, like a propeller on a fishing line, others with it, all those fine threads finally bringing the stainless steel shaft to a halt. How many of the other electrical wires? *Every wire in the boat,* Ned finally forced himself to say, his voice now a sort of whiskey-falsetto.

We were, then, without engine, sail, or electrical power; floating without steerageway down a narrow canal with traffic of every kind barreling past us. I called Danny and told him and Christopher to jump into the whaler, which is the ship's dinghy, start the outboard engine, and tow Cyrano back to the yard. They did so eagerly, and Christopher gave a powerful yank on the starter. So powerful that the 40-horsepower outboard, which had not been properly secured, leaped up from the transom and dove to the bottom of the canal.

At just this moment, a sight-seeing boat with about a hundred people on it trolled by. One of the tourists recognized me, and shouted my name in greeting. In the general clamor, the pilot of the boat slowed; and then reversed his engines to permit his guests to take a picture of Mr. Buckley and his friends cruising peacefully aboard his yacht. No one had any reason to suspect that Mr. Buckley and his friends and his yacht weren't going anywhere at all for the simple reason that there was nobody around to push them. They must have thought it genial of me to stop my boat to allow the whole world all the leisure they wanted to take our picture. Noblesse oblige. Under the strain of posing unselfconsciously for a dozen cameras, it was difficult to continue with our war game. But Ned finally volunteered to row the dinghy to the far bank and then to run back to the boatyard to get the yard tender to tow us in. *Don't let that electrician go home,* I growled.

A half hour later the electrician, who moonlighted for the yard— his regular job was to install navigational gear for National Airlines—not only volunteered genially to sail with us to Lauderdale, which would give him the necessary time to splice together the forty or fifty severed lines, but to lend us his own beloved 30-horsepower outboard provided we would agree to treat it as one of the family. Pat contributed the observation that unless I agreed to treat it much better than one of the family, the engine was surely doomed. He had meanwhile pulled the wires out of the way of the drive shaft, so we were at least able to start our engine, and now, as we slid down the canal, every half hour or so an additional electrical installation would begin to work as, on his back, the electrician worked chirpily away in what proved to be dreadfully uncomfortable weather with heavy swells.

We could not get stability from our sails because the wind was from the south, and Mrs. Taylor began to vomit regularly, causing Pat, who has never quite believed that I don't secretly control a weather switch, to stride back from time to time to the wheel to accuse me of *deliberately* trying to kill her mother. Suddenly the wind swung right around, and we quickly lifted the mainsail. Ned proudly fastened a brake strap to the drive shaft, to prevent the propeller from turning unnecessarily while the engine was turned off. An hour or so later, Christopher and the very young first mate began to lower the dinghy, the electrician's precious family outboard attached thereto, into the water, so that it would be readily available to us on coming into the harbor in Miami. At this operation they were unskilled, with the result that the flowing water suddenly caught the edge of the dinghy, swamped it—and the second outboard flew out into the water.

Without a second's hesitation, the young mate dove overboard. "Keep your eyes on him!" I shouted to Christopher, tossing over the life ring. I then started up the motor and slipped the boat into gear. Mrs. Taylor roused herself from her comatose state to point out in a weak voice that smoke was coming up from directly under her. "Great God!" said Ned, shouting to me to put the gear back into neutral. He had forgotten to loose the strap. He disappeared below, and in due course told me I was free to engage the gear. We hauled up into the wind, dropped the sail, and in ten minutes were abeam of the mate, who said proudly he was certain he was still swimming directly over the outboard engine.

The electrician, smoked out from his ghetto below by the drive-shaft fire, was marvelously stoical about the separated member of his family, but took careful bearings—depth of water, bearing on points of land, etc.—and said that the next day, in the daylight, he would venture out with his son and try to find the motor with a scuba outfit; and so we resumed our way, dropping anchor in Biscayne Bay forty-five minutes later, feeling as if we had crossed the ocean. Ned hung out a kerosene anchor light of which he was very proud, fastening it on the headstay, and Mrs. Taylor began to revive as her daughter and friends began to joke about our maiden voyage. She did not, however, say anything; until, finally, she looked at me and said, "Bill, dear, is there supposed to be a fire up there?"—pointing to the bow of the boat.

The kerosene light, for reasons unknown, had fallen into the collapsed Genoa below, which was now beginning to light up like a bonfire. Ned Killeen rushed forward with a fire extinguisher. The electrician, who had finally emerged sweatily from his completed task, a Coke and a sandwich in his hand, continued eating. "You know," he said, "I've been doing marine electrical work for years, but this is the first trip I've ever taken except on my fishing dinghy. Is it always like this?"

I knew she would be the first to speak, even though I'm fast at the draw . . . "Yes," said Pat, calm as Ethel Barrymore. "Oh, yes. In fact, tonight was one of the more *peaceful* sails we've ever *had.*"

But you move quickly to other extremes (as even Pat would agree). A few weeks later, we cruised over Christmas, our first prolonged family experience with Cyrano. I wrote about that cruise at sufficient length to convey at once some of the properties of cruising . . . on Cyrano . . . in the Caribbean . . . with me.

Friday, December 19. We arrived at Antigua airport, and that was an achievement. J. K. Galbraith says you shouldn't use pull unless you need to. Well, I needed to get to Antigua because I decided to go there for Christmas aboard Cyrano—that was two months ago —only to find all the airlines booked solid for December 19 and for a day or two bracketing that day. I tried everybody I knew—or almost everybody I knew—and finally got Mrs. Julie Nicholson, who with her husband and family dominate Antigua more firmly than Horatio Nelson ever did, to help. She and her husband are yacht and charter brokers, and can get you a ticket from anywhere to anywhere, anytime. It was only ordained that we should make a stop at San

Juan. There, waiting for us, were the three Finucanes, who had come in from Los Angeles, joining three Buckleys and Danny, and the seven of us arrived at Antigua. At the dockside was our own Captain Ned Killeen, and a half dozen partygoers, at the center of whom was Mrs. Nicholson herself, who greeted me warmly, and, as I slipped away in the tender, demanded to know what comes after *Gaudeamus igitur*. My memory failed me, and I felt dreadful, after all the Nicholsons had done for me. However, I did not forget to bring her Barricini chocolates and ribbon candy, which you must not forget to do if ever you find yourself coming from where you can get Barricini chocolates and ribbon candy to Antigua at Christmastime. I have made a mental note to let Mrs. Nicholson know what comes after *Gaudeamus igitur* as soon as I find out. Let us therefore rejoice. What *would* follow naturally from that? At this point, I could only think: *Quam ad Antiguam pervenimus.*

Saturday, December 20. Cyrano is nowadays based in St. Thomas, and it was Ned Killeen's idea that it would make for a pleasant cruise if he "deadheaded" Cyrano to Antigua, permitting us to cruise downwind back to St. Thomas. To deadhead means to take a boat without payload. It took him two long nights, into mid-morning, to ferry Cyrano 220 miles from St. Thomas to Antigua. Ned likes daytime landfalls. I like nighttime landfalls. Ned usually prevails. Ned always prevails when I am not aboard. Interesting thought. How much should we charge charterers to deliver them Cyrano in Antigua, should they so desire it? Ned suggests two hundred dollars for the two days, which is less than one half the $265 per day that we get for the use of Cyrano; but his point is that at $100 per day we are not actually losing money, and a little noblesse oblige on the high seas is always in order. I say something dour about how I wish the bankers would show a little noblesse oblige and acquiesce in the arrangement.

My beautiful Cyrano. Built in the Bahamas, in Abaco, to an old fishing boat design. Sixty feet long, fifty-four feet at the waterline, with an extraordinary eighteen feet of bowsprit (which I reduced to twelve after Captain Crunch, by going under the fixed bridge, allowed me to start *ex nihilo*), seventeen and one-half feet of beam, tapering back to about thirteen feet at the transom where two stout davits hold up the tender. Acres and acres of deck space. And below, an upright piano which Art Kadey, the previous owner and skipper, banged away at to the great delight of his passengers over the three years between the construction of the boat and my purchase of her.

What was needed, I thought on first looking the boat over, was a great deal of impacted luxury, plus complete instrumentation and rerigging for ocean passages. The latter was obvious enough: running backstays, loran, radar, automatic pilot; that kind of thing. The former is, I think, less obvious. I had done a fair amount of chartering, not a great deal. But I had come to a few conclusions. They are:

1. Sleeping quarters should be small and public quarters large. One needs in sleeping cabins only privacy and room to turn around in.

2. Every room should have a port, which should be situated at about eye level when your head is down on the pillow. Why not? All my life I have been on steamships which require that, in order to see through the port—presumably there for you to see through—you stand on tiptoe, which is hard to do while going to sleep. I got my ports. Three of them on the starboard side, one for each of the cabins, and three of them on the port side in the saloon—all of this *in addition* to the picture windows.

3. Color, color, and more color. More boats are ruined by monochromatic dullness than by careless seamanship. So every room was decorated by my wife in a chintz of different color, of congruent patterns; so that we have the red cabin, the yellow cabin, and the green cabin, a green carpet, and a glazed cotton print for the settee and couches, a pattern taking off, in reds and blues, on an old Spanish sailing map.

4. Chairs, settees, and couches must be *comfortable*. I rebuilt the main settee three times, so as to make it, finally, slope back steeply enough and extend out far enough to make sitting in it truly comfortable for the slouchers of this world—who are my friends and clients. Opposite it, two club chairs, facing my three ports. Wall-to-wall carpeting is right for a boat; kerosene and electric torches, of course. Then I persuaded my friend Richard Grosvenor, the excellent New England artist who teaches at St. George's School, to do three original oil paintings of boat scenes which exactly fit the principal

Cyrano's saloon.

Crew's dining table. Background, aft entrance to engine room.

exposed areas I wired to receive them. So that every picture is lit as in an art gallery, the three little overhead lights providing plenty of illumination for the entire saloon, unless you want to read, in which case you snap on one of the other lights. But with the oil paintings alone, the saloon now lights up in color and comfort, a beautiful room designed for total relaxation. When you are under way in a breeze, the seas sometimes rise up, covering the ports completely for whole seconds at a time. (Sometimes the moonlight comes in to you right through the water.) Abaft the piano is the bar and refrigerator which the former owner so thoughtfully installed to keep charterers from having to go back and forth to the galley quarters, a whole engine room away.

5. The deck area should be—well, perfect. There was no deckhouse. I had one designed and built, with two six-and-a-half-foot-long, four-foot-wide cushions, usable as berths, on either side. Between them, the companionway and then a well, where your feet can dangle while you navigate over a luxuriously large area (larger than a standard card table), or look into your radar screen or check your depth finder or a supplementary compass, and where you can even steer the ship electrically. That is, when you want to come forward from the wheel, to get out of the rain.

Cyrano's deckhouse.

Stepping aft, six or seven feet, an enormous settee. Once again, the accent on comfort. In the Mediterranean many boats have main cockpit settees on which you can sprawl out in any direction. The trick was to accomplish this and also convert the new deckhouse into dining quarters for fair weather. Castro Convertible came to the rescue—by the adaptation of its essential mechanism that permits the raising of a table. Then a custom-built tabletop which exactly fits the arc of the settee, so that when you are not eating, the table sinks down and three tailored cushions exactly cover the area, which now merges with the settee, giving you an enormous area of about four feet by twelve feet in which four or five people can stretch out and read or merely meditate on the splendid achievements of the settee designer. At mealtimes, remove the three cushions, pull a lever—and (hesto) a perfectly designed table rises elegantly into place, around which eight people can sit. At night, you can close off the entire area with canvas, giving you something of the feel of a large Arabian tent.

6. The crew must have living space. Under existing arrangements, it is never necessary for guests to occupy the old dining quarters in the after section. There the crew has its privacy, adjacent to the Captain's cabin, the main navigational table, the galley, and the lazarette.

7. Noise. Somebody, somewhere along the line, told me that the biggest, most expensive, generators make the least noise. Ned came up with an Onan so noiseless you can hardly tell if it's on or off. It provides all the power you need, including 110-volt AC outlets. And finally,

8. Coolness. I know it is costly and difficult to install. Even so, air condition, or die. I reason as follows. If you live in the Caribbean the year round, perhaps you can get used to hot temperatures. But if you only *visit* the Caribbean, you get hot in the middle of the day— just as you can get hot in the middle of Long Island Sound in the middle of the summer. Turn on your air conditioner and life changes for you; or it does for me, anyway. I shall never be without my air conditioner. If the bankers one day descend on me, I shall go on national teevee and deliver a Checkers speech about my air conditioner. They will never take it from me.

I am staring at the chart as we cruise out of the tight little entrance

40

to English Harbor. What do you say we go to Nevis? I suggest to Ned. Nevis is about forty-five miles west, and it is already noon. The wind is as it should be, east northeast. Ned, so wise, so seasoned, suggests that perhaps we would be better off just going west along the coastline of Antigua, instead of striking out for so distant a goal so late in the day. I am glad I gave in.

Sunday, December 21. I said I was glad I gave in, and I suspect that I gave the impression that where we did spend the night, which was in Mosquito Bay in Antigua, was unique. Not really. It is a very pretty cove (there are no mosquitoes on it, by the way), shallow, and if you want to know when the tide changes, it changes exactly when it changes in Galveston, Texas, for heaven's sake; and not even Ned knew instinctively how to figure *that* one out. I mean, if the *Tide Book* says: "*see* Galveston, Texas," and you find that the tide begins to ebb at Galveston, Texas, at 1900, at what time does it begin to ebb at Mosquito Bay, Antigua? You will immediately see that conflicting hypotheses are plausible. You may find yourself reasoning that when it is 7:00 P.M. at Galveston, the tide also begins to change at Mosquito Bay: which means you have to figure out the time zone for Galveston. Well, figure Galveston is two hours behind New York and we are one hour ahead of New York; ergo, it changes at Mosquito Bay at 10:00 P.M. Right? Not necessarily. Maybe it means that just as when it is 7:00 P.M. local time at Galveston the tide changes, so when it is 7:00 P.M. local time at Mosquito Bay, the tide changes—what's implausible about that?

The time has come to note a further complication, which is that when I sail Cyrano in the Caribbean, I go on what we call Buckley Watch Time, the only eponymous enterprise I have ever engaged in. What you do is tell all hands on board to move their clocks up by one hour. The practical meaning of it all is that you can start the cocktail hour as the sun is setting and eat dinner one hour later, at eight o'clock. Otherwise, you start drinking at six o'clock and eat dinner at seven. The former offends the Calvinist streak in a Yankee; the latter, the Mediterranean streak in a yacht-owner. Anyway, in order to avoid digging into the fine print of the *Tide Book*, we decide to fasten on the fact that, after all, the tide here is less than one foot anyway; so we throw out the hook 150 yards from the beach rather

41

than crawl up further, as we might have done if we had been absolutely sure that Galveston had another hour or so to go before the ebb began. No matter. The sunset was beautiful, we swam, ate— ate very well, thanks to Rawle, a native of St. Vincent who is a superb cook, and who has the prestige of a real-life shipwreck under his belt. Then we played 21, and I won consistently. The tape-player is the arena of a subtle contest between the generations. When one of *us* goes by it, we glide into the tape cavity something melodic. When one of the seventeen-year-olds goes by, quite unobtrusively he, or she, will slip in The Cream or The Peanut Butters, or whoever. I acknowledge to myself that the war will be formally declared by about tomorrow, lunchtime. ("Will you please get those screaming banshees off the air, children?" "Mother, can we put on something that isn't Marie Antoinette?") I am right. We go to bed, and my wife and I can see, outside our porthole, the full moon and the speckly light it casts on the waters—our waters, because there is no one else in sight.

Monday, December 22. I must make myself plain. I am glad I took the advice that we make the shorter rather than the longer run to Nevis because I know enough now about other people to know what suits the general taste in a cruise. I am accustomed to a more spartan schedule, which, however, is not what cruising-chartering is about. I remember, in talking with Art Kadey, the disbelief with which I heard him say that the typical charterer travels approximately four hours every *other* day! I thought that (and still do) rather on the order of spending a fortnight at your fishing lodge and going out to fish only every other day. It takes time to adapt, if you have raced a boat in ocean races, accustomed to day and night running. Some come easily to the change, and indeed find it easy to oscillate from furious, implacable racing, day after day—week after week, in such as the Transatlantic or TransPac race to Honolulu—to strolling about for a few hours on the same boat you often race, going perhaps no further than ten or fifteen or twenty miles in a single day. Moreover, Cyrano takes long sails in stride. She is a shoal-draft boat, built for the Bahamas. She hasn't even a centerboard—merely a long keel stretching the entire length of the hull to a distance of five and one-half feet from the waterline. The result is a certain stodginess in coming about, as any boat has that isn't equipped with ballet shoes;

42

but with that great beam and with whatever it is the designer did to effect those numinous lines, she achieves a glorious seakindliness that makes ocean sailing dry, fast, and stable.

It isn't easy for everybody to relax on a boat. I adore my boat: and every boat I have ever had. But I feel, somehow, that I am always, in a sense, on duty; that I must be going from here to there, and if there is a little bad weather or whatever, well, isn't that a part of the general idea? The point, as Ned and others have patiently explained to me, is that there is the wholly other use of a boat, the use which is absolutely ideal for charterers, and that is the totally comfortable, totally unstrained cruise. So that if you decide this morning to go from Antigua to Nevis but the wind isn't right, why you simply go somewhere else! You don't have any obligations to meet the New York Yacht Club Squadron at Nevis at 1700, and nobody will tell the Commodore if, instead, you ease off to St. Kitts—I mean, some people come to total relaxation in boats more easily than others, and they do not feel any constraint to harness their boats to an instrumental objective, like getting from here to exactly there, and There had better be a good distance away from Here in order to give you the feeling that you have accomplished a good run and earned the quiet hours of anchorage. All I say is: There are those of us who are driven, and if you are one of those, you will have to speak firmly to Ned. To say nothing of your wife.

St. Kitts is absolutely ravishing. We arrive rather late and do not disembark, simply because we cannot be bothered to register the boat. Why, oh why, don't the islands issue a triptyque, or whatever the Europeans called that document with all the coupons that they used to issue which facilitated car travel in postwar Europe. Hunting down the Immigrations and Customs officer, giving him (on one occasion, at Virgin Gorda, *six* copies of the crew and passenger list). Why not a bond that every boat owner could buy, the possession of which would grant free passage everywhere during a season, with a severe penalty if you are caught smuggling, or whatever, guaranteed by the bonder? How easy everything would be if I were given plenipotentiary power over these matters.

The run to St. Bartholomew (St. Barts) is quite long—forty miles or so—and I suggest to Ned that we take off early, at nine o'clock, and sail under the great rock which they call the Gibraltar of the Caribbean. Surely you mean after the crew has breakfast? says Ned. What the hell, say I, why not get started under power, and *then* have breakfast? We weigh anchor and proceed, and two days later I notice in the ship's log the stern entry, "Got under way before the crew had breakfast." A brilliant day, strong winds just abaft the beam, poor Christopher is seasick, the only time during the whole trip, but by two o'clock we have pulled into the exemplary little harbor, so neat, so thoroughly landlocked, so lackadaisical, where the rum is cheaper than the water and the rhythm of life is such that the natives never go to work before breakfast, and not always after breakfast.

Tuesday, December 23. The proposal is to make a short run for St. Barts, which my materialistic family favors, sight unseen, because the guidebook says that the prices there are even a little bit less than those at St. Maarten. The sail is a mere fifteen miles. We considered dropping by St. Mart and then proceeding four or five miles west to Anguilla, perhaps to decolonize it, now that history has taught us how easy it is to do. But the iron schedule (we must relinquish the boat to charterers in four days) makes this imprudent. I feel very keenly the loss, inasmuch as during the few months of Anguilla's independence, when the rebel government took a full page ad in The New York *Times* asking for contributions to revolutionary justice, I slipped the government a five-dollar bill in the mail and got back a handwritten letter of profuse gratitude from the Prime Minister. (Another day.)

The idea is to spend a relaxed few hours at St. Mart, and then make the longish (one hundred-mile) sail to the Virgins, touching in at Virgin Gorda. St. Mart is half Dutch (the lower half) and half French. A very large harbor, almost the size of Provincetown, with beaches and calm and lots of picturesque boats. We swim and water ski, and then head out for dinner at the Little Bay Hotel, which is a Hilton type, with casino, triple-air-conditioned bar, so-so restaurant, and higher than so-so prices. We did not get to gamble because the Casino opened at 9:00 P.M. and we forgot that Buckley Watch Time wiped out the gambling hour we had counted on; so we went back to Cyrano, and started out.

I took the watch until 0200, along with Bill Finucane, Pat's exemplary sister, while my wife and her brother-in-law played gin rummy and the boys and my niece lazed about on deck forward, discussing no doubt the depravities of their elders. I felt constrained (I am that way on a boat) to go forward every twenty minutes or so to make an aesthetic point—single out the moon, for instance, which was about as easy to miss at this point as the sun at dawn—and say casually, "Have you noticed the moon?" The kids are so easy to ambush, because it never fails that they will look up from their conversation, stare about, focus eventually on the moon, and say, finally, "Huh?"

It was an uneventful overnight journey, except that at 3:00 A.M. I was roused from my cabin by my wife, who reported that my apprehensive brother-in-law desired me personally to confirm that the lights off at one o'clock were not (a) an uncharted reef, (b) an unscheduled island, or (c) a torpedo coming at us at full speed. I came on deck and peered out at the lights of what appeared to be a tanker going peacefully toward whatever it was going peacefully toward. A good chance, though, to show off my radar, which immediately picked it up at six and one-half miles away, heading toward, approximately, Morocco. I went back to sleep, and awoke when Ned at the wheel was past the famous Anegada Passage, down which the Atlantic often sweeps bustily into the Caribbean, but which on this passage had acted like a wall-to-wall carpet; and now we were surrounded by tall, hilly islands, such that by contrast we felt almost as though we were going through a network of rivers, calm, warm, but with breeze enough (finally) to sail. And we put in, at eleven, at Spanish Town, in order to regularize ourselves with the government of the British Virgins which, on Christmas Eve, was most awfully obliging, after the first mate and I completed the six forms registering the names and affirming the nonsubversive intentions of the tired but happy crew and passengers of the schooner Cyrano.

Wednesday, December 24. We head now for a bay, particularly favored by Ned, in Virgin Gorda. Getting there is a minor problem, requiring a certain concentration so as to avoid Colquhoun Reef. In nonnavigational language, you proceed like up, over, down, back, and up, so as to avoid the long reef. Look it up in any of the books or guides, and it is abundantly charted. The rewards are great because after you nestle down there you see along the reef, a few hundred yards away from the anchorage, the beautiful blues and greens you have been missing thus far, where the water was deep. It is strictly Bahamian here. They say, by the way, that the Virgins are vastly to be preferred to the Bahamas "from the water level up." This is shorthand to communicate the following: The islands are infinitely more interesting in the Antilles—the Virgins, the Windwards, and the Leewards. Every island is strikingly interesting and different, both topographically and culturally. St. Kitts, for instance, has Mt. Misery, an enormous volcano rising to 4,300 feet. Nothing of the sort happens in the Bahamas, where the islands are almost uniformly low. But the Bahamian waters are uniquely splendid in coloration. The sandbars and reefs, which are so troublesome to the navigator, repay the bother to the swimmer and to anyone who just wants to look. Anyway, Virgin Gorda is that way, and on shore is the Drake's Anchorage hostelry, which just that morning had changed hands. The previous owner of the little bar and inn had sold out to— would you believe it?—a professor at MIT. The bar and dining room were Somerset Maugham-tropical, and were all dressed up for Christmas. The talk was of the necessity to persuade somebody to come down and take over the exciting underwater tours of the departing owner, who specialized in taking adventurous spirits for scuba diving in the Anegada Passage to poke about the wrecks at Horseshoe Reef, not all of which have, by any means, reposed there since the eighteenth century. The flagpole at the hostelry is the corroded aluminum mast of the *Ondine*, which foundered there just a few years ago.

Having reconnoitered, we went back to Cyrano, at that point almost alone in the anchorage, just in time to see a smallish sloop come gliding toward us, brazenly avoiding the circumnavigatory imperatives of the guidebooks, treating the reef we had given such studied berth to as familiarly as if it were the skipper's bathroom. We watched in awe as a dignified lady with sunbonnet directed the tiller to conform with the directions given by the angular, robust old gentleman up forward handling the anchor. The landing was perfect, the motor never having been summoned to duty, and they lodged down, fifty yards away from us. I discreetly manned the binoculars, peeked for a while, and said to my companions, "By George, I do believe that is Dr. Benjamin Spock."

I know the gentleman slightly, having sparred with him here and there in the ideological wars. I wondered what, under the circumstances, would be an appropriate way to greet him. I thought of sending Ned over to his sloop, instructed to say, "Dr. Spock, compliments of Cyrano, do you happen to have anything on board for bubonic plague?" But the spirit of the season overcame me, and instead I wrote out an invitation, "Compliments of the military-industrial complex, Mr. and Mrs. William F. Buckley, Jr. would be honored to have the company of Dr. and Mrs. Benjamin Spock and their friends for Christmas cheer at 6 P.M." The good doctor rowed over (I knew, I *knew* he wouldn't use an outboard) to say Thanks, how was I? Mrs. Spock wasn't feeling very well, please forgive them, they were pulling out anyway within the hour, come back soon, once you've sailed the Virgins you can never sail anywhere else; and rowed back. We struck out in the glasshopper (all-glass dinghy) with the kids to explore the reef, which they did for hours on end. I returned to Cyrano (I enjoy skin diving, but a half hour of it is fine by me), mounted the easel and acrylic paint set Bill brought me for Christmas, and set about industriously to document, yet again, my lack of artistic talent. The girls were working on the decorations, and by the time the sun went down we had a twinkling Christmas tree on deck and twinkling lights along the canvas of the dodger; the whole forward section was piled with Christmas gifts and decorations, and when we sat down for dinner, with three kerosene lights along my supper table, the moon's beam, lambent, aimed at us as though we were the single target of the heavens, Christmas music coming in from the tapeplayer, the wine and the champagne and the flambéed pudding successfully passed around, my family there, and friends, I persuaded myself that nowhere on that evening, at that time of day, could anyone have asked for any kinder circumstances for celebrating the anniversary of the coming of the Lord.

Thursday, December 25. Intending to go to a church service on Christmas Day at Road Town, the capital of the British Virgins, we pull out earlyish, on the assumption that there is a Mass at noon. We arrive at 11:45 and come in European-style at the yacht basin.

47

European-style, by the way, involves dropping an anchor, sometimes two, about thirty yards ahead of where you intend finally to position your boat. Then you back up toward the pier (usually stone or concrete) while someone up forward, the anchor having kedged, is poised to arrest your backward movement by snubbing up on the anchor line the moment you give the signal. You back up the boat to about ten feet from the landing. At the right moment, you toss out the port stern line diagonally, and the starboard stern line ditto. Obliging passersby secure these lines on the pier, and you have— you can readily see—a very neat situation. The stern lines are acting as, in a way, spring lines, restricting the boat's sideward movement, sideward being where other boats are lined up, leaving, very often, no more than a few inches of sea room. Then, when you are safely harnessed, you motion to the gentleman on the foredeck to ease the line to the anchor, while the two gentlemen aft take up on *their* lines, bringing the stern of Cyrano gently aft until the davits are hanging quietly over the pier. You have now only to take a step over the taff-rail, touch down easily on the ground, and without equilibratory gyration (something you should practice), stroll on toward the nearest *taverna*. I don't know why the custom isn't more widespread in American harbors, the economy of space and motion being so very obviously advantageous. Of course, you need to have a sheer situation off the pier, which isn't always the case, for instance, in many New England snuggeries. But even when there is water, the habit is not practiced by American yachtsmen. So much is it the drill in, for instance, Greece, that pleasure craft of any size carry gangways that extend from the transom to the pier, including stanchions and life-lines to serve as bannisters for milady to hang on to as she descends daintily to earth. I remember a year ago in the Aegean seeing a hedonistic triumph called the *Blue Leopard*, an enormous yawl which, miraculously, ejected its gangway—it would appear electrically—from just beneath the deck level where it is stowed, like the dictation slide that pulls out of a desk—right down onto the pier? No, dear. To six inches above the pier, contact with which it was protected from by two special halyards which quickly materialized and were quickly attached to the far corners. The purpose? Why, to spare the *Blue Leopard* the fetid possibility that a restless rat might,

48

seeking a tour of the Aegean, amble up the companionway, it being acknowledged that healthy rats tend to board a floating ship.

We linger only an hour or so. The gentleman who owns the bar, the Sir Francis Drake Pub, is moved by the spirit of the season and does not charge you—Merry Christmas!—for your first drink, and we feel rather sneaky ordering only a single round and then returning to Cyrano for lunch. Christmas lunch. Rawle could give us anything, beginning with lobster Newburgh and ending with Baked Alaska. We settle on a fish chowder, of which he is surely the supreme practitioner, and cheese and bacon sandwiches, grilled, with a most prickly Riesling picked up at St. Barts for peanuts. Then we wander off to the Fort Burt Hotel, which is built around the top of the old fort, providing a 300° view of the harbor and adjacent islands. There is another hotel there, dubbed the Judgment Day Hotel, which has not been completed, even though it has been abuilding, lo, these many years, and is therefore the butt of many local jokes, seniority going to the one about how it will finally open only on Judgment Day. The attitude toward progress in the Antilles is ambivalent. On the one hand, the natives recognize that "progress" is both ineluctable and commercially desirable. On the other hand, the agents of progress are the presumptive disrupters of the natural order, and when bad fortune befalls them—as with the builder of the phantom hotel—the natives take pleasure in their fugitive alliance with adversity.

Off we go, to swim and to spend the night off Norman Island, which is reputedly the island Robert Louis Stevenson described when he wrote *Treasure Island*. It is, needless to say, just like any other island (except that it lies adjacent to fascinating grottos, complete with bats, into which you row wide-eyed). On the other hand, needless to say, like the other islands it too is captivating: a beach; a fine, protected cove. I remember a few years ago when, intending to pleasure him, I took Christopher, at fourteen and having done exceptionally well at school, with me cross-country, to San Francisco and Los Angeles, where I was to record television programs. My son was the prodigy of the McLuhanite dogma, but I was determined *not* to raise my voice in criticism—he was at my side (a) because I adored him, and (b) because I sought concrete expression of my admiration of his academic work. But finally—after *four* hours of flight, during which, earphones glued on, Christopher merely stared at the ceiling, even as his overworked father fussed fetishistically with briefcases and papers—I lost control, turned on him and said, acidly, or better, acidulously (if the word has uses, let it now pull its oar):

"Christopher, just out of *curiosity*, have you *ever* read a book?"

He moved his right hand slowly, with that marvelous impudence the rhythm of which comes so naturally to the goddam Kids, dislodging his right earphone *just* enough to permit him to speak undistracted, but not so much as to cause him to lose the musical narrative of whatever rockrolling fustian he was listening to: and replied in Peter Fonda-drawl, "Yeah. *Treasure Island.*"

Back went the earphones. The eyes did not need to revert to the ceiling of the plane. They had never left it.

It was our final night aboard Cyrano and we felt, although we did not sentimentalize on it, the little pang one always feels on approaching the end—of anything. The night was fine. Calm, peaceful. The moon made its appearance, though later; grudgingly, it seemed. I think we all lingered more than usual before going below.

Friday, December 26. We stopped at Trunk Bay, St. John, to skin dive. St. John is the island most of which was given by the U.S. government to the Rockefellers, or vice versa, I forget which. In any case, you must drop your anchor well out in the cove, because the lifeguards do not permit you to come too close. In fact when you come in on the beach with your dinghy, you are required, if you have an outboard motor, to anchor it fifty yards from the beach and off to the right, away from the swimmers. If you don't have an outboard, you may beach your dinghy. But if you do beach your dinghy, you may not attach its painter (the boat-word for the leash of a dog or tether of a horse) to the palm tree up from the beach, because you will be told that people might stumble over it, which indeed people might do if they are stone-blind. Then you walk to the east side of the beach, put on your face mask and fins, and follow the buoys, ducking down to read, underwater, marvelously readable descriptions of flora, fauna, and fish, the reading matter engraved on stone tablets which tilt up at a convenient angle and describe the surrounding situation and the fishes you are likely to come across.

50

The tablets I saw did not describe the barracuda that took a fancy to me, whose visage was fascinatingly undistinguishable from Nelson Rockefeller's, but then my eye mask was imperfectly fitted. We got back to Cyrano and sailed on down past the Rockefeller Hotel at Caneel Bay, to Cruz Bay, where we officially re-entered the United States of America. Embarrassing point. My wife thought, it being the day after Christmas and all, that it would be pleasant if I took to the lady who transacts these official matters a bottle of cheer. I went to her with Ned at my side, and found her wonderfully efficient and helpful. She completed the forms and then, rather like Oliver Twist making time with the headmaster, I surfaced a bottle of Ron Ponche, and, with a flourish or two, presented it to her, trying to look like Guy Kibbee playing Santa Claus. She smiled benignly and then explained that she could not, under The Rules, accept such gifts. I was crestfallen, embarrassed, shaken, and returned feistily to my wife to say, See, that's what you get trying to bribe American authorities, to which she replied, Trying to bribe them to do what? Which stumped me, and I took a swig of the rejected Ron Ponche, which tasted like Kaopectate, perhaps explaining the lady's rectitude.

We travel under power to St. Thomas, a mere couple of hours. Yacht Haven at St. Thomas might as well be Yacht Haven at Stamford, Connecticut, where Cyrano would spend next summer. Hundreds of boats, harried administrators, obliging officials giving and taking messages, paging what seemed like everybody over the loudspeaker, connecting pallid, sleepy northeasterners with their snowflaked baggage and then with wizened boat captains. Only the bar, which opens at 8:00 A.M., made it obviously other than Yacht Haven, Stamford; and, of course, the weather. About 82°, and sun, sun, sun: We had not been without it, except for an hour or two on either side of a squall, during the entire idyllic week. A charter would board the next afternoon, and the preparations were accordingly feverish. The adults obliged by taking a couple of rooms at the Yacht Haven Hotel. The boys stayed on board to help. We had yet to consummate a dinner cruise around the harbor, and our scheduled guests were my libel lawyer in New York, Mr. Charles Rembar, his wife, and son. They arrived (an hour late—a serious matter inasmuch as they had not been indoctrinated in Buckley Watch Time), and we slid out in the darkness (the moon would be very, very late), and cruised about, under power this time, bounding off the lights of the five great cruise ships that lined the harbor and its entrance. St. Thomas is not unlike Hong Kong at night, except, of course, that its hills are less high. But the lights are overwhelming, and the spirit of Christmas was everywhere, so that we cruised gently in the galaxy, putting down, finally, the anchor; had our dinner, pulled back into the slip, said our goodbyes, and left my beautiful Cyrano, so firm and reliable, so strong and self-assured, so resourceful and copious, and made our way back, in stages, to New York where, for some reason—obscure, after the passage of time—our ancestors left *their* boats in order to settle down there, so that their children's children might dream, as I do, of reboarding a sailing boat and cruising the voluptuous waters that Columbus hit upon in his crazy voyage five hundred years ago, because he did not have Ned aboard to tell him when enough was enough.

Switzerland, February 1974. I was hacking away, lost in pleasure as I always am when I do the two things I do worst in this world, the pleasuring of the Lord apart: play the harpsichord and paint on canvases. I was painting a sailboat in the huge, disorderly study-atelier where I work. The record machine played galvanizing jazz from the 30's. Van's wife Bootsie and my wife Pat had long since gone upstairs to bed. It was then that I asked Van whether he would make a commitment to an Atlantic crossing. There had been very vague overtures. He asked now, how long would it take?

About thirty days, I said, guessing. I told him I proposed to sail from Miami to Bermuda, then on to Lisbon. He puffed out a big ring from his small cigar, swallowed from his glass of brandy, and said, "Count me in—from Bermuda to Lisbon." I was both pleased and disappointed; but before the week had ended, Van had begun asking himself whether he would feel the full satisfaction of an ocean-crossing if he began it one-quarter of the way across; it was rather like doing the last three of four laps in a race. Two days later, with a conspiratorial wink—which implied that we shared a bit of information withheld from our wives for the time being—he said that, barring any emergency, he would do the whole trip.

I decided, along about then, that I should attempt to evolve a doctrine establishing what is, and what isn't, an *emergency* in such circumstances. I was raised by my father on the doctrine that, for busy people, there is "no such thing as a convenient time for a vacation." That being so—my father deduced—take a vacation *exactly* when you want to; and let the chips fall where they will, since chips are going to fall in any case. A burst appendix the night before setting

53

sail falls clearly on the legitimate side of the line. But what about a business deal that is getting hot and might fructify at a moment when, alas, you cannot meet the impulsive buyer at 56th and Park, because it happens that you are at 37° north latitude, 37° west longitude, mooning over the wind and the waves and the stars, four hundred miles from the nearest atoll?

In due course I brought the matter up candidly with Van, and later with Peter and Reggie, and we agreed that chickenshit emergencies would be—er—discountenanced, as they put it in the world of business. Christopher and Danny were at the lucky age where emergencies of the borderline sort do not occur, except romantically, and these were *categorically* excluded from consideration. I have said that a successful cruise requires elaborate attention to exactly who is on board, and that the more successfully that fore-planning is done, the more critical its success. Van and Reggie and Peter warranted that nothing short of a truly unmanageable problem would keep them away: and so I there and then set the date.

We would leave at 10:00 A.M. on the morning of May 30, 1975 from Miami. We would arrive—by now I had calculated the distance —on June 30. Not in Lisbon: studying the coastline persuaded me that the trip south from Lisbon into the Mediterranean, where Cyrano would charter during the summer, was pointless. Though awesomely prescient in political matters, I did not at that point foresee that sailing into Lisbon harbor in June 1975 would be like sailing into Haiphong in December of 1972. No, we would go to Gibraltar. Much later, I saw the sense of making that Marbella instead—around the Rock, and up the Spanish coastline, thirty-five miles. We had fifteen months in which to prepare the boat, discipline our calendars, and train lovingly our vast and ardent constituencies to do without us for an entire month. For me, the huge labor of preparing Cyrano and planning the trip was minor alongside the major problem that lay ahead. Telling Pat.

Pat is (I assert the distinction, the Equal Rights Amendment not having yet been enacted) the most feminine woman I have ever known. She moves almost entirely by intuition. Her intuitions are sometimes worth portfolios of precisionists' calculations. As when, many years ago, she calmly announced to two doctors that their diagnosis was quite wrong, that she did not care about the statistics they quoted, that in fact she was suffering from a specified disorder, which, in due course, like the preceding one, would have to be dealt with by surgery. Two weeks later she was vindicated, to use the word with bitter correctness. It is, however, a blessing that many of her insights prove to be maladjusted. I developed, some five years after we were married, the skill to continue reading a book equanimously right through one of her routine warnings that she smelled smoke and would I get up and look to see where the fire was. I am required, to be sure, to record that I *did* listen, twenty years after we were married, when she gave me the old song and dance, because although her warning did not enable me to keep the house from burning down, it did give me an extra few minutes to remove books and things before the house burned to the ground. She *knew* that she would never walk again, after her awful ski accident, nine months before she was dancing; but she was correct in supposing that the injury was graver by far than the doctors had let on. Mike Mitchell used to sail with an old friend, the owner of a racing boat, and the friend's freshly taken wife. The bride flatly insisted that there was no reason at all for a sailboat to right itself after being knocked over on its side, with the result that, whenever the boat heeled over sharply, she would don her life preserver, recite her prayers, and prepare to abandon ship—a comprehensively distracting performance in a Sunday afternoon's race. I told Pat, who shared the same suspicion, that Mike's friend had finally taken his wife to a psychiatrist for help. The psychiatrist, himself a sailor, ended by treating the husband rather than the wife. He explained that the problem with his patient was not neurological, nor psychiatric; merely common-sense-psychological. He prescribed for her one of those roly-poly dolls little children amuse themselves with. They knock it down, only to see it bounce up again. It is Wimpy-like in shape, at bottom full of sealed-in bird shot. Even if you tilt the head right down to the floor, the center of gravity remains so situated that, the head released, it responds to the weight of the bird shot which, exerting themselves to make an honest woman out of the law of gravity, easily overcome the unweighted head at the other end, rolling the doll back on her feet.

Thus, the doctor explained, a sailboat. If you have ten thousand pounds of lead (exactly what we had on *The Panic*) at the end of six feet of keel (the depth of ours), and the boat is pushed over on its (rounded) side, then, assuming the boat is on its side, you have sixty thousand pounds of force agitating to right that boat.

Meanwhile, since the boat's mast, in the hypothesis, is now parallel to the water, or almost parallel, the sails have obviously lost the air power that knocked the boat over. Accordingly, with sixty-thousand-foot-pounds insisting on rectitude vs. zero pounds insisting on distortion, the boat will right.

"Why do some boats sink then?"

"Other factors," Mike's friend snapped.

I was finally able to persuade Pat early in our cruising career (she resolutely refused to race), even without the roly-poly, that a sailboat *will* right itself. But the second day out on *The Panic*, I noticed a two-inch section of that omnipresent plastic tape on which you punch out labels and the like. It was pegged on the circumference of the boat's inclinometer, a two-dollar piece of hardware you tack on the cockpit bulkhead. Its loose-floated pendulum indicates on an arc the angle of the boat's heel at any given moment. It read, opposite the 25° point on the scale: "PATSY GETS OFF."

For *years* I whispered in her ear the safety features of ocean-going sailboats. I even told her, regally, that—in a sense—the *smaller* the boat, the *greater* the safety, as witness that a cork, bobbing on the water, is indestructible; whereas a destroyer clearly isn't.

That was a mistake; and thereafter she rejoiced at any opportunity to lavish on her friends my implied preference for riding out a storm on a cork in preference to the *Queen Elizabeth*. In my flying days, before we were married, and before I learned to say I'm-going-to-do-it-anyway, I tried telling her that gliders, which I had recently cultivated, were actually safer than motored airplanes, because something could go wrong with the plane motor, but the glider depended only on gravity. That became another of her favorites, and she has several times suggested, with radiant scorn and preferably in large and disgustingly appreciative company, that I should communicate my insight to Pan American which, by doing away with its motors, would increase its safety record and save a lot of money.

And it is true, I have had unpleasant experiences at sea. One or two of them with her aboard; one I tried to conceal from her (a humiliating fiasco). But the time had come to tell her about my resolve, and as the plane circled Dublin, in March, late one afternoon, in a mood of mutual affection, I whispered to her, "Darling, you know something? I'm going to take Cyrano across the Atlantic a year from June." Her answer was reassuringly conventional. "If you do I'll leave you." So far so good. No further mention of the trip for six months, until I was making arrangements for a weekend aboard Cyrano, with Peter and Reggie. "Why?" she asked. "To go over the plans for June." She accepted it; though, like a dying tropical storm, there was static aplenty left to discharge.

How dangerous *is* it?

My first misadventure happened in the spring of my second year at Millbrook School. I was sixteen. My father, four years earlier, had transported me and two of my sisters, much against our will, to boarding school in England for a year, complaining that during the preceding five years (Father was given to exaggeration), he had not understood *a single word* spoken by *a single one* of his ten children, and he could think of no other therapy than to remove us to a culture where, when people speak, *they open their mouths*. It was not at that point feasible to disengage the four oldest, two of them at college; and in any case, all of them had done time at English boarding schools five years earlier. The three youngest had not yet graduated from the nursery, so that left three victims. I detected a bargaining position, and asked my father if he would give me on my return from England a sailboat. He was better than his word, giving me not only a sailboat, but a sailing instructor, who spent the summer with me. I kept the 17-foot Barracuda-class sloop (the design was a wartime casualty) at Lake Wononskopomuc, seven miles from our home in Sharon, Connecticut. It is also known as Lakeville Lake. It is very beautiful, surrounded by high, wooded hills, spring fed, about one square mile, with two landmarks. At one end was Hotchkiss School, at the other, Wanda Landowska.

We raced twice, three times a week, a ragtag fleet of six boats, each of different design. The dictator of the fleet was a retired martinet who had served in some nautical capacity or other during the First World

War and had never got over it. He rejoiced at any infraction of the rules, because it permitted him to schedule, at his lakeside cottage, a court-martial of sorts, which he conducted with great gravity, managing nearly full attendance by the primitively effective expedient of giving all the boat owners a great deal of whiskey to drink, to help them endure the discipline of his ruling, which, after much exegesis, he would eventually divulge. The other five boat owners ranged in age from twenty-five to fifty; I was thirteen, never before (or since) devoted so completely to any single enterprise. Seventy-five races per summer for three summers may strike some as a few races too many. It struck me as too few races by far, and I would go to bed Tuesday and Friday and Saturday nights in delirious anticipation of the next day's drama on the water, waking early to see how the wind was blowing. *Sweet Isolation* (I named the boat in honor of my father's political preferences in 1939) did very well in all but the lightest and heaviest airs. Two of the three years I won the trophy for scoring the most points during the summer. It had been donated by the Lakeville Community Chest—cost, retail, $12.50 —and I still have it. Somewhere.

It was well before the racing season, a cold spring day early in

The author, 1939, and friends, aboard *Sweet Isolation,* on Lakeville Lake.

May. I took out for an afternoon's sail my sister Patricia; her English tutor, Miss Reilly; and a classmate from Millbrook, David Cates. A sudden puff swept down from the surrounding hills and we capsized— it was not unusual to capsize in the lake; it was more a nuisance than an event. A motorboat would tow you to shore, you would bail out the boat, and relaunch her. Though the water was cold, it wasn't paralyzingly cold. But after a few minutes it dawned on us that (a) there were no other boats in sight; (b) we were exactly in mid-lake, and therefore unlikely to be spotted; (c) we had only two life preservers on board; and (d) Miss Reilly did not know how to swim at all and David Cates not at all well.

I decided to leave Patricia (Trish) in charge of the boat; she and David could stay afloat by hanging on to it. Miss Reilly must don one life preserver. I would set out with the other and swim the half mile to Hotchkiss School and get help. A hundred yards along the way I abandoned the life preserver, which was slowing me down. A hundred yards further, I abandoned my shoes, socks, and pants. When I finally reached shore I was bitterly cold and frightened about the condition of the crew. I rushed up the huge lawn that slopes up from the Hotchkiss Boat House, spotted a door in the nearest building and opened it, interrupting a full faculty meeting of the Hotchkiss School presided over by a legendary and terrifying headmaster, learned, austere, caustic, and widely known for his impatience with schoolboyism. I had trouble, shivering in my dripping shorts and T-shirt, making sense; but the Duke, as they called him, emitted calmly a cluster of instructions, which resulted simultaneously in a motor boat's being dispatched to the middle of the lake, my being led off to the infirmary, and a telephone call being placed to my parents. Later that night it was all the subject of great excitement. As is almost always the case, the shock came a little later. David Cates, Trish told me—and he later admitted it—could not have held out much longer.

It was five eventful years later that I took *Sweet Isolation* on a trailer, again with Trish, and my sister Jane, and Richie O'Neill, who would be my roommate at Yale when we matriculated the following month, for a weekend of sailing off Edgartown. During those five years I had graduated from prep school, done a half year at the

59

University of Mexico, basic training in the infantry, then officer's school, then platoon leader in infantry basic training centers, while Richie, a native of Lakeville, graduate of Hotchkiss School, and a boyhood friend, had fought in the war in the Pacific. We all felt terribly grown-up arriving at Martha's Vineyard until the first evening, when the waitress refused to serve the grizzled veterans a beer. Our drivers' licenses betrayed us as being just short of twenty-one— only Jane, freshly graduated from Smith at twenty-two, could order from the bar. After dinner, we took a ride around the harbor in the Edgartown Yacht Club launch, which we boarded as though on our way to our own yacht. I had never before seen an ocean-going fleet of boats—the New York Yacht Club fleet was in. I looked about me with admiration and envy: the trim, exquisitely maintained boats, ranging in size from thirty-five feet to seventy-two feet, with owners and crew comfortably aboard, chatting, drinking, washing the dinner dishes, the little anchor lights almost perfectly integrated with the stars above, the dark profiles softened by the blurred yellow of oil lamps below, the moon highlighting the cross-currents that plague that harbor, causing asymmetrical anchoring patterns, always changing, as the local vectors change to reflect fluctuating strengths and direction of current and wind. I had crossed the Atlantic ten times before the war in big ships, and though the hurricane of 1938, experienced at sea on my way to school in England, was exciting, I was unhooked by the lure of blue-water sailing. But I sensed that night that some time, years away—exactly nine years, it proved—I would be back in the harbor, boarding my own boat.

It was blowing hard the next day as it so often does, and the Yacht Club had its own race going out in the Sound. We launched my little open boat, boarded our lunch, and set out downwind, along Chappaquiddick. A mile out, the mainmast suddenly lurched crookedly aft. The headstay, which connects the top of the mast to the bow, had parted at the turnbuckle, and the foot of the mast, unsecured, slipped proportionately forward along the boat's bottom. The mainsail had to come down and as I loosed the halyard, Trish reached for it, slipped, and fell into the sea, quickly separated from us as we went ineluctably downwind. I reached for a heavy prewar outboard motor, seated it with difficulty on the transom mount, and quickly threaded the starting

60

cord. I pulled it once, twice, ten times. By now Trish was barely visible astern. We could not tack our way back to her without re-rigging the headstay, which required straightening the mast. Richie tried starting the motor. My heart beat in an agony of frustration. It was then that, with great poise, a launch suddenly materialized, and a moment later we could see Trish being hauled out of the water. The launch then came to us, threw out a line, and towed us back into the harbor. Everyone was talking when we were reunited at the dock, and I was cursing the outboard motor and the defective turnbuckle, and, exhaustedly, we trudged back to our hotel. Late in the afternoon I returned alone to attend to the boat, sitting now in a boatyard, and concealed behind its hull, I wept, hysterical at the thought of what had very nearly happened. I had very nearly drowned my sister. It was, to use the word formally, a genuine trauma. It haunted me into my twenties. I rehearsed a thousand times what I should have done. It was as simple as instantly—by reflex action—tossing out a life preserver. *The moment someone goes overboard.* It sounds axiomatic. But at sea in an emergency very little is axiomatic that you have not silently drilled yourself to do, like straightening your wheels when you begin skidding in the snow. Man-overboard is the single most dangerous menace of the sea.

It does not exactly classify as a misadventure of the perils-of-the-sea variety when your ship sinks and you are not in it, but it is the kind of thing that creates apprehension in people like Pat, and even in people unlike Pat.

It was only two months before our first Bermuda Race, and the office operator told me the boatyard was calling. (I have, by the way, long since discovered how, if you want to get through on the telephone to otherwise unapproachable people, you do it to yachtsmen. You simply tell the operator you are calling from the boatyard. No yachtsman in the history of the world has ever been too busy to talk to his boatyard.) It was Miss Swann. Miss Swann is imperturbable. Her voice is high, but softly pitched. But what she had to inform me of this morning simply could not be done equanimously. It would have been a violation of taste, a confession of—insouciance.

"Mr. Buckley, I'm afraid I have some bad news."

"What is it, Miss Swann?"

"*The Panic* sank."

"Sank?"

It transpired that, going down to the dock that morning, the yardmen had seen, in the space previously occupied by a forty-four-foot steel cutter, only fifty feet of mast rising straight, indeed, proudly, one supposes, out of the water. Everything stopped, and the whole force of the yard was mobilized to pump out the boat and bring her slowly to the surface.

The damage was unspeakable. When the seawater reached the level of the batteries, the acid drew out. Since the hull was made of steel, the entire boat was converted, so to speak, into a huge magnetic field which corrosively began to gnaw away at the wiring, reducing it in a few hours to copper filigree.

Miss Swann having prepared me, she put me on to Mr. Muzzio, the volatile, peppery, omnicompetent owner of the yard.

We would need, he said, new wiring throughout, a rebuilt engine, a new generator, all new upholstery, a new radio direction finder, a new radio telephone. He was sure the sails had survived—they had been quickly washed in fresh water. The gas and water tanks he thought would survive. And he did not know whether all that work could be completed in time for the Bermuda Race, but he would make every effort.

"What happened?" I managed to ask.

"I don't know," he said. "We checked all the sea cocks. They're okay." If Mr. Muzzio didn't know what happened, it was unlikely that anyone would know; but even as the work began, I found it endlessly disconcerting that the boat, sitting jauntily at the dock one night, three days after it had last been sailed, should simply . . . sink. I have found that there is something less than an unquenchable intellectual curiosity among professional boat people. The insurance company had to pay out ten thousand dollars to put *The Panic* right, but I found it impossible to engage the company's inspector in anything like an exhaustive discussion of what might have been the cause of it all, even though Stamford, Connecticut, does not lie within the perimeter of the Bermuda Triangle, where one Isn't Supposed To Ask What Happened. The reason there are so many mysteries at sea is that nobody bothers to try to solve them. This particular mystery, continuously disconcerting—I was half afraid to leave *The Panic* at anchor alone for the balance of the year—was solved, quite accidentally, under circumstances more hectic than the sedentary, regal sinking in the womb of Muzzio Brothers Yacht Yard.

It was over a year after my family had rechristened my boat *The Ti-panic*, and we were racing from Annapolis to Newport. All night long we had tacked against a relentless southerly, fighting our way down the Chesapeake. At ten in the morning I was off duty and sound asleep, with Mike Mitchell at the wheel, when Reggie woke me. In his calm way he told me to look down at the floorboards. They were underwater. I jumped up, tore open the floorboards and saw a mass of water overflowing the bilges, rushing up into the lockers with every leeward roll of the ship. Reggie and I could feel no water coming into the boat from the engine water-cooling system or from the stuffing box. A quick investigation of the sea cocks showed them to be in good working order. Two crew members were mobilized to work the big hand pump. Working steadily, they managed only just to keep pace with the leak. I raced back to the cockpit, and Reggie, Mike, and I conferred. The water is shallow in the Chesapeake, and in the southern section there are stretches of mud and sand at depths of two feet. We decided the only thing to do was to head for a sand shoal and beach *The Panic* before it sank under us. I took the wheel and a bearing, bore off the wind, and headed for shallow water about a mile away, while Mike jumped into the bilges to have his own look. Seven or eight minutes later he ambled up, a smile on his face and a beer in his hand. "Let's get back on course. I found the trouble."

The electric bilge pump, which Reggie had switched on even before waking me, was of course the first mechanism I checked, and it was humming away industriously, though its capacity was insufficient to keep up with the flow of water coming into the boat. But Mike, unsatisfied, unscrewed the hose from the pump, thinking that perhaps the rubber impeller had burned and if he replaced it, we might get some relief. He found that the pump was working fine, except that instead of drawing water from the boat into the sea, it was drawing water from the sea into the boat. Astonished, he turned the switch off; then on again—and suddenly the flow of water was in the right direction. In a minute or two he could see the water level receding.

Here was the mystery solved. An electrical pump sucks water from the bilge and pressures it up a hose that becomes a copper pipe rising above the water level outside the boat. The pipe elbows around, and the water falls by gravity down the pipe and out to sea through an open sea cock.

We could now easily reconstruct what had happened. A piece of mud or sponge or whatever had been sucked up from the bilge and was rising under pressure up the pipe just at the moment, some time during the night, when the bilges were last checked, and a crew member, finding the bilges dry, had turned off the pump. There the foreign matter lodged, beneath sea level, like a cork, sustaining the weight of the water above it. In due course, the cork began to dissolve, and the dammed waterfall poured into the bilge creating a suction sufficient to bring a continuous flow of water up from the sea to the elbow. And now, by the law that specifies that water will seek its own level, Chesapeake Bay was happily filling up the cavity in the hull of *The Panic*. And of course the more water we took in, the lower the boat sank, guaranteeing a disparity in water level until our boat's decks were level with the sea. At this point water would cease flowing into our bilges, a point of only academic comfort since the boat would then sink like a full bathtub. When Reggie turned the electric pump on, the impeller was set into motion, but the pressure of the water flowing down redirected the innocent pump's energies, which now added mechanical pressure to the gravitational pressure bringing seawater into the boat. It was instantly clear what had caused *The Panic* to sink the year before: but on that occasion, it had taken two and a half days for the clot in the pipe to disintegrate.

It was simplicity itself to guard against a recurrence of the problem. You merely snip out a tiny section from the pipe that moves down to the sea cock; so that if a reverse flow were started, it would abort at that air hole.

End of problem. But there is always the scar left over, causing you to wonder: How many other causes are there, potentially, for boats suddenly to drown? And isn't it strange—and disturbing—that there wasn't a diagnostician around after it happened once to *The Panic?* Why didn't the mechanic put in an air hole? Five years ago? Ten thousand dollars ago?

Three months after every Bermuda Race and every Annapolis-Newport Race, which run on alternate years, comes the last of the season's major ocean races, the annual Vineyard Race, in which I had made my debut the year before. This time I was the skipper. We had rounded the lightship and were headed now 130 miles almost due west, to the finish line at Stamford. Mike was at the tiller when I went below to sleep. The spinnaker was flying under a stiff northeasterly, the fog was pearly thick, and we posted a member of the crew forward to listen hard, away from the distractions of cockpit-talk and grinding winches, while every few minutes we sounded our own foghorn and occasionally looked up for reassurance at the radar reflector, designed to attract maximum attention on the radar screens of the big boats.

I slept fitfully, and in due course was summoned to relieve Mike. It was nearing midnight and, always the competitor, he was very excited. *See over there!* he pointed ahead. I could make out a few lights through the fog, a stern light, and masthead light, and perhaps a flashlight. "We're overhauling that poor bastard!" Mike exulted, handing me the tiller. He stepped up from the cockpit to experience from the deck the special pleasure of sliding by a competitor. Mike was right. We were getting closer and closer. I checked the compass —dead on the course I had stipulated. I eased the bow the slightest bit up to make certain we would be comfortably to windward of the boat. Then came the screech, the ricocheting crunch of steel bouncing over rocks and, in a moment, motionlessness.

There is nothing to match the motionlessness of running solidly aground. It is as if concrete had suddenly hardened around you. Now that we were no longer moving downwind at eight knots, the wind on our backs was eight knots stronger. A hundred yards away was the boat we were pursuing, now plainly visible. Two forlorn street lights, one mile north of Point Judith. We were two miles off course.

I looked down at the compass in dismay. Even now it pointed us in the direction I had charted. All in due course. Meanwhile there was urgent work to be done. Already Reggie had the tide tables out. He told us in his matter-of-fact way that we were one hour and a half past low tide, that the water would be high just before five in the morning. We called Peter, who was thirteen years old and asleep in the forecastle, but there was no rousing him. We pulled up a hundred yards of chain past his ear, and two hundred yards of line, and he heard nothing. The boat's steel hull ground away on the rocks, and he heard nothing. We eased our heaviest anchor into the dinghy and rowed out a hundred yards astern. After attaching our nylon mooring line to the anchor, we let the anchor drop into the water, rowed back, and attached the end of the line to a bridle we rigged from one to the other of our heavy Genoa winches, situated across from each other above the cockpit. Now we had a harness of sorts, allowing us to apply simultaneous pressure on both winches. Thus prepared, we began working the boat aft, using also the reverse power of the engine at full rpm. We succeeded in moving about five yards, but we came then on something like an underwater stone wall, over which, under the careening force of eight knots, *The Panic* had leaped. She was not about to leap back over even at the urging of a couple of No. 4 winches. We finally stopped and I cut the motor.

It was the moment to call the Coast Guard.

To my astonishment, the Coast Guard station at Point Judith, which, after all, was almost within hailing distance, acknowledged our distress signal immediately. After a considerable conference at the other end, we were advised that we lay in waters so pockmarked with rocky shoals that no Coast Guard vessel could approach us to bring help without endangering itself. The officer recommended that we wait until the next day and get a barge from Newport to float us out. We were not, after all, in any personal danger, the Coast Guard reminded us—all we had to do, to start out life afresh, would be to abandon ship and walk to the beach. And, to be sure, wake up Peter.

There was nothing to do except to make a massive effort at exactly high tide. To lighten the boat, we emptied our water tanks (we had 120 gallons, which at about eight pounds per gallon is a lot of weight). It was then, I think, that, noticing the spotlight weakening, I decided to put a fresh battery into it to be ready for the big effort at four-thirty; but I couldn't find the spare battery. Mike poked around. "Here it is," he said, opening the binnacle box. I removed the battery. "Do that again," Reggie said, "—and look at the compass." The battery removed, the compass changed its heading eleven degrees. I can't remember exactly what I said. I think it was "Sheey*it*." I had recently read *The One Hundred Dollar Misunderstanding*, and was much influenced by its idiom.

We made it, but it was close. If the wind had been from the southeast, we would not have had the protection of the peninsula opposite, and the waves during the night would have battered the boat to pieces. A wooden boat would probably not have survived. As it was, the damage to the keel and rudder was extensive.

That was the episode I thought we could safely conceal from our families without any problem at all, and so it was agreed all the way around. There was, theoretically, no need to conceal it from Peter, who was entirely unaware of it, waking relaxed at about seven. I would simply say that we had withdrawn from the race because our spinnaker had blown out, and there was no substitute. In the early afternoon, we stumbled into a marina in New London and docked. I went to the telephone and reached Pat in Vancouver, three thousand miles away. Her first words were peremptory: "What time did you get off the rocks?" At least she said it before listening to a vivid narrative about the decomposition of the spinnaker.

I could not tease out of her the sources of her intelligence until, home from her visit to her parents, she finally broke down, with great relish. She had been at a cocktail party while her father, at home, listened on the radio to the evening news on what must have been a very slow night: because the last item was to the effect that the Coast Guard in Boston had reported that the cutter *Panic*, owned by the writer William F. Buckley, Jr., was on the rocks off Point Judith, Rhode Island. My father-in-law was a heavy man of decisive mien and habit. He dispatched the chauffeur for his daughter, authorized only to instruct her that she was to return instantly to the house. There with great solemnity he gave her the news, and in due course the Canadian Admiralty in Ottawa was on the telephone to the Coast Guard in Boston, which relayed back a conversation with the Coast Guard in Point Judith to the effect that nothing more had been heard from *The Panic*, but that there was no reason to fear for the safety of the crew. Mike's father had heard the same broadcast, and welcomed his son home exuberantly with a new drink, "Point Judith Scotch" (on the rocks).

A misadventure. It taught me not only to inspect the compass area from time to time for magnetic distractions, but never ever to rely on a compass alone, if there was an alternative to doing so, in a fog anywhere near land. A radio direction finder, trained on Point Judith, would have alerted us to a deteriorating situation. There were, of course, weeks and years ahead of us to improvise on Mike's calling enthusiastic attention to boats we were about to overtake.

The most illuminating experience I had had at sea was in October 1958. Pat's brother Firpo and I (we were co-owners) resolved to cruise *The Panic* to Bermuda, leave it there during the winter, and in the spring charter it by the day to tourists who desired a cruise in Bermudan waters. We yanked Peter out of school, and assembled a crew, fine fellows all, but undistinguished as seamen through no fault of theirs. I picked the fifteenth of October to set out because on the one hand we wanted weather as warm as possible; on the other, we wanted to be on the safe side of the hurricane period. The United States Naval Oceanographic Office puts out a chart for every month of every year on which are tracked the major storms and the paths they traveled the same month during the preceding ten (or more) years. Our chart showed only one storm (hurricane) in the general area after the fifteenth of October, and it did its mischief comfortably to the east of Bermuda.

Docked at 23rd Street on the East River, we gave a little going-away party at noon on the fifteenth to which a dozen friends came. My brother John arrived with the most hilariously inappropriate gift: an eight-foot-tall potted palm tree. With much ado, we wedged the pot astern, between the lazarette cover and the cap rail and tied the big red ribbon that came with it around the little willowy trunk to the backstay. Eight days later, in an entirely different mood, we tenderly planted it in Bermudan soil. It had, in surviving the vicissitudes of the passage, become our talisman, and now we were paying it our last respects.

What happened, after three or four of the most beautiful days of sailing I can remember—crisp cool days, with the wind steady from the southeast, the Kenyon never reading below eight knots, the moon at night framed by clouds, tricked into providing us a kind of private, silvery superhighway, New York–Bermuda, Non-Stop, Reserved for *The Panic*—was, first, that we hit a most awful storm. It came on us suddenly. Clearly, though moving slowly, it had been building doggedly, until now it began to run. We had an anemometer (wind-speed indicator) on board that at midnight clocked winds of seventy knots, which is hurricane speed (anything over sixty-four is). Late in the afternoon, when it was blowing about fifty knots, I decided to heave to. I had never done this before, but this clearly was the time to see what that maneuver would do for us; so I gave Firpo the tiller and, with Peter, went forward, took down the No. 3 jib and replaced it with the storm jib, which we led back through a snatch block to the windward Genoa winch. We had already prepared the storm trysail on the track to the side of the mast, like a spare train, ready, by pulling the switch, to track up the mainmast. Now we pulled down the reefed mainsail and ran up the storm trysail. The storm trysail is what they call "loose-footed," which is to say the foot (i.e., the bottom side of the triangle), like the forward sails, is not fastened to the boom, so that the air can spill out between it and the main boom, to which only its clew (i.e., the corner furthest aft) is fastened. We then pulled the mainsheet as tight as possible, flattening the sail. Then, taking the tiller, I shoved it over as far as I could to leeward. The boat edged up into the wind . . . and wobbled into it, without the strength to come about, but with enough to cause the mainsail to luff: whereupon the jib, led aback, brought the bow once again to leeward. I could move the rudder back a little from its extreme hard-left position, or I could ease slightly the mainsheet. I tried the tiller, and now the effect was eerie. The boat came to virtually a dead stop, both sails hard. I looked about me in triumph. We could have played a game of checkers in the cockpit, except that the checkers would have blown away. I took a piece of line and made a becket, securing the tiller in place; about as complicated as tying a shoelace.

Here is what happens when you heave to. To begin with, you hoist only enough canvas (made out of the toughest material) as is, on the one hand, necessary to dictate the boat's movement; and on the other, not so much as to challenge the storm's machismo. Less sail

69

than the two storm sails, there isn't. If the wind is too strong to allow you to keep even them up, then you do something most appropriately named—you "run." Downwind. Always in a bad storm your objective is *to reduce your speed in the water*. *Pace* Pat, the bobbing-cork idea is the objective.

Bear in mind that the wind does not distinguish between an obstacle made of canvas and one made of steel or wood. So if you run, even without so much as a handkerchief hoisted, you are still—as far as the wind is concerned—an obstacle, which is the square measurement of everything that lies above the water and is exposed to the wind. If you take a picture of a sailboat, sails furled, from dead astern, you will note that this is a considerable area. Add to the obvious transom that much of the freeboard that swells out before reaching the lee side of the beam, the area of the mast, the cockpit bulkheads, the cockpit coaming, indeed, the helmsman's back, and you see that there is a great deal that stands up against the wind. Enough, in very strong air, to generate dangerous forward speeds. Dangerous because there is no practical means of synchronizing your movements and those of the waves, which are in any case irregular and sometimes highly erratic; so if you are running at, say, eight knots, you will soon find the bow of the boat submarining into the bosom of a huge wave, causing great havoc. It is in such situations that some boats can even pitchpole, i.e., do an entire vertical somersault, the mainmast, for a moment or two, pointing down like a surrealistic fin centerboard, and the keel up, like the dorsal fin of a whale. People have survived pitchpoling; but no mast has done so; and one must assume that there are people who have not survived pitchpoling—which by the way is likelier in a centerboard boat than in a keel boat. Short of pitchpoling, there is the dangerous yaw, the bow digging into the water, the stern bouncing off, leaving your beam for the wind and waves to work on. How do you, then, if you are running, keep down the speed of the boat? By trailing lines (the easiest way) —each line is an anchor of sorts, and you can keep tying them together so as to form a huge bight. By trailing a sea anchor, which is like a huge canvas parachute designed to brake the boat's motion by dragging underwater (sheer hell to retrieve); and you can even use reverse engine power.

70

Moreover, you can also let the boat travel backward, if your boat is the kind that does that more comfortably, i.e., trail your lines forward, and haul up into the wind. But beware the rudder. Sudden backward movements with the rudder off-center can wrench and disable the rudder. It is better, of course, for the great breakers to attack you from the bow of the boat than from the stern, because they will be partly dissipated by the cabin trunk before reaching you. You can, when things have come to such a pass, put a can of oil in a bag filled with rags, punch a couple of holes in it with an ice pick, and trail it from a point on the boat as far forward as possible—for example, in Cyrano's case, off our twelve-foot-long bowsprit. The instant slick of the oil is said to prevent most waves from breaking under its umbrella, at the center of which is you. I have never had to run or use oil.

When maneuvering to heave to, you are fine-tuning right-left oscillations in the heading of a boat to the point of rendering them nugatory. It is as though you brought your right and left hands steadily toward each other, with a swinging pendulum in between making its strokes shorter and shorter and shorter, causing, ultimately, immobility.

The wind catches the little trysail aft, and, because the tiller is held over to leeward, the boat's bow swings up into the wind. But no sooner has it done so than it exposes the forward sail—the jib—to the wind. To lead a jib *aback* is to lead it, not to leeward, where it belongs, but to windward. In that way you reach out for the wind, catching it before you are headed directly into it. The wind's force is now trapped by the jib, propelling the bow back to leeward; but the moment it has moved a mere matter of inches, the aftersail has again caught the wind, reversing the swing. A well-balanced boat, perfectly tuned, will heave to in such a way as to make the oscillations imperceptible. The wind is, quite simply, stymied; and you have become like the cork. There *is* forward motion (otherwise your rudder would be inoperative); but we are talking about two knots or so.

It was eerie primarily because of the contrast. The noise from the wind tearing through the shrouds and the lifelines was a continuous howl, reaching a screech, like a tightening violin string, when the wind came in furious puffs. The waves rise and fall a dozen feet above your head, and you rise and fall, but the waves do not break over you. The dodger, a canvas windscreen of sorts over the companionway, protects totally the faces of the two men who nestle at that end of the cockpit, and it occurred to me that there was no reason for three men to stay on watch. There was nothing to do except sit there, wait it out; and so we ate something, and went through the night. I rested with some apprehension, always alert to the sibilant wind and roaring seas, and wondering what possibly could go wrong and what would I do in the chaos if something did go wrong, trying in my mind to match problem with solution.

Nothing did go wrong. The next morning, at about eleven, I made a mistake. The wind had slightly abated. It was back to fifty knots, and I was growing restless. We were pointed southwest, and Bermuda lay southeast. It occurred to me that we should try to resume course and sail on a broad reach under storm jib alone, making at least a little progress toward our destination. So I loosed the becket and took the tiller in hand, and ordered the storm trysail brought down. The windward jib sheet was eased inch by inch and the strain taken on the leeward sheet. It was in tight when I said: "Here we go," and brought the tiller up to take the bow downwind. We suffered an immediate knockdown.

A knockdown is when the boat suddenly goes from vertical to horizontal, or nearly horizontal. I have had only three honest-to-God knockdowns in my life, one of them at the start of the 1958 Bermuda Race. Generally they hit you when your boat is practically at a standstill. If you are moving along, a sudden gust of wind will cause you to heel over, but the forward movement of your boat absorbs the suddenness of the blast and distributes it into its component parts, absorbed by keel, sails, and rudder.

I did not believe that *The Panic* could be made to suffer a knockdown when flying only a storm *jib*. But it did; and it was so severe that we were on our side. A huge wave from abeam bulldozed into us, wrenching the entire binnacle stand from its mount on the cockpit floor, heaving it over toward the sea. Peter lurched out and grabbed it a second before it fell into the ocean, his torso stretched over the lifeline. Firpo grabbed him around the waist and kept him, and the binnacle, from going over. I yelled to loosen the

Chaotic start of Bermuda Race, 1958. *The Panic* recovering from a knockdown. WFB at wheel.

jib sheet, but it was almost immediately unnecessary. We were righting on our own inertia, the sixty thousand pounds of pressure on the keel asserting themselves, roly-poly-doll-wise. The cockpit was half under water; we loosed the jib sheet well out, and within a minute were making five knots toward Bermuda.

I especially remember, during the next six hours, the waves. The wind kept abating. But the waves, as if sullen at the wind's default, grew hilly, then mountainous. Not since the storm in 1938, viewed from the porthole of a cabin in the S.S. *Paris*, had I seen anything like them. They rose thirty feet high. But *The Panic* was untroubled, and in due course we shook out our reefed mainsail;

and then our No. 3 jib. At noon the sun was briefly out, and I snatched a latitude and established our position as on a line that ran seventy miles north of Bermuda. The trouble was, I did not have any close idea of our longitude, and the sun wasn't out in the afternoon to permit me a running fix. Our radio direction finder began picking up a commercial station in Bermuda, and the crew was lighthearted in anticipation of arriving perhaps a little bit after midnight. The off-watch declined its privileges, preferring to stay up now to the end. At about 6:00 P.M., a Bermuda patrol boat cruised up to us in the ebbing light. I shouted out: "Give me a course to Gibbs Hill!" He shot back: "A hundred and twenty degrees." I was putting the information on the chart (Bermuda has to be approached with extreme care—it is like a starfish of coral reefs), when Firpo told me to come up and look at the extraordinary horizon. It was certainly extraordinary. We were completely surrounded by low, low clouds, not much higher than a steamer on the water's edge, black as pitch. The wind was suddenly gone. The skies grew grayer as the light faded and the black noose began to tighten, and I felt a sudden touch of air in my face, cold, undecided. I gave orders to bring down *all* sails. Something was going to hit us imminently from somewhere. In five minutes the storm was back and, laboriously, once again we hove to. The wind was not as heavy as before, but it rained now from time to time, hard, passionate rain, and the direction of the boat kept changing as the storm danced around us. No one slept. The next day was gray and lumpy, and now the serious question was, *Where are we?* Miraculously, the sun appeared at about noon for exactly as long as it takes to get a single sight, and I put us at forty miles north of Bermuda—but once again, longitude uncertain.

It was about 7:00 P.M. that I became creepingly aware that the crew was demoralized. No one would eat. The dishes were piled up from the last three meals. There was no conversation, no unnecessary motion. I saw such a scene once before, in the infantry, when a company of soldiers completing their basic training was ordered to storm a hill to seize imaginary enemy installations. It was noon; the temperature, 110 degrees. At midnight the night before the trainees had been made to crawl on their bellies under barbed wire and tracer ammunition, only to be awakened at 2:00 A.M. for a forced march.

They started up the hill: and then, as if rehearsed, they all stopped and sat down. Nothing mutinous. They simply could not move on. Discipline was out of the question. Our shrewd battalion commander was called in by walkie-talkie. He looked at the men only briefly, then dispatched four trucks from the base, loaded the men onto them, and took them to a lakeside, where they swam.

A crew member slightly more alert than the others came back from the emergency storeroom with two large tins of hardtack. I reached into the tangle beside the icebox and got out a bottle of port. Hardtack looks like dog biscuits, but tastes slightly better, I think. Port goes well with hardtack. Soon everyone had a glass of port and was munching a biscuit. And beginning to talk. I told them there was no point in trying to make progress under sail tonight. We could not approach Bermuda without a more specific idea of where Bermuda was, because of the shoals. Under the circumstances, we would set only a No. 3 jib for stability, and more or less hold our own on an easterly course. Two men would stay up, but only for two-hour watches. The other five would sleep.

The next morning the recovery was complete. It was a brilliant blue day and we spotted a cruise ship, obviously headed toward Bermuda. In a few hours I had a running fix, showing that the storms had taken us forty miles west of Bermuda. We began to slog against the easterly, tacking, tacking. At 4:00 P.M., a Coast Guard plane buzzed down and, obviously, recorded our sail number. At seven we saw Gibbs Hill Light. (The radio direction finder was 40° off calibration.) Still there was five hours of tacking left to do before, a few minutes after midnight, we rounded the shoal area, easing, exhausted, into St. George's Harbor—seven days out of New York.

The radio telephone had not worked. My wife's anxiety mounted, and telephone calls between her and her mother in Vancouver grew in frequency. That very morning, her mother acted. She telephoned Pat and announced calmly, imperiously: "Tell the Coast Guard to go out and find them. And to send *me* the bill."

The airplane, that afternoon, had done its duty.

Never permit an off-duty watch to stay on duty.

Better to cease purposive motion altogether, if necessary, to restore a crew, than to flail about with an overtired and demoralized crew.

Do not depend on the accessibility of sun and stars if you are near land.

You need at least one other navigational instrument.

It was after that trip to Bermuda that Reggie designed, and I wrote up and published, a Consolan chart. But Consolan, the cheapest, neatest little off-shore navigation system ever devised, is defunct now. I mourn its passing, but I have useful things to say on the general subject of ocean navigation; soon now.

As to *Suzy*, I can remember every variety of mechanical misadventure: The only thing I can think she forgot to contract was teredos in her aluminum masts. Though, always, her specialty has been eating Westerbeke engines for breakfast. The kind of thing that goes wrong in boats I have something to say about, of an iconoclastic sort. But perils-of-the-sea-wise, the ill-timed crossing of the Reversing Falls at Saint John is relevant. I had traversed them before, with Peter and Reggie and Bruce (RIP), on a crazy sail from Digby, Nova Scotia, across the Bay of Fundy, in a cold fog. Crazy because having no radio, I navigated by dead reckoning, carefully precalculating the tidal vector across the forty-mile passage. It was fog all the way. Reaching land (we had a hundred yards' visibility), we could not discern where we were. After an hour's Braille-close, snail's-pace investigation of the looming, eccentrically-lit presence we had been keeping away from, we established that it wasn't land or a fort, but a large cargo ship at anchor. We approached it and motioned that we wished to come aboard. The officer, relying on hat and fingers, was obliging, and we expressed our desire to look at the position on his chart. There was the difficulty that he spoke no language any of us knew, including pig Latin, and he led us exuberantly to the infirmary. Eventually we devised, through an ad-hoc revision in the rules of charades, a means of telling him what we wanted; and, lo, it transpired that we were exactly where we were headed for, at the mouth of the Saint John River.

I resist as somehow extraneous the temptation to describe that river (the most beautiful in the world) and the sensation of passing through the falls from the typical fog and wet of Saint John into the sunny fairyland of New Brunswick. The point of this story springs from the Reversing Falls' being a natural phenomenon of sorts. What you have on the one hand is the Bay of Fundy, with its famous, gargantuan tidefall—forty feet is typical. Enough power, rushing in and out twice a day, could it be harnessed, to generate electricity to light the world; or so they say. And what you have on the other hand is a four-hundred-mile-long river with a tidefall of one inch that debouches into the Bay of Fundy. When the Bay is flooding, and before the bay water rises to the level of the river water, all of the Saint John River is falling into the Bay, and the transitional mile between the river and the bay looks something like the runway to Niagara Falls. No boat could survive in those rapids for a moment; indeed they are so spectacularly scary, tourists come from all over just to sit and stare. When the Bay is ebbing and before the bay water falls below the level of the river water, all of the Bay of Fundy is pouring into the Saint John River, the transitional mile between the river and the bay looking exactly the same as usual—except that the rapids are running in the opposite direction. Do not ask why, but it happens that exactly two hours and twenty-five minutes after high tide, and three hours and fifty minutes after low tide, the Bay of Fundy and the Saint John River fight each other to an irenic stand-still; and then the water is as smooth as a skating rink.

For ten minutes.

Which is when you power across.

One night, Pat on board, she begged us to wait until the morning, but we cooed her into a resigned silence, marked time with a lengthy, gourmet dinner, and took off at 11:02. We were two minutes early. I do not know whether our time was off or even whether through some inexplicable miscalculation we had taken the time from the wrong table. Reggie was below, leaning over the navigation table atop the icebox, as arranged, to feed me quick-fire navigational instructions. But the current scooped us up, and while Reggie was intoning calmly, *"Keep at 295° for exactly four minutes, toward the fixed white light,"* I was headed at 020° toward an Esso station which I would land on in about two minutes. When the current is taking you faster than your engine drives you, the rudder has no effect. Reggie, intent on his assignment, crouched over his magnifying glass, was saying things like: *"On your right, you should be seeing a flashing green approximately abeam."* Meanwhile a surge of yellow-gray foam lunged toward us, like sea lava about to overtake us. It proved to be the discharge of pulp deposits from a mill that lets it all go just as the tide begins to turn. We were within a hundred yards of the filling station when, gradually, like the feeling that creeps slowly into your hands after a frostbite, the rudder began to respond. The equilibrium was finally upon us, and the amphibious operation against Esso Petroleum was aborted. The lessons are too obvious to expatiate upon. I have in fact wondered why the city of Saint John does not indulge itself a navigational light that turns green from red when the precious ten minutes begin. Perhaps they have to provide an occasional wreck to maintain tourist interest.

Again Pat was on board when we were racing with the New York Yacht Club, destination Block Island, sailing out of New London. It was blowing hard, and we were tacking with the No. 2 Genoa.

The sequence had its comic side. Van has friends in Paris, a couple who maintain an apartment with a tiny terrace in full view of the Eiffel Tower. During the summer months, whether there are guests there or not, the couple proceed through a balletic sequence that gives them the greatest pleasure, day after day, year after year. At exactly twelve seconds before nine (they have an ornamental, but Houston-Control-accurate chronometer), Wife says to Husband, "Darling, don't you think it would be nice to put on the lights?" "Why yes, of course, dear," Husband replies, proceeding to walk at a torturedly rehearsed pace over to the veranda door, reaching to one side, flipping a switch—and, lo! all the lights *on the Eiffel Tower* flash on. Lighting the Eiffel Tower lights in France—like starting the bullfights in Mexico—is the only thing that is done there with Apollo-like precision. The effect on guests is, needless to say, electric.

Leigh Seaver (who succeeded Peter as first mate) was standing on the windward side of the mast, trying to catch my attention. The wind was too noisy to shout, so he waved his hand. I saw him, and he directed my gaze down to a stanchion he wished me to know was loose. He leaned down in a didactic gesture—he would show me what was wrong with the stanchion—and yanked it up from its mount. It was like the Eiffel Tower story, whose generic grandfather is the

78

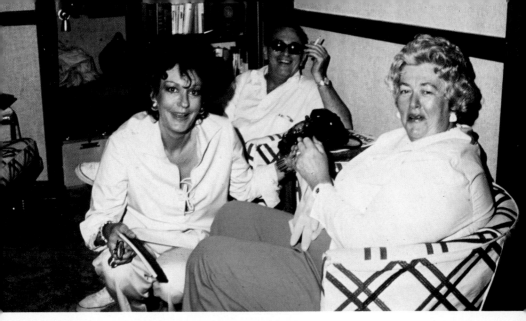

Pat and Marvin seeing us off

View from the crow's nest

Departing Miami

Arriving in Gibraltar

Piloting

Maintenance

children's joke about unscrewing the belly button and the posteriors falling off. In that instant the entire fifty-foot-tall mast broke off six feet up from the deck and splashed into the churning water, a mass of lines, cable, wood with huge jagged splinters, and six hundred square feet of sail.

There are few things worse that can happen to a sailboat. Dozens—hundreds—of boats have been dismasted without loss of life. It is not quite like losing the wings of an airplane, because you are not thereafter required to sink. But the feeling of helplessness is total. In such circumstances one takes the emergency cable cutters and snips away, as required, to float out the jagged trunk and prevent it from penetrating the boat's hull. Several crew members busied themselves doing this, bringing in sail and line, while Reggie called the Coast Guard. He gave them the bearing from the boat to the Coast Guard station, taken from our radio direction finder. When, an hour later, the Coast Guard cutter had still not arrived, we called again—and learned that the CG had sent the cutter on our bearing out to sea, i.e., in exactly the opposite direction. If I say to you over the radio: "You bear ninety degrees from me," and you decide to come to where I am, you must set out on a course of 270°. (Moral: Be extremely, childishly, explicit, when making emergency communications.)

What happened? I have demonstrated that the support of the mast is the supreme obligation of a boat's standing rigging. Where a shroud reaches the deck, it is attached to the boat by what they call a "chain plate." This should be the single strongest part of the boat and, accordingly, modern chain plates are regularly made out of stainless steel. They are usually invisible to the naked eye, but they reach down as far as two or even three feet, sometimes as a fork, the better to distribute the strain. They are bolted through the sturdiest cross-planking in the boat. It is inconceivable in any well-designed boat that chain plates would pull out. One of ours, holding down the upper shroud that passes over the spreader to the masthead, did. Rather, it broke in two. I retrieved the pieces and gave them to an engineer to inspect. He discovered a bubble in the casting. Courtesy of Hong Kong. The boat had sailed thirty thousand miles since being built, and the bubble hadn't burst. Now it did. Who knows what was the proximate cause. Metal fatigue, probably. Yielding, perhaps, to a sudden snap of the mast, if the corresponding leeward shroud was a little loose. They call this a "latent defect." I have not inquired whether there is insurance against latent defects; in any event, our insurance company came through. Incredibly, a boat-manufacturing company, owned by a friend of Reggie, putting its assembly line at our disposal, had us four days later racing again with the fleet.

Several times, Cyrano has run aground in Bahamian waters. Running aground on a sandy bottom in a rising tide is nothing much to worry about. Running into coral heads is very worrisome. Bahamian waters are, of course, the worst-charted, worst-lit waters in the traveled parts of the world, so the first time I cruised in them in winter I was glad to hear the captain chosen by Ned Killeen to relieve him (so that Ned could spend Christmas week with his family) confess, through his endearing shyness, to knowing "Bahamian waters like the palm of my hand." Accordingly, I yielded to Frank Roepken the navigational responsibility, and as we were returning the last day out to Nassau, late in the afternoon, seven or eight miles southeast of the harbor, *CRUNCH!* that unmistakable, heart-stopping noise: wood against rock. The boat stopped dead. We pulled down the sails and gunned her into reverse. Slowly she began to move, and everyone cheered. She had no sooner picked up reverse speed than—*CRUNCH!* We hit to the rear. Evidently it was not an isolated coral reef we had first hit. After extricating ourselves, I gave instructions to throw out anchors forward and aft: We would remain in the area overnight, notwithstanding that Ned was waiting on shore and the charterers (friends) were to pick up the boat, spick-and-span, two days later. Cyrano is built like a battleship; even so, we had sprung a leak forward, and a night watch was maintained in case it got worse. Before going to bed I wandered back to the steering area. Captain Roepken, sprawled out on the aft companionway, gangly as J. K. Galbraith, was listening to a portable radio. The news announcer, out of Nassau, was reporting on a visit he had just had with a prisoner in the death cell, who would be hanged in the morning.

"I know just how that poor bastard feels," the captain sighed.

I cheered him up, but recommended he restudy the palm of his hand.

Don't sail in the shallow waters of the Bahamas when the sun is too low to illuminate coral reefs.

We hurried to port the next morning, dodging through the reefs, plainly visible now, and turned the derelict over to Killeen, who implored a boatyard to make emergency repairs. I left a propitiatory note for my former college roommate Tom Guinzburg and his party. The yard, after promising to have the boat back in the water in two days, took four. My friends, adrift in Nassau, did not let me off lightly. Telegrams arrived what seemed every few minutes.

"IS BOAT ON CHARTER THIS WEEK ADVISE WHERE TO MEET CLIENTS NED CAPTAIN."

"IS BOAT'S NAME ALWAYS SUPPOSED TO BE BELOW WATER LINE WHERE ARE PLIMPTON AND DUCHIN? WORRIED. TOM GUINZBURG."

"CANNOT FIND PLIMPTON CAPTAIN OR FOR THAT MATTER CYRANO PLEASE ADVISE. PETER DUCHIN."

"CANNOT FIND NASSAU PLEASE ADVISE. GEORGE PLIMPTON."

In June of 1971, Peter, now president of the Starr Broadcasting Group, chartered Cyrano for four successive nights, to give dinner cruises up and down the Hudson to advertisers. On the third night, the guest list completed as the thirty-second reveler was checked aboard, Peter instructed the captain to set out. Everyone was standing about or seated on the raised decks or chairs, drinking cocktails and nibbling hors d'oeuvres. It was seven o'clock and the sky was sunny and smogless as they headed north from the 79th Street marina, the captain at the wheel. Marvin Hayes, a young black advertising executive, was sitting on the lifeline just aft of the gate, talking to two friends who were seated on the raised afterdeck. Suddenly the stainless-steel rubberized cable collapsed under him and he fell over backward into the water. Though there was instant commotion, there was no sense of alarm: Marvin would get an unscheduled ducking, was the obvious attitude of his companions. It took an estimated seven seconds before Peter Starr, standing on the port side, noticed the cause of the commotion and rushed to the wheel, taking control from the captain. Cyrano, under full power, was doing a little better than eight knots: fifteen feet per second. They were therefore over a hundred feet from Hayes before Peter could begin his turn. A U-turn on Cyrano, at cruising speed, that brings you back exactly to the point where your turn began, requires fifty-five seconds. Before the ship's direction has actually reversed, the distance between the man overboard and the boat necessarily increases, and probably at that point—about thirty seconds after the turn begins—Cyrano was 250 feet from Hayes. Everyone's eyes were trained on him, but suddenly the chatter ceased. Hayes was not swimming, but flailing his arms. At just about the point when the boat was fully turned and headed toward him, he disappeared. He was discovered at 65th Street, five days later. Poor Marvin Hayes did not know how to swim.

The Coast Guard helicopter was there within about ten minutes, but it was soon obvious that Hayes had drowned.

Nobody who does not know how to swim should sit on a lifeline. On the other hand, the lifeline should have withstood force—up to three thousand pounds. Exhaustive investigation established that the rigger had applied the wrong kind of crimp to bind the cable to the fitting that secures it to the stanchion. The Coast Guard, after conducting an investigation, exonerated the ship and its crew of any charge of negligence. Hayes's widow sued Starr Broadcasting —her late husband's hosts—and Caribbean Enterprises—the owner of Cyrano—for a total of $1,800,000. Interesting legal footnote: $1,500,000 was sought in compensation for income she would lose over the course of her lifetime in virtue of her husband's untimely death (happily, Mrs. Hayes is remarried and has children by her second husband), and $300,000 in damages for the pain her husband endured during the minute in which he drowned—a discrete tort action, I am told. Caribbean's policy amounted to $300,000 total liability; Starr's to $5,000,000. The latter company (needless to say) took the position that Starr was in no way liable. The former took the position that since the insured (me) had warranted that there would not be more than six passengers on board, and there were thirty-two, the policy was null and void. We maintained that a dinner guest is not a "passenger." We took that to arbitration, and won. Four years later, two months before the beginning of our transatlantic voyage, the case was set for trial—to begin *three days before our scheduled departure*. A galling coincidence, because Peter would be required as a witness. The morning of the trial, the suit was settled—for $350,000: $290,000 from Cyrano's insurance company, the balance from the rigger's insurance company and from the manufacturer of the ill-placed fitting. The uninsured lawyer's fees (protecting Caribbean and Starr) came to over $25,000.

It is a mistake to assume that all young men aged twenty-seven know how to swim. You cannot easily avoid taking nonswimmers on such a boat as Cyrano; but you can be conscious of the question. It is impossible to know whether, if it had happened that the captain saw Hayes fall into the water and had there and then tossed him the horseshoe life preserver that sits at the side of the wheel, Hayes would have been able to swim the distance necessary to reach it. A swimming teacher, hearing the story, told me that from Peter's description he concluded that Marvin Hayes made the pathetic mistake most nonswimmers tend to make in such circumstances. They seek to *climb* out of their difficulty: by climbing up a mythical ladder. If they tried instead to "climb a ladder horizontally," as one might struggle with a broken leg to the door of a room, they would stay afloat. I never met Mr. Hayes, nor had Peter, before the fateful evening. But Peter recalled that as the crew tossed out the dock lines, Hayes said to him, "This is a very exciting night for me, Mr. Starr. My first on a boat of any kind."

And, finally, a month before we set out, Cyrano was on charter— to a middle-aged man as host, along with wife, and an older couple and a male friend as guests. The host and his wife, enthusiastic scuba divers, insisted that we provide two tanks. We keep one on board for hull emergencies, and Danny let us have his personal set. Off Nassau, the couple dove into the water, not far from Paradise Beach. In about ten minutes, the husband surfaced, gestured agitatedly to Phil Jr., the captain's son, sitting in the whaler waiting for the divers' return. Phil Jr. zoomed over to him, and was instructed to take the tank from the diver's back and speed off to the beach to bring out Nassau police divers, because his wife was "in trouble." Within fifteen minutes the police were there. They dove and found the woman, lying on the sandy bottom forty feet below the surface, dead. There was no explaining it. No heart attack. She had drowned. There was nearly a half-hour's air left in the tank. The regulator was working perfectly. She was a certificated diver.

A peril of the sea, to be sure; though not, except tangentially, related to the life and hard times of sailing boats. Still, it happened, and she had slept the night before on my bunk, and expected to sleep there on the following night. We won't permit scuba diving again off Cyrano, if that is any consolation to the bereaved.

Those were highlights from experiences of my own and of boats I have owned. I have read a lot, and listened a lot, and doubt that many seasoned ocean sailors would disagree with the following propositions:

1. The chances of a well-rigged, well-sailed, well-constructed boat going down in the open sea (you are safer there than near land) by reason of ocean conditions are so small in the safer months, in the safer latitudes, that you should not become obsessed with the question of physical survival. On the other hand, you must make emergency arrangements. (A 42-foot ocean-going cutter was abandoned on the run from Bermuda to Cape Hatteras in a hurricane that began the day we landed in Marbella, concerning which Van will say apt things in due course.)

2. I have mentioned the danger of man-overboard; the gravest danger, in my experience.

3. The other danger is from fire.

Astonishingly, the race from Newport to Bermuda, which has been conducted every other year for over fifty years, has brought death by drowning to only a single human being. Several boats have been destroyed on the rocks around Bermuda, but the crews were saved. The exception was the large yacht in which a fire got out of control. The distress signal was sighted by another craft, which powered in to render assistance. One by one the refugees jumped aboard. One man —the cook—slipped and fell into the seas in between the boats, and not knowing how to swim, drowned immediately.

We maintain, on Cyrano, two large and two small fire extinguishers, handily located. A diesel engine is indispensable to one's peace of mind. Although all the electricity is wired to circuits, in fact we once had a fire aboard Cyrano, at the 79th Street marina, which did extensive damage. Central electrical switches are available to cut off, and then isolate, short circuits. Needless to say, the gas cylinders for the stove are stowed on deck.

Reggie agreed to serve as chairman of sorts of a Safety Committee for what we now regularly referred to as The B.O. (Reggie even had stationery printed: THE BIG ONE.) We pooled our knowledge, and decided to gear up for two kinds of emergencies. There is a third kind, but you needn't bother about it: A whale eats you, say, or a steamer runs you down in a storm. We defined as Emergency A any development that would result in Cyrano's sinking within two minutes (the whale barges into you, let us say; or an iceberg). Hanging on the davits was our unsinkable Boston whaler. It was packed with emergency food and water for ten people for ten days. It could be lowered into the water in about fifteen seconds. Sheathed knives were strapped alongside to cut any lines that might foul. Forward of the cockpit-cabin area we kept a twelve-man life raft, neatly tucked into a small barrel—also with emergency food and medicine, and a radio with strength to emit, for seventeen hours, emergency signals to over-passing aircraft; and, for night use, flares. That life raft was equipped with a kind of Arabian tent to protect us against the sun's rays. It would inflate immediately on hitting the water. But one hundred feet of light line would keep it attached to Cyrano. That line could be cut (a) from Cyrano, by a knife handily situated for that purpose, or (b) from the raft, by unhooking a snap hook. I know personally of two shipwrecks—one of them off Bermuda in 1956, a boat that was only a few hours ahead of us—in which the life raft was thrown overboard with no thought to what would then happen to it. What happened (in both cases) was that the life raft drifted out to sea and was of no use to anyone. Always, there should be a painter tying the life raft to the boat.

The right-hand locker next to the steering wheel was filled exclusively with life preservers. To each was attached a waterproof flashlight, a whistle, and dye marker (a substance that, once punctured with your teeth, dissolves and oozes out at a tiny rate, coloring the sea red, and permitting you, by following its track, to come eventually on the source of distress. Excellent for man-overboard).

We would work in prestipulated pairs, one senior, one junior partner. In Emergency A, only the whaler, the life preservers (also tied loosely to one another, and jointly to the boat), and the twelve-man raft would be unloaded. Every crew member was responsible then for causing his partner to jump overboard, for following him in, swimming then to the life preservers, donning them; then swimming either to the whaler or the life raft.

In Emergency B, we would know the boat was going down, but that we had *five or more* minutes. The life preservers would be donned first in this case. The captain would work until the last minute, giving our position and a distress signal on the radio's emergency band. Two additional eight-man rafts, tucked into cavities just beyond the pillows of the berths in the cockpit section, would be hauled out, automatically inflated, and trailed alongside. We would fill them with as many supplies as we had time to gather together. In a raging sea, schematic arrangements of this sort are sheer fantasy, and you simply do what you can. But in a moderate sea, losing ground, say, against fire or an uncontrollable leak, you have time even to remember the corkscrew.

In other words, take precautions. "For," thought Starbuck, "I am here in this critical ocean to kill whales for my living, and not to be killed by them for theirs."

I touched on the subject of danger in a memorandum I published in *National Review* the week before setting sail:

Memorandum to All Concerned.

From: WFB

Re: My imminent departure for thirty days.

I plan to sail the Schooner Cyrano beginning at 1000 EDT May 30, from Miami to Bermuda, to San Miguel (the Azores), to Marbella (in Spain).

During that period I shall be virtually incommunicado, although the ship has an excellent radio telephone for outgoing calls which, I pray, will be few in number. I shall serve as captain and navigator, and if I call to say, "Where am I?" I would appreciate a non-derisory reply, even if it offends the stylistic preferences of my colleagues. I shall write three of my newspaper columns before setting sail (careful readers will note in them a certain detachment from highly contemporary affairs); and then I shall take my two weeks' annual vacation from the column.

I have been hoping to make such a trip for a very long time. It has been a busy winter and spring with, in addition to the usual things, a novel (Doubleday, February), and another collection (Putnam's, September). In November, *NR* will be twenty, and I'll be fifty. It is unsafe to put off things like sailing across the Atlantic forever. For those of you who have been kind enough to express a concern over my physical safety, a reassuring statistic: for $500, Lloyd's will be giving us a million dollars' insurance. And remember, there is always the silver lining. Since our policy is in favor of *National Review*, if the ship goes down, you'll have two entire years without a fund appeal.

5.

We were off. Not at 10:00 A.M., but at 7:22 P.M. The covenant was that we would all keep journals. Christopher (C.) and Danny (D.) performed dutifully, magnificently. Van (V.) dutifully, a little perfunctorily, his bubbling wit ruthlessly suppressed. Reggie was too busy fixing things and being kind, and worrying about his companions. Aunty Bill keeps saying she can't understand why I haven't received hers, since she mailed me copy after copy (read: she didn't), but she knows she has nothing to fear. She is above criticism). WFB, as noted elsewhere, finds journal-keeping impossible. He writes cryptic *notes* in his journal at night, which remind him of this and that . . .

But indeed we were off, after fifteen months of planning. The leave-taking was hectic.

Danny and Christopher meet me at the airport in Miami, on the eve of departure. Christopher's picture.

[C] Reggie and I took the car out at 11:30, announced we'd be back in ½ an hour, and returned at 2:30, with 36 cans of Nutrament, 100 Space-Stiks, and an assortment of dried fruits. This little cache of protein-laden goodies will, by our estimation, keep nine people alive, happy, and starvation-free for 10 days. After that, it's a matter of sieving plankton with your teeth. Hell, old Captain Bligh kept 18 men alive for two months in a longboat with six inches of freeboard. He covered 2,100 miles and also managed to chart the coast of New Holland a/k/a Australia.

[V] A last and final delay was due to a lack of grapefruit juice, which P. [Pat] remedied.

[C] Danny and I had bought a bottle of $4.28 Taylor New York State champagne, with no other intent than smashing it against

89

Cyrano's prow. A bubbly baptism for a voyage that promises a great celebration. Namely WFB's 50th birthday. The bursitis kid hits the Atlantic. But when we tied the cork to a piece of shock cord and mentioned

    our intentions,
El Capitán said,
    Screw it, let's get on
        with it.
So be it.
So was it.

[C] Now that the Dream has passed through the eggshell dividing all fantasies from realities, let us consider what we have left behind: Burger King, Biscayne Boulevard, those Wonderful people at Miamarina, Mrs. Hayes, $350,000, the Coast Guard and their very wonderful gunboats, sand, trees, Stamford, Connecticut, Mrs. Buckley, Marvin Liebman, 15 relatives of Van Galbraith who traveled from Little Rock and Tallahassee to see us off, Manny the mechanic and his refractory drive shafts, Cuban carpenters, Sambo's restaurant, the reporter from the *Miami Herald* (who wanted to know what kinds of food Mr. Buckley liked to eat), and The New York *Times*. Let Americans live and love, work and play, screw and get screwed without us. Or, as Mr. Kadey's magic cordite so eloquently puts it, "Phoomp!"

                        ◇

Art Kadey, the original owner of the boat, had volunteered to remove Cyrano's propeller and replace it with the spare, properly pitched. Manny, the mechanic, had observed that we did not achieve the proper rpm with the present propeller, and would eventually strain the engine with it. But there was no time to haul the boat, so the replacement had to be effected underwater. Art Kadey, the scuba team having failed to pry the propeller loose, volunteered to wrap some cordite around it, detonate it, and blast it loose. ("No sweat. I've done it a thousand times. Well, a hundred times.") Phoomp! as Christopher said. Then the darkest moment of the day. The scuba diver reported that the propeller was indeed loosened, but that the drive shaft had been bent. That would have meant at *least* a day's delay, perhaps two days. But he was wrong. The reflection of the water misled him. However, no more cordite, ever; even if I did embrace Art.

∽

[V] First dinner—it smelled good in the cooking, but nobody liked yams. In any case, everyone was too pooped to wax over anything. We started the official log with gusto and thoroughness but je me demande si on va continuer aussi diligent que ça.

∽

Indeed. It is ever so, I have found, in the absence of a ruthless monitor. Entries are reduced from one an hour, to one every two hours; toward the end, to one every four hours, at the change of the watch, unless something extraordinary happened. It doesn't make so very much difference, actually; again, especially if you are not racing. It is the barometer one has to watch carefully; but ours—Van soon established—wasn't working. "How do you find out if a barometer is working?" he asked in the log when, after two days, it had recorded no changes. I remember asking, the first day out on an ocean run from Bermuda to Stamford, a green friend of Firpo's to give me the barometer reading from below, as I scribbled on the log. He bounded happily down, and came back with the information: "It says Fair and Warm."

Yes, everyone was pooped. But the moment was not lost.

∽

[C] 0300. Two very contented Cheshire cats [Danny was on watch with Christopher] are sitting on the poopdeck, absorbing. I marvel at the autopilot and the steady helm. It's so . . . nice when things work.

> I must go down to the sea again,
> To the lonely sea and the sky,
> And all I ask is a tall ship
> And a Benmar autopilot to steer her by.

Sing, my 32-volt muses!

0330. Nice feeling, sitting here by the transom of the Slowpoke Express, with a can of beer and the silvery moon. Danny's walking up forward to check on Phil Jr. and Augustino to make sure they haven't rolled off the deck. The cassette player is singing and so is the wind. So far, no ships have pierced the circumference of our horizon. Uninterrupted solitude. At times like this it makes sense that man once worshipped the moon. Even two millennia after the death of Diana, we still pay her homage. Our pleasure is the moon; may she never wane.

$\backsim$

Phil Jr., tall, brawny, laconic, is Captain Campagna's son, a college senior and aviation student, on board as cook. Augustino, the world's most obliging Argentinian, was on as steward. When the weather was hot, they elected to sleep on deck forward, rather than in the crew quarters aft or in the forecastle cabin.

The long process of settling in begins.

$\backsim$

[C] 0400. Not able to sleep. I switch watches with Van. Reg and I (with the redoubtable WFB and Danny) put up the main, took down the main; put up the Genoa, took down same; put up forestaysail, Gollywobbler, mainstaysail; took down forestaysail and rigged main-

Cyrano slides out of Miami, under the Rickenbacker Causeway.

staysail to windward. All in a night's work. WFB says to Danny: "Try to get some sleep."

∽

Van, a couple of days out, and euphorically unseasick, records the thoroughness of his precautions, plagiarizing his seven-year-old son, who, since the Galbraiths live in London, uses English terminology: "Have been diligent about 'poo-in-the-loo,' as Evan would say."

Danny, like Skeezix, will accommodate to anything, eat or drink anything, any time. He has the delicacy to put this particular breakfast together when senior members of the crew are absent and need not therefore contemplate it. "This morning I slept through breakfast so went without. Beer and M & M's will do fine."

Christopher records with (voluptuary?) thoroughness the kind of vexation that can madden a man at sea. His account is not entirely filial:

∽

[C] WFB lost his wristwatch. Captain Campagna was telling me about the deterioration of discipline in American Catholic schools when WFB, dressed in one of his 18 blue Lacoste shirts, and shorts, comes out on deck. Poor guy. He went to take a shower, removed his wristwatch, and now he can't find it.

"I'm going mad. It's taken me 52 minutes *not* to find it. I looked under the chair, on the bookshelf, on top of the settee, under the settee, on my bed, in the sink, in the head, in Reggie's cabin, on top of the hurricane lamps, in the camera-locker, through the cassette shelf, and if I don't find it," he says, his voice now a well-tempered, exasperated whine, "*I'm going to commit suicide.*"

My father, who is capable of handling every crisis from people drowning off his boat to global asphyxiation, is not ordinarily so frustrated by something that, to thee and me, is an everyday crisis. But, you see, he has not lost a watch in 15 years; and his movements during the period in which the watch disappeared were confined to ten feet from the shower; and, most important of all, he will not be . . . happy . . . until he finds it.

"We" finally find it in his drawer, nestled comfortably with the 18 blue Lacoste shirts and the 15 white socks. I fancy it was sleeping comfortably, ruing the moment it would be found and pressed back into service. Its brother was meanwhile strapped around the wrist of a man who once lived in a large white mansion on Pennsylvania Avenue in Washington. Now he lives in San Clemente and probably has little use for instruments that measure out his final moments of life. How large a burden that small watch must be!

∽

I had once mentioned to Christopher that the only wristwatch I had ever seen that was exactly the duplicate of mine, which Christopher's maternal grandfather gave me years ago, was worn by Richard Nixon.

But the lost wristwatch was piffle. A son's capacity for exasperation with his father, like a father's capacity for exasperation with his son, is endlessly variable, like their relationship; a complement of their capacity to love each other.

∽

[C] There are times when I'm right and times when I'm wrong. Usually, I admit when I'm wrong. WFB, it seems, does not subscribe to this. I ask him if he threw away the top yellow sheet of a legal pad attached to a clipboard. "Yes," he says, "I thought it was a shopping list." When I tell him it was an *inventory of the ship's supplies* and *where they are stowed,* he just tells me I should instead have written the inventory in the log. "Well," I say, "it indicated quite clearly things like 'Cabin A: 2 cases Bud.' "

"I don't read what's on odd pieces of paper," he says.

"Then I guess it's my loss," I say. Horseshit. He then, when he has me up with him taking a noon sight, gets mildly impatient when I tell him the sun is still rising according to my sextant. His indignation— he says the sun has passed our meridian and begun to sink—is wonderfully juxtaposed against a six-degree error he made with the sextant one hour ago. But that doesn't figure in his calculations.

WFB later tells me his six-degree error was a paper miscalculation, a fact which mitigates the triumph of my last entry. Nonetheless,

94

I don't think it's too much to ask that you glance—however periph-erally—at a piece of paper before you throw it into the permanent wastepaper basket of the Bermuda Triangle.

∽

Probably he's right; even as it isn't too much to ask that pieces of paper one desires to preserve be removed from the hugger-mugger of the navigator's working area. A six-degree error, by the way, *has* to be a mathematical mistake. A navigator with advanced Parkinson's Disease could not err by six degrees shooting a falling star. A sight six degrees off-target would put you three hundred and sixty miles off course.

Christopher had another disillusionment that day:

∽

[C] A sad story: When I went to the toolbox to get a screwdriver last night, I saw it was half empty. Danny scoured everywhere. Our conclusion: One of the mechanics ripped off a whole load of ham-mers, Allen wrenches, screwdrivers, drill bits. . . . Perhaps the defini-tion of a wise man would be the man who, upon finding his tools missing in the middle of the Bermuda Triangle, would smile and say, "But, of course!" I find myself lacking this wisdom. I would gladly remove the fellow's head with one of the hacksaws he saw fit to add to his own collection.

∽

On top of the conventional aggravations that grow out of ocean sailing, by the third day out Christopher was rapidly decomposing, head to toe.

∽

[C] My morale is so-so. Got about ten minutes sleep before going on watch at 2400, and today was by no means marvelous. I whacked into the companionway step with my nose. It's swollen, and I can't breathe through it. With the fungus on my foot, the acid indigestion,

the broken toe, and the nose, it's been one of those . . . days. Fortunately, the ship's store is well-stocked with iced beer.

⌣

Feeling ill at sea is infinitely worse than feeling ill ashore. Perhaps
there is a law of nature on this point, reaching out toward sym-
metry—because when you feel fit at sea, you feel fitter than ever you
do ashore. Fair enough?

There is only one thing to do. Van wrote: "Sleep is an omnipresent
factor. People drop off around you during the day as if they had been
suddenly gassed."

⌣

But sleep apart, if you are sick, there is Aunt Bill:

⌣

[C] Aunt Bill sleeps soundly in Cabin B next to her medicine
chest. The sum knowledge and technology of the AMA, the California
Red Cross, and Blue Shield all tucked, compressed, and compart-
mentalized into a deep-sea fishing tackle box.

⌣

But, soon, body health returned; and Christopher was now pre-
occupied with his role as ship's photographer:

⌣

[C] A cross sea, 2–3 feet, slaps occasionally against the starboard
topsides. Took two more rolls of film today. Experimented with Pola-
roid and blue filter. I'm beginning to feel like a one-man paparazzi
corps.

"Excuse me, but I couldn't help noticing that your pose is just
so . . . right. You daguerreotype quite nicely, yes, indeed."

⌣

And his mind wandered over to consideration of his sudden economic importance:

∽

[C] It makes me feel . . . warm . . . inside to know that if Cyrano is swallowed by a kraken, my mother will be richer by $1,100,000.
"Uh, before you leave, would you mind signing this?"
"Of course not. Do you accept American Express cards?"

∽

He undertakes to track a conversation during a watch:

∽

[C] Reg and I had the midnight to 4 watch. Things we talked about: the Big Brother program he works at in Gainesville; the 16-year-old who molested an eight-year-old girl and later sold his body to over 100 farmhands; the Martin Luther King Center in Newport and my experiences there; MIT; Yale; friends; China last summer [Christopher traveled there with a dozen other "student leaders"]; Bermuda Races (Reg tells me after he skippered *Suzy Wong* back to Stamford, he'd dream he was raising the mainsail and wake up raising the venetian blinds, or dream he was taking a piss over the side and wake up peeing next to the bed, or dream he was winching in and wake up falling backward over tables and chairs); Charlie Lindsay; Teddy Tucker; shark fin soup and Chinese chili peppers; my tattoo; cocaine and marijuana; sea urchins; about the time a skate lashed him in the hand with its tail (he had to soak it in boric acid for ten days); the stars; how beautiful it is to be alone at sea; our dreams and what they portend; hypnosis; The Manchurian Candidate; the taffrail log; and how quickly our watch had come to an end.

∽

I note a passage, four days out, which I can only assume is so written for the purpose of pulling one's father's leg, or perhaps, as he

97

would put it, "testing WFB's alertness." Christopher as The Old Man of the Sea:

～

[C] Only one more hour. We put up the fore and main staysails to steady the ship, but it didn't work. They're batting about from windward to leeward. "Whores," says Danny. The engine room is purring with 1600 rpm's. Looks like a squall line is moving down on us from the north. If we do get a storm . . . well, we get wet and scramble. *I take out the corncob pipe. I found it in the pocket of my foul-weather jacket. Soggy and worn, the rim is burned black from hundreds of matches. I bought it years ago, in San Francisco, before the* Fernbrook *sailed for Manila. That pipe kept me good company on many a watch. In the Pacific, South China Sea, Strait of Malacca, Bay of Bengal, Arabian Sea, Indian Ocean, and the South and North Atlantic oceans. I was glad to find my old friend.*

～

Just to begin with, WFB comments, "years ago," Christopher hadn't been born. . . . But the voyage he touches on was a supreme experience, undertaken after graduating from prep school. Five months as a deckhand aboard a Norwegian vessel, the *Fernbrook*. I remember driving with him to Brooklyn after a lachrymose dinner with his mother, arriving finally at the strange, empty, forbidding vessel berthed at a remote dock, the father's ritual pain on the son's inevitable rite of passage; my son's newfound stoicism (the tears were his father's; what seemed only a few months before, returning to boarding school after the vacations, they had been his).

And reaching, finally, equilibrium-at-sea.

～

[C] My head hurts. Danny has drifted off. Keeping me company are: this journal, a flashlight, pen, packs of Rolaids, autopilot, shroud light, down parka, corncob pipe, and the sea. Quite a crowd.

～

There was an unpleasant incident today. The captain was asleep, the generator conked out, Danny put oil in it, the captain awoke and lost his temper. On which failing I have recorded my feelings. Here are Danny's:

〜

[**D**] . . . we exchanged angered phrases, but he won by reiterating what a complete "fucking ass" I was and bla bla bla, whereby he withdrew his eminence, slandering me all the way deckside. I think to myself how odd he didn't burst a blood vessel around his already thin temples. Passé as it seems now, I still wonder.

Two hours later we were in the close quarters of his luxury engine compartment helping each other with suggestions and "remedies." Numero Uno having given up, I rallied to blow up his confidence. Low of me to do so, but feeling good having done it, I emerged an hour later weighing less by 5 pounds, but happily exclaiming my accomplishments and being rewarded by sheepish smiles made my day.

〜

Danny has a green thumb in matters mechanical. Like his prose style, it is untutored. But it doesn't seem to matter. Even machines like Danny.

〜

[**C**] Off watch, finally. Reg and Dan spent 20 hot, oily minutes in the engine room, dealing with a leak in the overflow injector system. Danny's prowess in that goddam room amazes me. He's a cranked-up dervish. His blood is one part battery acid. He hooks the jumper cable to a grounding plug on the engine, shouting directions above the roar of the generator. Sparks fly. "You mother humper!" he shouts. He readjusts the cable and the engine kicks over lethargically, with an anthropomorphic grunting of pistons, as if to say, "Jay-sus, here we go again."

〜

Danny had worked since January on Cyrano, helping to make her fit. Augustino came on a fortnight before the sail. They have become

99

friends. No doubt unjustly, the boss man is usually the victim of their complaints. See, e.g., *The Nigger of Narcissus.*

～

[**C**] Danny tells me Augustino has approached him. Phil Sr. and Phil Jr. have been treating him like a dumb Mexican wetback, he has complained. "Cristobal, te voy a decir una cosa. Le agarro a Danny, me entiendes? I *lof* him. Es un chico rarísimo." ["Christopher, I'm going to tell you something. I dig Danny, you hear? I *love* him. He is a rare one."]

"Sí, Augustino. No hay dos Dannies en este mundo." ["Yes, Augustino, there *aren't* two Dannies in all this world."]

～

There is routine. Time to think about time.

～

[**C**] We've been out three days now. Three days and all we've seen are two ships, one plane, and Melville's "great shroud of the sea," rolling on as it did 5,000 years ago. *Moby Dick*, unlike *Jaws*, was not an instant bestseller when it appeared in 1851. Solzhenitsyn has said he believes his message will be most powerful when he lies in his grave.

～

And fantasy:

～

[**C**] As for me
I just long to see
One of the Soviet
Subs,
With Captain Fyodor Ilyitch
Manning the conning tower
"Soviet sub two points to starboard, skipper."

"Right. Bring down the Gollywobbler and get me the .222.
Those Russkies try something I'll blast 'em right back to Odessa."

∽

Danny, deserting the engine, gives the muse her head:

∽

[**D**] Last night was nearly as eventful as 6/1. I tried unsuccessfully a half-dozen times to sleep only to be needed to set sails, drop them or both in a short period of time. If I found myself getting mildly frustrated I needed only to look around and the enjoyment of all this lovely sea and night breathed fresh sentiment to me.

∽

And again:

∽

[**D**] We had a small squall early last night. The wind perked up, it rained and we all scurried around dropping the mainsail, Genoa, and staysails while it passed and then up again after all the weather seemed to have gone—then down later when we lost all wind and up two hours after that. Ah! sailing is a man's sport; like a good woman you love it, tolerate it, and never forsake it. Sailing is one of the very few pleasures left that is individualistic. There are nine aboard, nine opinions, nine feelings, nine hopes, nine happinesses. I feel elated, a part of each wavelet I see.

∽

And, finally, Danny as the poet, untethered:

∽

[**D**] Can't you see I enjoy the sea
All its beauties surrounding me

101

I doubt each day whiling by
More pleasant Kingdom than sea and sky
Don't forsake a feeling true
Like mine for this blue.

∽

And there is Bermuda.

∽

[C] Wrote two letters tonight, one to M-g-g and one to Blythe. With land coming into sight, there comes a nervousness, a restlessness, a longing, once the landfall is made, to return to sea.

As a general principle, it is unwise to encourage the clans to gather, before one goes to sea. Probably it is even wise (amiably) to forbid it. I suppose it would not matter greatly if one were Onassis going out to sea. Onassis doesn't worry about the missing grapefruit juice or about preparing the plotting sheet for the first day out. What is distressing about people who come to see you off is that they are (in my experience) uniformly charming—so that you *worry* about your neglect of them, which causes you to worry about yet another matter. Moreover, an ocean cruise is to an ocean race as a taped television program is to a live television program. Somehow, even as studios are *always* ready for a live show, you *always* make it to the starting line of the race on time—even if you are up all night, as once we were before a Bermuda Race, trying to devise a means of extracting the through-bolt at the top of our mast that had broken in two (we even meandered up Narragansett Bay to the nearest friendly American naval base in search of a quiet battleship with a turret fifty feet high, whence someone could exert sufficient purchase to pry the bolt out). You *never* set out on time for a cruise, even with fifteen months' notice. Danny, with his invincible optimism, told me the boat would be ready to sail forty-eight hours before the hallowed hour we had designated. But at the appointed hour on Friday morning at ten, we faced the need of replacing our propeller (*op. cit.*); the loran (long-range navigation) was suddenly not working; the radar was not working; and the new automatic pilot was not even definitively installed. Never mind the grapefruit juice.

Fifteen years ago I wrote a detailed article raising the question of just how much expertise an ocean sailor can genuinely rely on.

Expertise being a word that is precisely used by a total of about twenty people, I pause to define it as meaning *a body of operative knowledge*. It isn't synonymous with *expertness*. One cannot be an expert except in a field in which there is something to be expert in: i.e., in which there is *expertise*. A radar technician can be expert *only insofar as there is room for expertness*. Beyond that he is extemporizing. In due course, when I discuss celestial navigation by computer, the distinctions will be pragmatically elaborated. Better, an attempt to do so will be made.

It is, of course, one thing if a particular product is defective or if it is defectively installed; another if that product presumes to standards of performance it is not scientifically justified in presuming to. The gentleman who (finally) installed our automatic pilot effected an installation which, during that day's midnight watch, came apart; and Danny put it back together, using bolts rather than screws; and *his* installation held. But not the pilot, which suddenly stopped working when Captain Campagna started the return voyage. Six thousand miles without the automatic pilot. There are grounds for believing the installer sloppy, or inexpert, in installation; but the machine's breaking down after one month suggests defective design. Or else there is—a mystery. Mysteries abound at sea. I had an autopilot on *Suzy* that worked with exquisite precision for three years. One day it stopped working, and I assumed a need for spare parts or even for replacing whole units. Over the course of four years, six technicians, three yards, and finally the personal mechanic for the president of the manufacturing company tried to make it work again (at this point every component unit had been replaced). It never did; never has. Come see.

The gentleman who looked at the radar fiddled expensively with it and succeeded in decocting from it only the faintest signal, eclipsed in less than a day at sea. The gentleman in Bermuda tried to fix it and couldn't. The gentleman in Marbella fixed it for six hundred dollars, 25 percent of the original cost of the instrument, and it lasted about a week. Now this is a Japanese machine about which it is boasted that there are six completely discrete and replaceable components, so that the problem is supposed to be as simple as identifying the delinquent part, throwing it away, and inserting the new part. That turns out to be hogwash. One never quite knows whether it is intentional or inadvertent hogwash. Perhaps there is an individual in Japan who, with his

104

little tool kit, could have set the radar right in minutes. The question seriously arises whether that man's skills are thaumaturgical rather than mechanical. Or is he an artist? Artistic jury-rigs are feats of individual achievement, and one cannot deduce from them an expertise that sustains them.

A gentleman exhorted me there and then to buy a brand new loran with the latest gee-whiz digital scanners that automatically seek out the two relevant transmitting loran stations and their slave stations, and track them automatically and continuously, giving you second-by-second fixes which you then situate on your chart. The same gentleman installed the radio telephone and the whip-antenna aerial on the mast. The new loran set stopped working a half hour after we left Miami, was not revived even after a half hour's telephone conversation with Reggie at sea, at which he was given minute instructions by the expert; did not work even after a replacement unit was installed in Bermuda; and in the storm we went through on the way to the Azores, the antenna came clattering down. Not quite, actually. It hung above our heads, describing large circles and parabolas, like a huge ice pick, for about a day, during which the roll from the storm's afterbirth made it too risky to go up the mast to cut the wire it hung from. (Thereafter, we used the emergency antenna, rigging it on deck.) Again, the defective installation of an antenna is traceable to sheer inexperience. Even though we were dealing with a graduate of the Naval Academy with impressive credentials in electronics—still, like the electrician at Fort Lauderdale who had never been to sea, perhaps his experience had only been in aircraft carriers or battleships, and he knew not, nor ever imagined, the trials mere sailboats are put to in storms. Of course this does not explain the fiasco of the loran itself.

In the briefest conceivable experience with physics at college, I remember the professor saying that it was not possible to "define" electricity. This does not, of course, mean that there is no expertise in the field of electricity. It is, however, limited. One summer—the summer with the English captain—I noticed that he was keeping the boat's generators working eighteen hours a day. I informed him that this was unnecessary; that even on a day when we used the engine not at all, sufficient power was developed by the generator in four hours to sustain the electrical system for twenty-four hours. He replied that

I had only to look at the voltage indicator to discover how wrong I was; and, indeed, the batteries were being dissipated after one hour without the generator. I told him that something was wrong, inasmuch as four years' experience with the boat had *positively established* that we were equipped to take care of our maximum needs with four hours of generator time.

He spent the entire summer consulting electricians. Anywhere Cyrano berthed for over two days, the local electrician would be consulted: like a diseased man, wandering around the world in search of the man who might cure him. They would all start at the beginning— check the batteries, check the voltage, check the alternator, check for a short circuit. Four months later we were *still* running the generator eighteen hours a day, and it wasn't until we decided (for other reasons) to replace the generator that a modest electrical contractor in Fort Lauderdale informed me, in a handwritten letter, that the silver coil in something-or-other, which should have been wrapped clockwise, had been wrapped counterclockwise during the spring tuning, and that that had been the source of our difficulty.

The trouble with concluding that all this means is that Cyrano had been coincidentally examined by a dozen incompetent electricians is that indictments of such a categorical character are unconvincing. Expertise presumes (a) that the knowledge is there; and (b) that the knowledge that it is there is *widespread*, readily available. Just because, during the Second World War, it happened that there was a wild British don who succeeded in cracking the German code, we are not entitled to deduce that cryptographical science was sufficiently developed to crack the German code. The distinction, as well as being interesting, is important. When buying a piece of equipment one should know just how widespread is the knowledge of how to keep it operating; and, certainly, whether such knowledge exists in the first place.

A day out of Miami, the nightmare revisited us. Our batteries were brand new, the voltage and the generator were producing to capacity, yet after one hour without engine or generator, our 32-volt supply would sink to 15 volts—you could see the lights in the saloon darken in front of your eyes. The captain and Reggie spent day after

106

day trying to find the source of the problem. So did the most schooled electrician in Bermuda. We thought we had it licked, but a day out of Bermuda the trouble recurred. Suddenly, five days out, the batteries began to display their vaunted potency—and ever after were entirely normal. The captain came up with the theory that the batteries, being new, required day after day of redundant charging before, so to speak, dropping their testicles and achieving potency. Quietly, Reggie dismissed this as fiddlesticks, pointing out that the batteries had received a full charge day after day when plugged into the shore power in Miami for two weeks before we sailed.

So it went; so it almost always goes. There are problems that beset what one might call middle-sized boats. The big boats have their engineer and electrician on board, who can fix or replace almost anything that goes wrong. The very small boats don't have radar or loran or automatic pilots. Cyrano is in the class between, and perhaps for that reason there is an insufficient expertise to provide reliable electrical or electronic systems for her, though it must be observed that the little commercial fishing boats use the same kind of radar and loran that is offered to the sailboats, with, however, the significant difference that such boats are always operating under power and their instruments no doubt adjust to, or are designed to adjust to, regular operation, rather than the episodic operation of the sailor anxious to conserve his electrical power.

Since mystery does indeed attach to electronics, and even to electricity, it is worth pausing over a purely mechanical example of the sort of thing that seems to happen especially to boats.

It was three years earlier, just after the Republican Convention of 1972, and we had been cruising, laying over a day and a half in Cat Cay, and were setting out now for Bimini. It was the kind of afternoon with which the Bahamas are so frequently touched, which causes the heart and the memory to flutter: a steady balmy breeze, lengthening shadows on sugarbeaches, ten shades of blue and green between Cyrano and the mouth of the little harbor, only forty yards away. We were on the leeward side of the dock, tied up alongside, and so we had only to release the lines to the pilings, float clear of the Hatteras behind us and the Hatteras ahead of us, back gently under power out into the channel, then hard right rudder, a lazy 90-degree turn, and on out by the inland passage to Bimini. We slid smoothly away from the dock; in due course I eased the gear stick into reverse, quickened the throttle by a few hundred rpm, and in seconds found myself dreaming the dream wherein you are trying desperately to run away from the monster who is chasing you, except that your legs, though they go furiously through the motions, fail to propel you. My beautiful 60-foot Cyrano, snotnose unflinching, was proceeding slowly, majestically, toward the stone jetty twenty yards downwind.

Only once before had I geared in and gotten zero response. The experience occupied an instant and secure place in my repertory of nightmares. It was Newport, the day before *Dame Pattie* would begin the first race in her competition for the America's Cup. Newport was crowded with sportsmen, sportswriters, enthusiasts, and celebrants. I was bound for Nantucket on *The Panic*, and proposed to my friends that before leaving the harbor we might have a look at the challenger. We powered into the U-shaped pier basin, slid slowly, closely, by the pier opposite *Dame Pattie*, and then turned sharp left, pointing my chubby steel bowsprit directly at the soft underbelly of *Dame Pattie*. Five or six seconds of that and I would be perfectly situated to slide into reverse, turn left again, and cruise quietly back out into the channel after enjoying a long, lascivious look at *Dame Pattie*. I moved the gearshift back. Nothing happened. Fifteen tons of *The Panic* were sliding, without room for maneuver, smack into the challenger at about five knots. Ten seconds later, at the speed we were going, we'd have precipitated the withdrawal of Australia from SEATO. Four or five young crewmen were relaxedly, adoringly, lying about their beloved *Dame Pattie*'s deck in the midday sun eating sandwiches, when suddenly they noticed the dagger approaching slowly but ineluctably the heart of their vessel. As if programmed by Balanchine, five bodies went into pandemoniac motion that climaxed with ten frozen hands interlaced over the side, each pair holding a fender or seat cushion, piled one on top of the other at the point in *Dame Pattie*'s midriff toward which our juggernaut was lumbering. It occurred to me to throw myself into the water and plead later, at the war-crimes trial, that I had suffered a heart attack when—suddenly, unaccountably, providentially—the propeller engaged.

At the exhaustive postmortem conducted secretly by myself, I was told cheerily by an expert that a *collapsible* propeller sometimes disdains to engage immediately in reverse gear at low rpm speeds. (I got myself a *non*collapsible propeller.) At Cat Cay, Danny—who had had, on the East River, the definitive experience with the nonengaging gear—was following us in the whaler under his own power, so as to be out of the way of our stern when we backed down. In a few seconds, with the whaler as tug, we were laced back along the pier, and discovered that the drive shaft had disengaged from the coupling.

This means that the rod to which the propeller is affixed, which rod must (obviously) itself be turned by something, had come loose from what turns it, namely, the engine. Frank Warren, the young professional captain of Cyrano at the time, had experienced this breakdown under tame circumstances a few weeks earlier. So he took the boat to a great shipyard in Miami, which put it in drydock, aligned the engine, tested the shaft, repaired the coupling, for all I know prayed over it, wished us happy cruising, and sent me a bill for about three thousand dollars.

We examined the shaft and found that a stainless-steel through-pin binding the shaft to the engine had sheared and that, moreover, the liberated member had rocketed aft, embedding the propeller in the sternpost forward of the rudder. A local mechanic meditated laconically on the situation, and in three hours pronounced it repaired. He used a galvanized pin, but suggested we exchange it for another stainless-steel pin, the collapsed one having been clearly defective, when the boat got back to Miami.

The next day, approaching Lucayan Beach in Grand Bahama, we had the identical experience.

This time the local mechanic pronounced comprehensively on the sources of our difficulty. The pin, he said, is not nearly strong enough to carry the load of the revolving drive shaft. The shaft should, *to begin with*, engage positively a key in the engine. This key had worn. We needed a new key. He would have one made up at the machine shop—perhaps that very Sunday afternoon!

Thirty hours and $125 later, he pronounced us totally fit. Not only had he put in a fresh key, and a fresh pin, he had capped in three setscrews. There was no *way* the drive shaft could give us any more trouble.

It was early afternoon, and the wind now was oscillating from south to southwest, in a dirtying sky, barometer, however, steady (at 30.02). Edgy to move on, we set out for the eastern port of Grand Bahama, beyond which is the bight wherein Deep Water Cay beckons. The *Yachtsman's Guide to the Bahamas* describes it as "an anchorage [which will] carry 6 ft. at L.W. while 4 ft. can be taken in over the bar. The Deep Water Cay Club . . . [is] an attractive fishing camp with space for four boats, gas and diesel fuels, electricity, water and ice in small quantities. . . . The bone fishing is considered among the best in the Bahamas. There is a 2,200-ft. grass airstrip, but buzz the Club and make contact . . . before landing as it might be soft." Would that we had been airborne.

Chart 26320 shows the shallow water along the southern coast of Grand Bahama tapering decisively ten or twelve miles before the entrance to Deep Water Cay to glorious depths of not less than thirty feet (we draw, remember, only five feet) right up to the beaches approaching the bight.

Six hours later the wind was stiffening, so we pulled down the fisherman. I noticed then that two (of the seventeen) lugs that slide up the groove in the aluminum mast, holding the luffline of the mainsail to the mast, had pulled out. Strange, they had never done that before. They are tough, one-inch by half-inch, hard plastic. Christopher tightened the halyard with all his strength another half inch to take the strain off the remaining members, but within minutes the rest of them had ripped out, and the mainsail was now sloppy, and in the whippy wind, very nearly intractable. Turning on the engine, sliding the gear forward, and turning the wheel to windward, I ordered the mainsail hauled down.

I cannot imagine what happened, in the all but total absence of stress—we had used the engine only in order to ease our way out of Lucayan Harbor—to the beautiful new key, to the setscrews, to the stainless-steel pin. But I was accosted by the distinctive purr of an engine in neutral. We were still three or four miles from the bight, but with less than an hour left of daylight, we needed to make way. I gave instructions to fasten on the storm trysail. As we wrestled with it, Peter Starr, having peered forward, rushed back quickly to the wheel. I have sailed with him 100,000 miles. His voice had the imperative ring to which one pays very special attention. *"We are,"* he

110

said quietly, *"about three hundred yards from a reef, breaking in the sea and stretching right out along our course."*

I looked up from the trysail operation. There it was, clear as pitch. A mile south of the shoreline, as far as the eye could see—exactly where the chart indicates a freeway. To the right of us was upwind. To the left, land. We rushed forward, fastened the sixty-pound Danforth (anchor), let down the headsails, paid out 150 feet of chain—and held our breath. The waves and wind pounded against us, and our twelve-foot bowsprit rose and plunged like . . . a bronco! But the anchor held. Danny took out a second anchor (the plow), attached to a one-inch nylon, on the whaler, out about the same distance, forty or fifty feet to the right of the Danforth. Frank Warren dove below to alert the Bahamian Air-Sea Rescue Station at Freeport, forty miles west, and reported that thus far we were not dragging, that we were a mile from the beach, that the mainsail was inoperative. Freeport replied that inasmuch as we were not in any apparent physical danger, they would not send out their rescue vessel, which in any event was busy right now with other emergency duty. I dispatched Danny and Warren in the whaler into the womb of Deep Water Cay to request a fishing boat to come to us to take the ladies—Pat and Aunty Bill—to the club, there to take refuge from what I knew would be a tossy, emetic, nerve-bruising night, manacled as we were in the way of a raucous wind and boisterous sea. The boys returned, three hours later, tatterdemalion, announcing that the alleged channel through which we proposed to pass had, even at high tide, scratched the whaler's eighteen-inch propeller shaft a half dozen times. That the club was inoperative. That there were no boats anywhere in the vicinity. That they had hitchhiked twenty miles to the nearest telephone, whence they had called Freeport once again, giving more exact details on our position. This much we already knew. We were guarding No. 2182, the emergency channel, and Freeport had called in to report that the boys were safe, and would spend the night ashore. Instead they elected to make their way back to Cyrano, where they now huddled, wet and exhausted. We sprawled about the huge cockpit, covered by canvas, looking past the six squat candles smug in their colored chimneys, gazing through the large windshields at the wind and the sea and the rain.

111

During that long night—as off the beach at Point Judith and off the reef at Nassau—our position didn't change. The anchor watch reported not a detectable foot of drag. The boat's continual yawing made sleep difficult. The gusts, though specially strident in our fixed circumstances, probably didn't reach more than thirty knots. We were not shipping water, and the reserve anchor, to judge from the tests we put it through on the forward winch, was itself nicely kedged. If it happened that both our anchors slipped, Cyrano would have floated toward the shore, on the safe side of the vicious reef, there either to be battered to pieces, or if we were lucky to hit at high tide, which would come just after midnight (and not again until noon the next day), to be lumpily beached, in chaotic fashion. We could briefly hold the boat away from the beach by pulling it with the whaler (and its 40-horsepower outboard); but in this sea, this would not have worked for more than long enough to try one time or perhaps two to resituate the anchor. We had on board, that far ahead of the B.O., just the two six-man emergency life rafts, which would have drifted our crew and passengers, a total of eight people, safely to the beach. We had repaired the mainsail by pulling the runners out of the trysail and stitching them in. The halyards were poised, ready to lift all sails. We needed a windshift, though not much of one. Forty-five degrees west and we could sail away from the reef on a starboard tack. Twenty-five degrees east, and we could sail back toward Freeport at a safe distance from the shore. Schooners are not designed to tack out of an acute angle.

But the wind held. Then, unaccountably, just after dawn, as I was listening gloomily to a weather forecast that gave no indication of any imminent change in wind or weather, a cutter approached us over the horizon, slowly, sniffily. (Through the wind I could hear the bagpipes.) But its purpose was so much unexpected, I found myself waving my cap, lest the cutter should ignore us or continue blindly on its eastern course. At least I could warn that if they wished to bone-fish in Deep Water Cay, they would need to portage their cutter into the harbor.

Within a few minutes we could see that it was a Coast Guard cutter, *Cape Shoalwater*, which soon came within hailing distance. Moments later, two men in a powered rubber life raft approached us—Chief

Green, an engineer, and Seaman First Class Mike Harvey. They required, first, to inspect our documentation and our safety equipment. We passed triumphantly. It transpired that at about 10:00 P.M., Freeport radio—without our knowledge—had called over to Fort Lauderdale to request assistance in our behalf. Within one hour, the cutter *Shoalwater* had collected its standby crew of twelve men, and started out on the 120-mile journey.

Chief Green inspected our drive shaft, and in an incredible forty-five minutes had it reconnected—a dazzling feat of virtuosity, which among other things required him single-handedly to slide the entire shaft forward with only the tools at hand. (Alas, it slipped out again twenty minutes later.) Captain Warren, outside my earshot, had meanwhile asked, wistfully I assume, if the cutter might tow us all the way to Miami, instead of merely to Freeport, since in any case the cutter was bound eventually for Fort Lauderdale. Within minutes, Mike Harvey's portable telephone relayed the request to the cutter, the cutter relayed it to Fort Lauderdale, and the request was approved. A very long hawser was slipped out over the *Shoalwater*'s stern, bound to our samson post forward, and we were off on a sixteen-hour trip to Miami, with Mike Harvey aboard to relay necessary signals on his radio. Sixteen hours later, averaging just under ten knots (we do ten and one-half maximum under sail) we reached Government Cut at Miami, and there a small tender took us over.

I pause in this drama of the malfunctioning coupler because I can't go through Government Cut to the marina without hearing again Danny's strangled cry. At my instructions he had leaped into the whaler when we got into the channel—as is our mode coming into port—to get the whaler out of the way when we docked. We could not see in the dark what had happened to him; we attempted to get the tender to go back and fetch him, but were told that would come later—first came the job of depositing Cyrano a mile down the line at the marina. As we drew into the dock, Danny was getting out of a car, smack in front of us. The huge outboard, the fastenings loosed by the long haul, had tilted up over the transom of the whaler, purred away under water for a minute or so, gurgling finally into silence. Danny, who is as resourceful as Robinson Crusoe and as buoyant as styrofoam, had used the water skis to paddle to one side of the cut, and bounded up, drenched, to flag a passing car. The driver instantly obliged. It developed that he was working on his twentieth can of beer. He asked Danny solicitously where he lived. Danny replied Stamford, Connecticut, at which the driver looked blearily at his Miami road map for the most direct route to Stamford. . . . No, no, Danny said. Miamarina, Fifth and Biscayne, would do just fine, and that was only twenty blocks away.

At the dock there were reporters and a couple of cameras. Evidently Dick Cavett had heard the news and observed brightly on his program that he hoped I had not run my yacht off the edge of the world. I was too tired to riposte that if the edge of the world had happened to be located in the Bahamas, the detail would have escaped the attention of the man who drew Chart 26320. The Miami *Herald* was already out with a report taken from Freeport radio, which was quoted as observing: "They either had no sail aboard or no one who knows how to sail." Peter Starr and I could not work up the strength to be indignant. Somehow, I mused, it would never occur to a newspaper to write: "Apparently no one in the Miami-Caribbean area knows how to connect a drive shaft." We settled for professing our gratitude to the Coast Guard.

One continues to learn. One learns and relearns the conventional things. For instance, that piloting in the Bahamas is a continuing act of brinkmanship, and unless you have on board someone who knows the waters personally, you are best off being skeptical of everything you read, doubting every reassurance you get, and treating all charts the way Little Red Riding Hood should have treated her alleged (as the newspapers say) grandmother. You relearn for the dozenth time the critical importance of super-rugged anchors and anchor lines, ready to go at very quick notice (it took us a couple of minutes: the chain was twisted around the windlass). That kind of thing.

At another level, you meditate on larger themes, like the eternal question of expertise, the limits of nautical expertise I have fussed over for years (though not purposively). I was angrier at the Miami shipyard after the first failure than after the fourth. If the mechanic at Cat Cay had fixed the drive shaft so that it had held, I'd have been blasphemously unforgiving about Miami. Again, if the meticulous

114

mechanic at Lucayan had fixed it, I'd have been irreconcilably critical of Miami. If Chief Green, after a few minutes of tinkering, had made it hold, I'd have dismissed the lot of them as incompetent. The next morning I met eyeball to eyeball with the head of the shipyard and his chief foreman. I heard the foreman say: "*I never did like that arrangement for the drive shaft.*" Question: Why did he not register his skepticism about it? To whom did he speak of it? (To his priest?) Why did he not recommend a different arrangement? Boat fixers are presumably not more evil as a class than, say, car mechanics, and probably less so than, say, newspaper columnists. The trouble is their failures magnify a problem most critically. Let the drive shaft fail in an automobile, and you miss your appointment. Let it fail coming in, say, to Cat Cay, and you are on the rocks. Marvin Hayes, who perched trustingly down on Cyrano's lifeline in the Hudson River, drowned. The rigger had not properly crimped on the lifeline cable to the shackle fitting. If you like, another coupling had failed. How is an amateur supposed to instruct a professional in such matters as how, soritically, to assure the linkage of a propeller all the way to the engine? How adequately to fasten an antenna on the main mast? An autopilot to the steering box?

I know there is no easy answer, any more than there is an answer, this side of a stony-faced jury that levies draconian penalties on the delinquent, to deficient motivation. But increasingly I attach importance—never mind how little of a technical nature you or your representative know—to someone's *being there.* We had people there on Cyrano that last day, but the circumstances were too hectic. On Cyrano that last day we had on board, at one point: Phil the captain, Phil Jr. his son, Augustino the steward, Reggie, Christopher, Danny, Aunty Bill, me, four of Van's relatives, three of their friends, Pat, our friend Marvin, two Cuban carpenters, the mechanic, the mechanic's assistant, the scuba diver, Art Kadey, Mrs. Campagna and her friend, the autopilot technician, the electronics specialist, and his assistant. On the slip, discouraged from actually boarding the boat, was a youngish lady in black, a stranger. She kept insisting on having a "session" with me, which I politely but tenaciously declined, weaving my way around her every time I needed to go ashore. I shouldn't have, because, frustrated by my inattention, the next day she traveled all the way to New York, where she ambushed my sister at our office to tell her her story, which was that she was plagued by a demon which had slipped from me into her when—she explained—our paths had crossed a year ago in Saigon, and she would only succeed in exorcising that demon by inhabiting with me, wordlessly, the same room for a half hour, during which the vibrations would reactivate which, alone, might chase, or seduce, the demon out of her body. I must assume that, in retaliation, she left a part of that demon on board to inhabit our loran and otherwise amuse himself with the radar, the antenna, the autopilot, the batteries, and—but that is for tomorrow—the Buckley Home Entertainment Service.

A workman must be attentively watched—both to encourage him and to ask the right questions. An acute eye can detect indecision; certainly it can detect sloth, and often sloppiness. Beyond that, a human circuit is activated, and clearly such a circuit needs to be revived between workman and boat owner. The nuts and bolts that occasionally get left behind in the jet engine probably wouldn't be, if the pilot had been there. His psychic presence doesn't appear to be enough. ("I never *did* like that arrangement for the drive shaft.") And as a matter of practice, I wonder if, when its services are summoned, the Coast Guard shouldn't be encouraged to conduct quasi-judicial investigations, the purpose of which would be to censure ignorance, incompetence, or outright delinquency.

The water is the last area on earth where total spontaneity of movement is possible. The odds are benignly in favor of the sailor. But the odds build on certain assumptions, such as that workmen will competently use such expertise as there is, and advertise the case when the expertise does not pronounce reliably on the solution to a particular problem. Certain of the sea's resources we cannot ever match—its occasional fitfulness, uncharted meannesses, occasional savagery. But the odds shouldn't close down against the sailor merely because those who are concerned with the sea become indifferent.

I feel *splendid* after saying all that.

Friday, May 30. I'll write notes in my journal once a day, when I go finally off duty. It is a fine opportunity, on a long voyage, to write belletristically in the log. Bill Snaith wrote about the joys of entering the daily log. He took a voluptuarian delight in going on and on in his logbook with the most entertaining, descriptive, informative sea prose by anybody in memory, at once the businesslike Joshua Slocum explaining just how it was, and the reflective Hilaire Belloc, explaining how it ought to be. I remember, after reading Snaith, resolving to expand on my anaemic entries in the log, bearing in mind the diffuser graces of rhetoric. But I came face to face with the unfortunate differences between Mr. Snaith and myself, every one of them in his favor. Writing is what I go to sea to get away from. But I did *try*, and a few years ago, taking *Suzy Wong* from the Chesapeake to New York, I got pretty talkative in the log the first two or three entries, but by the third watch I found myself writing, "Nothing new. Proceeding as above. Wind speed down, 2–5 knots." Then, remembering Snaith, I added, "Drank Coke." Six hours later, I observed that the intervening watch captain, Peter Starr, had scrawled alongside my entry, "So why do you think we care if you drank a Coke?" He led with his chin. I was able to write down in headmasterish script to my beer-guzzling young friend, "Go ye and do likewise." But, of course, that kind of thing really isn't what Bill Snaith had in mind.

Peter's withdrawal left us short one qualified watch captain, so that the idea of four hours on, eight hours off, will have to yield a little on the side of rigor. Every other cycle, the watch captains will get only four hours off between watches. I have made up watch rosters

117

for years, and sometimes they're like the inside of a Swiss clock. Racing, as I've observed, a crew member is on duty half the day. I use the Scandinavian system, 4–4–4–6–6. The six hours fall between eight and two, and two and eight, during the daylight hours. That gives everyone one longish sleep per day. Breaking up the day into five parts means you do not repeat a watch except every forty-eight hours. Nothing is drearier than to come on board and learn that you are on duty every single night from midnight to four. I have tried here to devise a system that will keep mixing us up, so that every watch captain (Danny, Reggie, myself, Campagna) will alternate with the watch assistants, Christopher, Van, Aunty Bill. Campagna and Van are out there now, having relieved Bill and me.

We are both tired, but quietly jubilant, and we talk of Pat's apprehensions, which seem just now so unreal, as we slide up the Gulf Stream, doing eight knots by courtesy of the wind, another two by courtesy of the stream.

We learned a month later that the nine-hour delay in leaving Miami spared us a quite unusual and idiosyncratic squall: violent enough to make the headlines in the Fort Lauderdale papers, which described fierce winds blowing out panes of glass that had hitherto withstood hurricanes. These winds were directly athwart our course, though it is probable that the incredible velocity of the tornado-type gust that did in the picture windows of Lauderdale was local; at least, there were no reports of ships going down, which might have been expected if the winds had been typhonic in reach.

The lights of Florida's gold coast will be visible through the night, since I have elected to stay in the stream until we are at the latitude of northern Georgia, and only then strike out for Bermuda. I calculated that the lift from the current would more than compensate for the extra distance run. I pointed out a couple of signals to Bill, one of whose enduring charms is that she is interested in everything, while affecting knowledge of nothing: though she is a grand master as administrator, world champion as friend and counselor. She is capable of graduating from a half-hour's conversation with a stranger as that person's suddenly discovered best friend. She still visits once a year the grave of Frank Roepken, who fell down in the captain's cabin and was driven by ambulance to the hospital five years ago. Bill and I got

118

word a few hours later and visited him there at midnight. Recognizing her, he was as shy, as embarrassed, as when years earlier he led us into the rocks, and felt, empathically, the disconsolation of the condemned man at the Nassau jail. Though only half-conscious, he groped for his toupee, which Bill located for him, under the bed. He died three days later, aged fifty-two, and Bill arranged his funeral in Los Angeles, where his surviving sister lives. The two of them were at the funeral service.

The wind is steady from the southeast, getting lighter. We ended by powering a little and clutching in the automatic pilot. Little ocean-racing sailboats now use, almost as a matter of course, autopilots that are governed by the wind. They are designed to maintain a boat's heading at a constant angle off the wind. The disadvantage is that they necessarily redirect the boat when the wind changes, which may happen when you are asleep. If you instruct a wind-vaned autopilot to keep you headed 90° off the wind (let us say), you could conceivably wake in the morning to find yourself going back home, if the wind changes direction by 180°. The wind-powered autopilots were developed primarily for the single-handed ocean racer, and the gentleman who won the transatlantic race several years ago records

Bill F. and Van in the deckhouse. The dark well leads down the companionway to the saloon and staterooms. WFB stands in the navigator's well.

that his own model was so marvelously successful that his hands were on the tiller for a total of only twenty minutes from Southampton to Newport, twenty-eight days.

Other boats use autopilots operated by power. These have the obvious disadvantage of—consuming power, offset by the advantage of maintaining a steady compass course irrespective of (a) whether there is any wind at all, and (b) where the wind is coming from. They operate through a compass of their own which, once set, sends out electrical impulses that keep the wheel turning in the indicated direction to maintain the stipulated course. They require a little mothering, but are splendid mechanical achievements.

Before sleeping, I asked Bill whether, since I feel lousy and am quickly losing my voice, I shouldn't take a little drastic medication; and she opened up her clinic, and gave me an antibiotic. In my cabin, looking out at the stars, I am content, though I sense, at my nerve ends, lingering apprehensions. I don't know what they are, and don't pause to excavate.

Saturday, May 31. I changed my mind about following the Gulf Stream this morning when we heard predictions of an easterly wind a couple of hundred miles north of us. If we waited until reaching the latitude of northern Georgia to wheel over toward Bermuda, we would run right into that wind. So we head right for Bermuda

Taking a sun sight from the top of the deck-house.

(course 072°, distance 891 miles). How do I know that is the heading for Bermuda? Because I had taken two sun sights (by now we had given up on the loran). That gave me what they call a running fix, which I'll explain in due course. Bermuda being as far away as it is, you can't get a heading in the conventional way. Regular charts (and plotting sheets) are what they call Mercator projections, and the lines are rectilinear, whereas of course meridian lines are not. After all, they all meet at the South Pole and the North Pole. But in between they fan out, squatmost at the equator. It is a fairly tricky business to figure out the course between two distant points, requiring you to consult tables that record the degree of curve between two positions, given the respective latitudes and longitudes. If, for instance, you are going directly south, there is no problem: 180° true is your course. Ditto north. If, however, you are going in any other direction, you need to apply yourself—even if your destination is on the same latitude. (Exception: if you are on the equator heading to another point also on the equator. This has never happened to me.)

Let us assume you are at latitude 45°, longitude 70° (A), and you wish to know the course and, while you are at it, the distance, to a point (B) on latitude 45°, longitude 50°—i.e., 20° closer to Greenwich. Without telling you how the answer is arrived at, I give it to you:

846.36 miles (nautical)
82.89°

Suppose one measured the distance but on to a point (C), another twenty degrees of longitude further away; then to yet another twenty degrees further (D). Again, the answers:

From lat. 45°, long. 70° (A) to lat. 45°, long. 30° (C):
1679.45 miles
75.57°
From lat. 45°, long. 70° (A) to lat. 45°, long. 10° (D)
2484.58 miles
67.79

Sailing from point A to point B due east requires you to travel 846.36 miles at 82.89°.

121

Sailing from point A to point C requires you to travel only an additional 833.90 miles and shaves 7.32° off your initial course.

Sailing from point A to point D requires you to travel only an additional 805.15 miles and shaves 8° off your course.

These are not proportional relationships that you can plot in plane geometry or on a graph.

One notes that the longer the distance, the more northerly the initial heading.

From a point at lat. 45° and long. 180°, headed to a point at lat. 45°, long. 100°, your heading is 59.32°. But to a point at long. 20°, it is 14°.

And to a point at long. 00.00°—you guessed it, the heading is 000°, or due north. But, obviously, on reaching the North Pole your heading would then become 180° (there is no other heading from there). Headings are constantly changing. You can only set an initial heading. That course is good in a sailboat—depending on a number of factors—for a day or so; after that, it needs to be modified.

How does one make such fine calculations? One way is by a rather complicated set of tables. The other is by Hewlett and Packard. For about eight hundred dollars, you can purchase their HP–65, and spend the rest of your life playing with it. It is the miniature programable computer, with one entire deposit of cards (they call it their NAV-PAC) for the flier or ocean navigator. You pick up a paper-thin flexible metal strip and ease it into a slot at the upper end of the wallet-sized instrument; an invisible gear clutches it, passing it quickly through, right to left, leaving it limp to the fingers at the opposite end. You grasp it and then slide it into the upper slot where it serves you as a dashboard, and what you see, imposed over eight rows of pencil-eraser-sized keys, is Great Circle Navigation: STD 03A. And under that the headings

LAT   LNG   calc dist   calc hdg

You enter the latitude of your present position, and depress the key (A) under "LAT"; then the longitude of your present position, and depress the key (B) under "LNG." You repeat this for the latitude and longitude of the point you are headed for. Then you push the key under "calc dist" (C). In a few seconds you have a digital

With Van and Reggie, using the deckhouse settee-table to plot loran lines.

display: the distance in nautical miles. Press the key under "calc hdg," wait another few seconds and you have: your course.

I had today my virginal experience with the HP as a celestial triangle-breaker, which is more complicated. It worked! But I'll keep plotting the sun to make sure.

Van fussed with the portable radio, trying to get more detailed weather information. He knew nothing more about meteorology than the meaning of the word, but several months ago bravely took on the assignment of Ship's Meteorologist, a duty Peter Starr was to have shared with him. He attacked the subject with the gusto of a non-scientist before whom such esoterica, as they do to me, reveal themselves slowly, grudgingly. He announced gravely at lunch, with the high self-amusement he brings to every subject: "I've got to teach Danny meteorology, in case anything happens to me."

At dinner time (1900), we were given a fine barbecue. Phil Jr.'s cooking is resourceful, painstaking, and nicely varied. The cassette player gave us Alicia de Larrocha's stunning interpretation of Albéniz's *Iberia*. The captain is at the wheel, the air just beginning to cool, the sunset tropical, the seas light, but the shoulders of the ocean are beginning to flex. We have a bottle of red wine and a bottle of white wine, and the rule is that the person who empties a bottle must write out—on a printed sheet marked, "ABOARD YACHT CYRANO, Miami to Marbella. May 30–June 30, 1975. If you find this message, please

123

Writing out a psywar message to put into the empty bottle.

mail it to William F. Buckley, Jr., 150 East 35th Street, New York, New York, U.S.A."—an anti-Communist message, insert it in the bottle, and throw it overboard. The fantasy is that, in about six weeks, several hundred bottles will lap up on the shores of Africa and Latin America, and, opening them, the natives will say to one another, sadly, "See? Verily, thus has the Congress of the United States reduced the CIA."

The discipline is that no anti-Communist message may repeat one that has gone before. This will prove exhausting before the trip is over. I began it, ninety miles from Cuba, with: "Oiga Fidel: Veniam Videbo Vincam." Someone contributed, since we were out of the reach of Senator Church, Congressman Pike, Anthony Lewis, and Harriet Van Horne, "CIA will guarantee one (1) free assassination upon retrieving this message." Van, whose instincts are bawdy, wrote: "Attention: Kommrad Kapitan SS Lenin subski (on special detail): Please stop fucking up our electronic gear; if not, we will invite you aboard and corrupt your morals." Christopher contributed: "Memorandum. From: Allan Dulles. To: All Cuban Operatives. Re:

124

Bay of Pigs Action. Have discussed proposal with JFK. Jackie wants to know if operation can be postponed until Father Joe's birthday (she promised him an invasion for his 70th). Advise if this presents problems at your end. Cariño. AD."

After dinner the great unveiling of the Buckley Home Entertainment Service. I am too dispirited to write about it. It forces me to be unhappy, and that is so hard right now. The moon is late tonight. But, of course—I had forgotten. We are headed 065° now. We sailed 170 miles in twenty-one hours and forty-five minutes—thanks to the current. We are a hundred miles out to sea.

June 1. Today is Sunday. Last night late, on watch together, Christopher asked whether I intended to conduct a service of some sort. I was surprised and pleased—and a little embarrassed. Upstairs, Christopher, Danny, and I are Catholic; Bill is a nonchurch-going Anglican (married to a Catholic) who (like her sister Pat) helped bring up her only child (Kathy) as a formally instructed, church-attending Catholic. Reggie is an occasional church-goer. I suspect that Van, like most Americans of his age and background, knows the inside of those churches in which his children were baptized, plus Notre Dame, Chartres, and Westminster Abbey, though there is something going on there. I remember someone asking Dwight Macdonald in my presence years ago: "What is your opinion of the Bible?" His reply: "I think it's the greatest book ever written. Of course, it has no religious significance for me whatever." *Of course* is the operative phrase . . . I shrink from religious ostentation. There is the further problem: If an improvised service of sorts were conducted, I would either invite Phil Campagna and his son, and Augustino; or not invite them. In the former event, a subtle pressure is exerted, intimidating, as between employer and employee. In the latter case, it is as if the veneration of the Lord, like free champagne, is a perquisite of first-class passengers. I end by doing nothing. Christopher did not bring up the subject today. I am displeased with myself: but then that, at least, is an oblation of sorts to my Maker, who has given us Christopher; and, tonight, quite the blackest sky I think I ever saw. The stars are visible, but nothing else. The flecks of white on the vast inkiness are visible as briefly as fireflies. I asked Van if anything was up on the meteorological front, and he replied happily that it beat the shit out of him. I told the relief watch to be very careful and to watch for any sudden freshening of the wind, and to wake me as a last resort; as a very last resort.

Oh, yes, the Buckley Home Entertainment Service.

When I bought Cyrano, I thought to dally with closed-circuit tee-vee, and did so. I bought one of those Sony jobs. The idea is that, at night in the islands, the children might get bored, or the charterers might think it amusing to show a movie. So why not stock an inventory of tapes with great movies pirated from the teevee channels, the commercials thoughtfully dubbed out? I remember one night, a year later, three hundred miles out toward Bermuda, lazy sailing conditions, a full moon, pleasant company, and I thought to ask my companions had they heard Horowitz's Carnegie Hall concert which had been televised that season as a CBS special? Well, no, they hadn't. Would they like to see it? The whole investment was worth that indelible memory, sipping brandy, smoking cigars, sailing at about eight knots out in the middle of the ocean, and viewing and listening to one hour of Horowitz doing Schubert, Chopin, Liszt, and Scriabin. There was another occasion—come to think of it—when an old

The attempt at closed-circuit teevee after dinner. Bill F., Van, Reg on settee; Danny at the television.

friend, an official of the New York Yacht Club, arrived in full regalia late one evening in Padanaram, in an advanced state of decomposition, to have another (yet another) nightcap with us. He came upon us lounging around our television screen. I informed him solemnly that I had requested the local television station to run *The Wizard of Oz* for us, and they had just now begun. "I'll phone and tell them to start it again from the beginning for you," I said gravely. I disappeared below for a few seconds, turned a couple of knobs surreptitiously, and *Oz* quickly rewound and started again. I returned to see my friend clinging to the mast in amazement at my extraordinary authority over the local station. On the other hand, he'd have been clinging to the mast in any case.

Our Important Visitor had been a friend for many years, and is widely beloved surely in part because of his total absence of starch, a substance not entirely absent among ocean-racing officials, some of whom take the rituals of the sport with a seriousness almost superstitious, for reasons not always communicable. I was once disqualified from a race because I forgot to lower the yacht club burgee from the masthead at the start—but that's okay, you gotta have rules, and even protocols. Sometimes, though, the tribal spirit spills over, and you get arteriosclerotic stuffiness.

Dear Mr. Buckley [a letter from a nabob in yacht circles, way back when Peter was still handling *Suzy*]:

At 3:00 A.M. on Saturday, September 19, 1964, an inebriated character climbed aboard my boat, while anchored off the Ida Lewis Yacht Club at Newport. Apparently he had taken someone's dinghy from the dock and started to row out to the *Suzy Wong*, where he said he was staying, but that you were not aboard. Inasmuch as the rowboat did not have oarlocks, only oars, he was blown in our direction rather than that of *Suzy Wong*.

He wanted to rest a while in the cockpit, which I permitted him to do, but when he tried to come down into our cabin, I gave him my only good set of chrome-plated oarlocks so he could get back to *Suzy Wong*. He said he would return them for sure by 8:00 A.M., which he did not do.

I think you should know of this incident, should endeavor to have my oarlocks replaced, and you might suggest to him that such unbecoming behavior does not add to the already dim view that many of us take of the crew on *Suzy Wong*.

Very truly yours,

J. . . J. . . J. . .

127

I found that last sentence provocative, and of course succumbed to the temptation to reply in kind:

Dear Mr. J. . . :

I greatly regret that you were inconvenienced. *Suzy Wong* was on charter between September 13 and September 22. My secretary has made inquiries and the guilty party has come forward, whose check for a new set of oarlocks I enclose, together with his apology.

I join with you in deploring the effects of inebriation on some people. The occasion calls, however, for qualifying that statement. I have never laid eyes on nor exchanged a spoken word with the offender. Even so, I confess that I would myself prefer the company of those who, under the influence of drink, occasionally walk off with a pair of other people's oarlocks to that of those who—presumably under the same influence—write letters waywardly assaulting the character of innocent people.

Yours faithfully,
(W.F.B.)

The reference by the oarlockless plaintiff to the "dim view" taken of "the crew" of *Suzy* was a grouchy allusion to an episode which for quite a while was the subject of much animated disputation in local yacht club circles. In a moment of exasperated exuberance during the 1962 Bermuda Race, after waiting a full half hour in a pitching sea, ear cocked over to the static-spitting radio speaker for the scheduled 6:00 P.M. weather broadcast from the Coast Guard cutter, which did not come, nor any explanation for the delay, Peter picked up the telephone mike and said, "This is *Paper Tiger, Paper Tiger, Paper Tiger.* Calling destroyer escort *Nautilus.* Goddammit, are you or aren't you going to issue a weather report?" Now the *Paper Tiger* bit was something of an inside joke. The yawl in question—a celebrated competitor, the favorite of many sportscasters to win the big race, had, at the starting line, "barged" on us (*to barge on, v.,*—that infraction of the rules of right of way effected when a boat coming in from the windward side requires a leeward boat, close-hauled on a course to the windward starting-line marker, to fall off to leeward in order to avoid collision with the windward vessel); and we had hoisted our protest flag, which is a routine, but formal, demand for the adjudication, in due course, of a complaint. During the ensuing days at sea, *Paper Tiger* was the object of amiable vituperation in all cockpit-stories that required a here-and-now hobgoblin. Peter, age eighteen, had prankishly blurted out *Paper Tiger* as our identifying signal, and no one on watch who heard him had thought much about it.

It was the day after the last boat had crossed the finish line in Bermuda, and I presented myself, as scheduled, before the Race Committee, obliged to press my formal charge against *Paper Tiger*, whose skipper, Charles Morgan, a boat designer and builder, I quickly learned on contact with him, is a man of extravagant amiability and calm, whatever his hectic practices on the starting line. He pleaded his case before the committee unsuccessfully—and I was awarded the first protest ever recorded in a Bermuda Race (or so the historians told me)—*Paper Tiger* was docked two whopping hours. Before I had risen to leave the courtroom, I found the officiating yachtsman abruptly announcing to the already-chastened Mr. Morgan that on top of the two-hour penalty for barging, he would be "expected" to disqualify the *Paper Tiger* entirely—for "breaking radio silence." For a few seconds I sat in dumb horror as Charles Morgan pleaded that it wasn't *his* boat that had broken radio silence, but *another* boat, using *his* boat's name. I rose shakily and said that, coincidentally, I was the very man to confirm this: It had been *our* boat, *Suzy*, using *Paper Tiger*'s name, that had made the transmission.

It is time to explain that there is indeed a rule of "radio silence," which applies in many races, including the Bermuda Race. Its purpose is to frustrate the cunning navigator who, ascertaining the position of other boats, might deduce the whereabouts and activity of friendly currents and winds.

That much, and so on and so forth, I knew. I hadn't ever assumed that radio silence would over the years achieve something of a doctrinal sanctity—proscribing the use of the radio even for purposes totally unrelated to the original purpose of the prohibition. It was like being accused of cheating after the exam is over. Even so, we had apparently (a) committed (to begin with) a capital offense—by using the radio-telephone; *and* (b) forged another man's fingerprints on the smoking pistol! I withdrew *Suzy* from the race (that is the prescribed auto-da-fé by which boats that have violated substantive rules atone), but only after extracting from the committee (which was extremely courteous) an official statement on the matter absolving the radio operator (Peter was then a sophomore at college, and I declined to identify him) from any extratechnical aspersion. When I returned to the hotel to join my crew for lunch, my mood was heavy with the emotional weight of the ordeal, and I felt certain—as the letter from the tormented gentleman with the chrome-plated oarlocks would soon prove—that the hardiest survivors of the episode would be the lip-smackers who would descry in the bumptious telephone call an insidious effort to disqualify a boat by means unspeakably foul. My spirits revived only when, after two hours of agitated conversation on every conceivable aspect of the matter, the bill for the lunch was brought in. There was the usual grabbing for it, won by Van who, with a flourish—after writing in a generous tip—signed the check, in the strokes of John Hancock: *"Paper Tiger."*

For years and years, during the decade I raced to Bermuda, I nursed a fantasy which I curse myself, now that it is too late, for never having consummated, even though it would probably have resulted in my being terminally drummed out of the yachting community. . . .

The major commercial yachting magazines regularly publish, in their post-Bermuda Race issues, half-page pictures of the three or four winning boats, sponsored by commercial yacht concerns. They were always the same. The crew is sitting on the deck of the victorious vessel, either in the cockpit or along the cabin top. In the center is the grizzled skipper, a huge silver cup in his hand. There are usually beer cans or highball glasses. Everyone, through his whiskers, is grinning, gazing at the trophy proudly, lovingly. The bold-faced, assertive affirmations ("My son, the doctor") inflexibly follow, e.g.:

AZURE BLUE. WINNER, CLASS C, 1964 BERMUDA RACE
Then, along the margins, the credits:
—SAILS BY RATSEY AND LAPTHORN!
—DESIGNED BY RAYMOND HUNT!
—BUILT BY NEVINS!
My idea was to publish an ad in the same issue, half-page, featuring me and my crew, exactly posed, exultantly seated in *Suzy*'s cockpit, smiles and beer mugs and all—with only the cup missing. In the traditional place the triumphant headline would appear:

SUZY WONG. NEWPORT-BERMUDA RACE, 1964

And, routinely:

—SAILS BY HATHAWAY REISER AND RAYMOND!

—DESIGNED BY SPARKMAN AND STEPHENS!

—BUILT BY AMERICAN BOATYARD, HONG KONG!

That's all. The entire yacht-minded community, aware that *Suzy* was, as always, one of the last two or three boats to cross the finish line, would stare at the picture for stupefied hours before the jape dawned.

That caper would have cost me about two thousand bucks in ad lineage, which is a lot of bucks even for a lot of laughs. My *ultimate* fantasy would have cost me about a hundred thousand bucks, but by God, it would have been one for the record. Dick Tuck, the renowned Democratic prankster, would have groveled at my feet. . . . We would start out together from the starting line at Newport, see? But about eighteen hours later, which is when you are generally out of sight of any boat, we would calmly come about and head for a pre-established cove in some little fishing inlet in Rhode Island. There a seaplane would be waiting. It would scoop us up, and deposit us two or three hours later about forty miles north of Bermuda, alongside a vessel, bobbing there waiting for us, ferried out by two deaf-mute sailors— an *exact replica* of *Suzy*, down to the chipped toilet seat and the loose spoke on the wheel. When the juggernauts from Class A began to appear on the horizon, we would hoist sail and head dramatically for the finish line, arriving there at about the same time as the A-boats, but with our seventeen-hour handicap. Oh, how the flashbulbs would pop! Oh, how the sportswriters would hail the greatest navigational upset in history! "Mr. Buckley, Mr. Buckley!—*MR. BUCK-LEY!*"—the microphones would obliterate my demure expression— "*HOW DID YOU DO IT*—a forty-foot boat coming in with the seventy-footers!"

"Wa-al," I would say, sort of Lindbergh-like, "we just figured— let's take a chance! Spent a couple of months studying the currents. Found out there are a few times, every hundred years or so, when a special current comes up at—well, guess we oughta keep that to ourselves, what do you think, Van?—and we figured, well, this is the year it oughta be there. Let's go look for it. Well, I guess we found it!"

My fantasy stopped short of the meeting a day or two later with the Race Committee, at which I would appear, unannounced, my huge trophy in hand. "Uh, gentlemen—about the race—I have to—admit—to an—infraction—of the rules. . . ."

But back to the Buckley Home Entertainment Service.

A year ago I acquired a cassette television cartridge player, many technological stages improved over the equipment I kept on Cyrano years ago. It occurred to me that it would not be unreasonable to borrow "War and Peace," which has 26 one-hour-long episodes, ship the cassette player to Cyrano shortly before the trip, and after dinner each night, watch a chapter. I mentioned the plan to Alistair Cooke a month before sailing, and he told me "W & P" was something of a bore, but that I should take "Upstairs, Downstairs." With much wheedling, my friend Warren Steibel, the producer of "Firing Line," borrowed the set from an easygoing television station, plus a few ballets and the like. Danny carted the set to Miami. We built chocks for it on deck and a waterproof canvas cover; and last night the great moment came—and the screen gave us only horizontal lines. Danny and Reggie spent three hours trying to fix it. And another three hours today. For a brief moment we got an image, with a kind of fauvist discontinuity, the faces babbling away, connected with the torsos only tangentially. What they said under the circumstances sounded especially silly. The episode is the one in which Milord's lady goes down in the *Titanic*, and Van deplores people who go out to sea in nonseaworthy boats. But even that ended halfway through the hour, and proved to be the final experience with the series: No one could figure out the problem. [Later, in Bermuda, Pat brought a fresh television set from home, retrieving the boat's—and that didn't work either.] It must be that the generator is producing slightly off-beat power, notwithstanding that the voltmeter, at all points of contact, shows pulse, heartbeat, vital organs, sight, vision, and reflexes absolutely normal. One more mystery. The ideal mystery at sea`is one that would announce itself before one goes to such pains.

I wonder: Will the absence of this hour, widely touted in my preview memorandums to the crew, pull out of the trip a little, but important, element—the Theater-on-the-Sea—substantially diminishing the pleasure of it all? I resolve to substitute a poker game after dinner; one hour, no extension. House limit on the betting—as if

Danny won't win it all anyway. . . . We did less than 170 miles during these twenty-four hours. A casual attempt at star sights proved unsatisfactory. I shall have to tighten my belt on this matter pretty soon. We are 560 miles from Bermuda. In a way, you relearn navigation each time out if a few months (or years) have gone by since using it. But your skills redevelop very rapidly. I must remember to shoot the man in New York who installed the astigmatizer on my sextant.

Monday, June 2. The sun was bright, but we were without wind and had to power the whole day long. At noon we stopped and swam. Christopher, the .222 magnum cocked, sat on the cabin deck, prepared to fire at any shark attracted to our flailings. Aunty Bill decorously stays below, so that we can do without swimming trunks. If the Atlantic is polluted, it is polluted other than at latitude 30°, longitude 76°, where the water is a cobalt blue, accepting as confidently as trained dolphins their dollops of fish, the traditional beer can you throw over the side, to observe and marvel at its endless visibility as it sinks into ocean water unmurked by the detritus of civilization. There is a great fuss this season about the danger of sharks, thanks substantially to the bestselling scare-story on the subject. There are, of course, sharks everywhere in the oceans, even as there are rats everywhere on land. Ten years ago, when I was taking instruction off the Virgin Islands in the use of scuba gear, my instructor, using an underwater chalk crayon on blackboard, wrote, "Hammerhead shark," and pointed to an object about thirty feet away which floated there, apparently as contented as a cow, more or less looking at us, but without any trace, that an amateur could detect, of greed. I followed my instructor along, as he went on scribbling on his underwater palimpsest, describing the underwater population, harmless for the most part but not entirely. There were several barracuda and one moray eel. On surfacing, he told me the experience was altogether normal, though spotting the moray eel was "a bit lucky"; and that the key to a serene relationship with sharks is simply this: Bear it in mind that they are so dumb, you can neither anticipate nor outwit them. Accordingly, you play the statistics, which are vastly reassuring. Avoid swimming in tandem with outflowing garbage—which one would tend to avoid doing for reasons entirely independent of the fear of sharks. Don't

133

swim if any part of your body is bleeding. If you swim at night, enter the water gradually rather than splashily—and look forward to a ripe old age, limbs intact. I respond joyfully to almost any permissive franchise and have never since given a thought to the danger of sharks, a serenity I have not communicated to Christopher, who, in guarding the ramparts, visualizes the enemy and loses his appetite to disport in enemy territory. It is all very refreshing, and the lunch tastes better; and we are less depressed by the absence of wind.

I am haunted by the matter of our fuel reserves. Four years ago, the inconceivable happened. We cruised to Bermuda in the fall and hit an anomalous three days without wind. Cyrano burns 3 gallons per hour at full speed (eight knots) and carries 275 gallons—so that we have a technical range of about 725 miles. But Ned didn't top the tank in New York and we pulled out with only three quarters of our fuel. We had an intimation of the problem a hundred miles from Bermuda when the windward tank gurgled dry—causing astonishment (we had never run out of fuel before). We reduced the speed to five knots, which doubles the efficient use of the fuel; but even then, twenty miles from Bermuda, we ran clean out. Two P.M. No fuel, no wind. I was solemnly committed to introducing Vice-President Spiro Agnew at the annual New York Conservative Party Banquet at eight, holding reservations on a five o'clock flight. Van had reservations to London at six, having convened for the next morning one of those crucial banking conferences that decide what we will pay for fried chicken next year. We telephoned the U.S. naval base which, having established that we were in no physical danger, politely advised that they could not offer us amphibian helicopter service. We then secured, through Bermuda Radio, the services of a powerboat which in due course arrived and raced us into Hamilton Harbor in a bronco-busting hour and a half, just in time to miss all our flights. Where there are no alternatives, the wise man says, there are no problems: So we spent a pleasant time in Bermuda, until the next morning, when the bill came in for the powerboat, after the paying of which I could only satisfy myself by writing a column, defending the island against charges of a synthetic modernization by documenting that, even now, piracy survived in Bermudan waters.

We have made extensive arrangements, this time around, to leave Bermuda for the distant Azores with ample auxiliary fuel. But Reggie and I paid insufficient attention to the possible demands of this leg. There are 440 miles to go, and there isn't, should the calm persist, fuel to go that distance. But I'll go another day before taking the drastic step of powering down to five knots. Meanwhile, in the calm, with our motor—usually so very quiet, a little noisier now than it ought to be on my silence-oriented Cyrano (something else to correct in Bermuda)—there is still the feel, somehow, of the sailboat: the rhythmed lilt, slowly, as we furrow through the lolling seas, dipping down ever so slightly, at the end of a great wave cycle; and in the long in-betweens, side to side, but ever so gently; restrained, perhaps, from seesawing action by the sheer weight of the masts. I turn off my reading light and calculate, ever so loosely. Seventy feet of mast. Weight, 1,200 pounds. The top ten feet, then, weigh about 120 pounds. 120 times 70 equals 8400. So there are—never mind the trigonometric refinements—about eight thousand pounds up there that resist instant righting of the boat; that slows the pendulum action. It amuses me to contemplate getting up, going aft, and with solemn countenance telling Danny and Christopher that the captain and owner of the yacht Cyrano desires that one of them should be always aloft at the crow's nest to add to this soporific leverage. If I had five minutes' more energy I'd do it, by God, just to see the reaction; but as it is, I'll sleep without even reading on into *Moby Dick*.

Tuesday, June 3. We had a squall today and its effect was tonic. It came on us slowly, late in the afternoon. We lost the sun. Then the

The wind rises.

Van at the wheel during a squall.

high clouds began to gather, and the seas to swell. There was a distinctive nip in the breeze, which stayed southwest. I ordered the Genoa struck, and a while later, the mainsail. That left us with the main staysail and the forestaysail. These are brand new—for this trip; and they are very tough, made of 10.5-ounce Dacron. A heavily built schooner like Cyrano should be be able to carry these two sails in all but very rough stuff. A lot depends, to be sure, on the course you are sailing and the condition of the seas. If you are close-hauled, the tendency to heel increases. And, of course, without a head-sail you are almost as helpless as Columbus pulling out of San Salvador—what you do is use power, just enough of it to supply the upwind bite you have lost with the headsail. When I bought her, Cyrano had no running backstay. Said fixture is a cable running from the mast at the top spreader to the windward deck. The point is that in an ordinary wind you don't need to buttress the mast with that extra support. But in a very strong wind and choppy sea, the running back-stay plays off the forestay to give you rigidity in the top one third of the mast. But, as is always the case in a sailboat, for every advantage gained, there is a penalty. When the running backstay is secured, the main boom cannot change its position from one side of the boat to the other—it hits the backstay. It ceases (in the graphic terminology) to be "self-tending." That means, as a practical matter, that there is yet another reason to avoid an involuntary jibe, which is what happens when the wind direction passes behind you, from five o'clock, say, to seven o'clock, causing the sails suddenly to slam over to the opposite side of the boat. Dangerous. For one thing, the boom coming over does so with great and sudden force, and would knock out Joe Louis if he were unaware of it, let alone lipped it. For another, the articula-tion of the boom at the mainmast is called the gooseneck, and it is a relatively delicate fixture. A very bad jibe can ruin your gooseneck, leaving you without the swivel apparatus to use your mainsail. That happened to me once on *Suzy Wong*, in a wild ride from Province-town to Monhegan Island, for which Pat has never quite forgiven me. It was downwind all the turbulent way, and we jibed quite unex-pectedly. Pat, sleeping in the forward compartment, was thrown from her bunk into the well below. She swears that Peter Starr, dispatched below with flashlight, moved her bleeding arm slightly to one side with nothing more than an "Excuse me, Mrs. Buckley," for the pur-pose of opening the drawer, removed the pliers and screwdriver I had sent him down for, and left her disordered body unattended and un-noticed. At Monhegan, a little island dream we miraculously came

The squall has come and gone.

upon in the wind and rain and fog, I asked at the pier for the local blacksmith. There was none; but the fisherman spreading his nets as he spoke to us volunteered that there *was*, on Monhegan Island, a very famous sculptor who worked in iron. In due course, battered gooseneck in hand, I knocked timidly at the door of Herbert Kallem. On being admitted, I found him listening, amused—as who would not be?—to a story being told by Zero Mostel. I cleared my throat and asked whether he would consider repairing our gooseneck in his forge. Rising to full height he said Yes—"provided you don't try to pay me for it." I promised. We have been friends ever since. I have three of his sculptures.

So—involuntary jibes are to be guarded against. The running backstay was now secured. When the mainsail was finally brought down, we were left with the staysails, which are self-tending. They too have goosenecks, however. The mainstaysail is a pretty big sail, so I had a preventer rigged. That is a line attached from the end of the boom through a leeward block on deck to a cleat—to prevent a sudden jibe. The line holds the boom to leeward.

Thus prepared, with foul-weather gear on, we watched. There was much nervous anticipation. It came in two waves. The wind speed rose to about thirty-five knots. And then, in blasts of rain and fury, to gusts of about fifty knots. The direction of the wind was fairly steady, requiring no adjustment in course. Our speed, under the staysails alone, rose to over ten knots. Express-train stuff. It lasted about an hour, after which the gusts began to yawn, leaving the seas with inflated, but aimless, energy. Christopher was everywhere, taking pictures. But no picture of a storm at sea begins to tell you what it is like. We decided to have our dinner buffet-style like our lunches, leaving the main table down so as not to wrestle with sliding dishes. We lit a half dozen of the colored-glass, fat-assed candle lights (a buck each at the A & P), and there was animated talk, a touch of the corporate experience. Everyone suddenly realized what Cyrano would do for us, and we were sorely proud.

After dinner, with some reluctance, I accompanied Bill to the telephone, at the use of which she has become masterful. We have experienced a lesion of interest in world affairs, and no one bothers to turn on the news broadcasts. But Bill has her personal empire to check on,

After dinner. The boys are on watch.

like the reclusive Philip II, and she makes the rounds on our powerful ocean telephone. We learn that her sister-in-law has pneumonia.
That the daughter-in-law of a dear friend has committed suicide.
That the son of another dear friend has been caught mainlining
heroin—the catch of a single hour on the radio telephone, while outside there are only the big seas; the steady breeze; and the boys on
watch, chattering and talking now about perhaps bending on the
Genoa—I peered over and looked at the Kenyon; we were doing eight
knots. "Go ahead," I said; and Bill and I, clutching the lifeline,
groped our way back into the saloon, where she told me matter-of-
factly what she would do to help her afflicted friends—it would not
have occurred to her, even five hundred miles out at sea, to think herself helpless to extend a hand. Since Van and Reggie weren't asleep,
I sat down at the piano and plunked a few chords from my Cheat-
Sheet Jazz Book, and Reggie in due course came and sang the lyrics,
hitting the notes about as securely as I hit the chords. After attempt-

139

ing "Two Sleepy People," it was universally agreed that we should go to bed. Van has gritted his teeth for the midnight watch.

Wednesday, June 4. This was the day the generator stopped, causing crises (a) mechanical, and (b) diplomatic. It was after lunch, and I was asleep. Fortunately, because otherwise I'd have had to rebuke Captain C. for losing his temper. Now it is over, and the generator is fixed. We have on board an emergency gasoline-operated generator, the purpose of which is to charge that crucial battery needed to turn over your engine needed to charge your batteries. We had to use it. It is what woke me, no such sound having been recorded since they tore down the 3rd Avenue El. Hardly what one associates with an irenic sail across the ocean. But it lasted less than an hour, subsiding in perfect synchronization with the Captain's temper.

I toyed a few months ago with the notion of sending out as one of my pretrip memorandums a casual proscription of beard-growing, to see whether I could get away with it. I don't like beards by and large—I tend to think they are for people with uninteresting faces. Men tend to look the same. I have always shuddered at the possibility that, by mistake, St. Peter admitted Karl Marx and barred Johannes Brahms. But I especially don't like easy stigmata. In this case, the ocean sailor's. In days of yore it was cumbersome, at worst difficult, to shave every day at sea. Now it is as easy as brushing one's teeth. Arriving in Bermuda, unshaven, at the end of the ocean race always struck me a little like the athlete on campus who wears his sweatshirt inverted, ostensibly to disguise the varsity letter—which, of course, accentuates that which it purports to cover; like men's bikinis. I once

"Christopher came on board looking like Peter Pan, and left looking like Charles Manson."

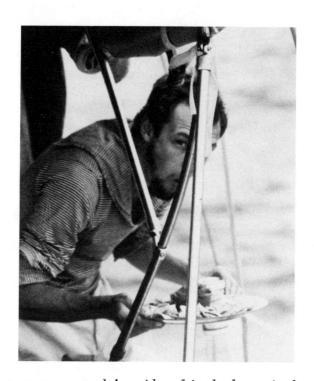

lunched at college—supreme example!—with a friend who arrived
·not having *quite* removed his parachute harness. I should have known
that my beloved beautiful Christopher would succumb to the temptation; which he has done—he began the trip looking like Peter Pan
and ended looking like Charles Manson—though his motivations,
whatever they are, are pure: He is the least exhibitionistic of creatures. But that which is natural has an allure for him. Even as a child,
Christopher, for all his worldliness, was the boy who would have
to get cotton candy at the circus, salt water taffy at Atlantic City,
shells at the beach. I am glad he didn't visit the Fiji Islands on his
round-the-world trip as a deckhand, else he'd have returned with a
ring through his nose. As it was, of course, he appeared home with a
huge tattoo. ("You don't like it?" he exclaimed, when, his arm bared,
his mother clutched the curtains to keep from collapsing. "It cost me
fifty-eight Hong Kong dollars!")

But, of course, I shan't say a word, not a word; nothing would so
much reinforce his determination to grow it down to his chest than a
wisecrack from this quarter (unless I asked him as a personal favor;

Christopher and Reggie compare progress. Note $58 (H.K.) tattoo.

but then he'd jump over a cliff if I put it that way, which is why I wouldn't: though I wish I had asked him, years ago, as a personal favor, to practice the piano). Well, maybe just *one* crack, sideways-wise. Let's see. . . "In the event of Emergency B, Christopher should paint his beard orange, to make it easier to see him in the dark." That could be entered in the Emergency Instructions page in the logbook; surreptitiously. It would be a while before he spotted it. I'll wait for the opportunity. . . .

Reggie's plastics company is collapsing. The firm he counted on for a critical order hasn't come through. Over the telephone there are negotiations, and the awful possibility arises that he may have to leave us in Bermuda. I will not think about it. Peter absent; and now perhaps Reggie.

Van advises that a shit-eating front is headed toward Bermuda and is likely to hit on Friday. I decide under the circumstances to supplement sail with power and race in, even at the risk of running out of fuel. I need a clear sky to home in on Bermuda, since we don't have electronic gear, except the squeaky old direction finder. Approaching from the south is a lot safer. Still, I want to be in St. George's before the front closes in. All this means we should pull into Bermuda sometime tomorrow night.

142

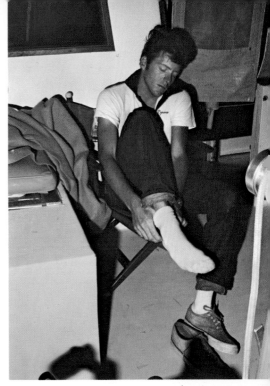

Reggie's fish

4:00 A.M. watch

Azores

Storm

Surcease

Camping out.

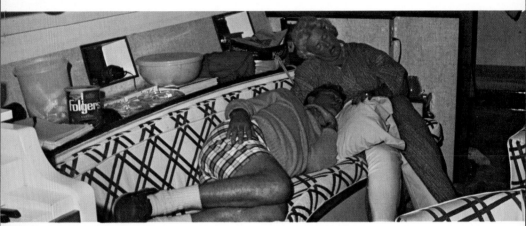

A long afternoon

The Party

Thursday, June 5. More properly, Friday, June 6. Because we tied up at 2:50 A.M. at St. George's harbor. Early this morning, the wind almost directly behind us, the gollywobbler up, we conducted a pool: At what time would we spot the light from Gibbs Hill? It is a powerful beacon. Within its twenty-five-mile radius three hundred ships are said to have foundered on the treacherous rocks during the high days of Bermuda's role as a way station to the Virginia colonies and points south. Even now, Reggie's schoolmate Teddy Tucker devotes himself full-time to locating wrecks and salvaging three-hundred-year-old cargo. He has found gold and silver and jewels, including a famous emerald crucifix, but mostly such stuff as lead and copper. For a while the Crown claimed the lot, but in Teddy *vs.* The Queen, a landmark case, it was settled that the discoverer gets one half.

I picked 8:15 P.M. for the landfall, and bets were taken ranging from 6:30 P.M. to midnight. At noon, after the sunsight, I decreed that our watches should move forward by one hour. When, at 8:10 P.M., the light at Gibbs Hill was spotted just off the port bow where it should have been, we were catapulted into a great legal controversy. *Danny et absolutely al. vs. WFB.* Danny had "bought" 7:15 P.M., and insisted that since the bets were made this morning before our watches were moved forward, he had clearly won the pool. I took the position that we were betting that morning on what would be the time *on our wristwatches* at the moment of the landfall. Van, as a graduate of the Harvard Law School, was consulted, and I suspect that that appeal to his vanity suborned him, after appropriate deliberation, to find for the plaintiff. The matter was economically moot at this point since Christopher, Aunty Bill, Reggie, and Van had already paid over their dollar bills to Danny. I reluctantly gave my dollar to Danny, sniffing something about the dangers of ochlocracy. "What's that?" he asked. I told him it was the only kind of government that would find for *him* in a dispute with *me.* Reggie then proposed a loser's toast—to my navigation, a toast I acknowledged with a graceful speech minimizing the complexity of my achievement. We were all in high spirits.

There is an underappreciated phenomenon at sea in a small boat. It is the exasperating length of time it takes, after spotting a major beacon, to pull into the wharf. The tendency, on seeing the light, is to

143

think the trip over. It took almost seven hours, even at 8 knots, to get in (against a tide of about 1.5 knots). Once, on a bizarre passage back to Stamford from Bermuda, with a crew that included Sam, a charming friend of Firpo's, a confirmed urbanite who was as useful on board a sailing boat as Mayor Daley, we got terribly lost, encountering every imaginable minor misfortune, and Sam got gloomier and gloomier as the days and nights went by—right past the baptism of Firpo's daughter, my godchild, and no telephone even. Finally, at 8:00 P.M. one night I spotted Montauk Light, and Sam was so relieved he embraced us all, drank deeply to our health, and went happily to sleep. When he awoke at six, startled to find himself still surrounded by seawater, he demanded an explanation and was told that it hadn't been Montauk after all, but a passing ship. There and then he wept. But Firpo led him gently up to the cockpit, where he could see that Montauk was, literally, just around the corner.

Those long hours are anticlimactic, and it is sensible to dampen the spirit of celebration. Usually, on making a landfall, the crew (except in a race) breaks out a bottle. If there are still six hours' sailing to do, that can make for a very wet landfall. Van, experienced in these matters, retired to his cabin to read a book. The boys eventually peeled off and went to sleep. Having given everyone advice, I failed to heed it myself—I cannot be wrenched from the wheel between a landfall and arrival. Coming in to St. George's is a spooky experience. One flows in through a deep but very narrow cut that becomes visible only as you become convinced that you are headed right into a hill. The placid lights of seventeenth-century St. George's are suddenly before you, and for the first time in six days the ocean swells were suspended, and we crossed the harbor to the slip as if skating over ice. And there was the customs official, waiting for us. And Pat and Marvin.

[**C**] Dear Bermuda: Thank you for:

The Lobster Pot and Fritz the nice Nazi; Little Venice; the Clams Casino, Veal Zincata, Ricolgi wine, 12 cups of hot coffee and the rolls that absorb Planter's Punch so well; 2001 Club, where John the Australian, Colin and I continued our discussion of Vietnam while Danny stalked the dance floor in search of Bermuda onions; the Princess Hotel and the swimming pool where we collapsed, singing in the rain at 5 A.M. after locking ourselves out of the hotel; the oil drums, which we fastened to the deck during our hangovers; the barnacles on the Kenyon fingers which Danny scraped off with my knife; Roy Cohn and his "SuperJew" T-shirt; Roy Cohn's friend and his gang-bang T-shirt; *Le Bistro*, where Alistair, Colin, Kathy, John, Danny and I had lunch, nursed hangovers, drank Bullshots and ate amorphous Reuben sandwiches; Diana Rigg and her amazing presence; Colleen, who entertained Danny in his moment of want; the Beatles and especially "Rocky Raccoon"; Steppenwolf and "The Pusher"; the Scottish dockmaster who calls everyone "mate"; his old, hunchback assistant, who tells cryptic tales of Bermuda circa Edward VIII and whom tourists consider "quaint"; Dung Ho restaurant and its blessed, nonalcoholic "Polynesian Delights"; the Rosemont Theatre, where I finally saw "The Paper Chase"; the companionway hatch, which crushed my two thumbs; the Edward VIII Memorial Hospital where a wonderful nurse set me at ease by telling me she really hated "syringing" ears and then proceeded to drill though my blackened thumbnails with a red-hot paperclip; my mother, who gave me a Percodan and worried; Marvin, who told her not to; my father, who

145

made the B.O. a reality; Gilly, who left me with sweet memories of a beautiful island tryst; and, finally, Cyrano, who carried me away on a rainy, windy, gray day in June.

P.S. Other acknowledgments must perforce go to:

The staff of the Princess, whose publicity department filmed my father and me while we strapped the tanks down on deck, and whose room service served us soggy pancakes and wooden toast; the Greek, American, and Italian liners entering Hamilton Harbor as we left it; the three destroyer-escorts sullenly hanging off St. George's as we set our course for Horta; the U.S. Navy tugboat and its skipper, who waved at me after I waved at him, both of us peering at each other through binoculars and achieving that special, prismatic, long-distance intimacy; the Mass at St. Patrick's, which reminded me how otherworldly that celebration is; the hibiscus blossoms on Bermudiana Road; the ice machine at the Princess; Teddy Tucker and his fleet of nimble (albeit unsuccessful) mechanics; and to Juan de Bermúdez, who got it all started in 1616.

P.P.S. And of course, final note to the Princess Hotel's 80-degree swimming pool, for providing cold, chlorine refreshment for two drunken first mates at 4 A.M.

Snatches of radio-telephone conversation:
"Franny, it's fine, it's O.K. I got the kid. Herb got the dog."

[C] Later. Surging along at eight knots, a strong wind out of the north, and a sky streaked with black, black clouds. I'm alone. Couldn't bring myself to wake up Danny, but I also have a feeling the sky is gonna open any second now with furious winds and boiling seas.

But *this* is sailing, eh. No matter that nothing works: so what that a new loran and new TV were flown down from New York and even these won't work; so what if the electrical system on this boat is a cogent argument for the return to gas and steam; because on a night such as this, your hull buried in the swells and your sails knifing the wind, the only things that matter are a steady helm, a clear head, and a warm jacket. On a night such as this, who needs the consolation of philosophy?

146

[C] 0900. We jump. Bermuda lies now to the west, 220 miles aft of the taffrail. The sun has been up three hours, the sky is dotted with cumulus clouds, the binnacle shines like gold . . . but what does all *that* matter, weighed in the scales of the New Testament?

Reggie is gone. His absence left us all sad. As Pup would say, the chemistry of the thing is changed. I'll only say that there are very few people around you can wake up at 4 A.M. and ask to help you pump out a bilge, raise the fisherman, or figure out why the autopilot box gets so hot. Few people who would smile and say, "Well, why not?" Few people have his kindness, soft-spokenness, generosity.

[V] So far the nights have been slightly eerie from the threatening squalls, the lack of moon and the unknown. Also I think everyone seems a bit uneasy without Reggie.

[C] My tic is gone, but replaced by a weariness that keeps me in my bunk practically every minute of off-watch time. After 7 hours of more-or-less solid sleep, I wake up feeling as though I've been at the helm for 12 hours. This could be either nightclub fatigue (which occurs after you've ingested 35 Planter's Punches and 4 packs of cigarettes over two nights and stayed up until 5 A.M. both nights), or, given it's been two days now, it could be that an arcane bacillus in my Clams Casino is this minute charming my central nervous system into a soporific trance. Yawn. Maybe I'll do another paragraph, but (yawn) I think I'll . . . get . . . some . . . sleep. . . .

[D] We have a lovely afternoon today, the sky clear, crisp, the waves rolling lazily one after another seeming endless. Sunset was unusual. Our western horizon sparkled crimson with faint shades of pink. The grand finale was 7 seconds long; the clouds acted their part as bursts reflecting the magnificence earlier. I had a restful night. WFB woke me about 3:00 A.M. with hot coffee in one hand, cookies in the other. "Don't work too hard now."

[D] Five A.M. is approaching quickly. What lies before me is this: a calm sea surrounds me, dark on three sides, and a faint reflection ahead. The sky to the east (straight ahead) has low dark clouds just

147

No wind. At wheel, talking with Captain Campagna.

now beginning to take shape in the light. Four or five shades of blue that are almost unique to the ocean are making a fine start of a new day.

If I could paint, which I can't, I doubt if ever I could reproduce the tones of the blue ahead. God has many kingdoms and too often we forget he exists except when we need some supervisions, what-have-you. No argument ever could convince me of any other fact other than God made this.

[**D**] Just as I thought, today would be the usually chilly, early morning; I received the rain on my unshaven face—two thoughts now demand attention. One, get out of the rain, and two, somehow bring myself to shave. Ah, I don't want to. Yesterday I cut my already scarred chin with that type of shaver that guarantees not to cut or your money back. Wait till I get to the Azores. I'll just walk to the nearest Grade A market and ask for a refund. Sure, Dan.

Beautiful Dreamer, la de la da, those rollers are huge.
Beautiful Dreamer, la de la da.
G-o-o-d Night.

[C] Both books I brought aboard, *The Everlasting Man* and *Moby Dick*, have been commandeered, the first by Danny, the second by WFB. I am forced to biography. *Kissinger* [by the brothers Kalb]. Two quotes so far stand out: "As a statesman, one has to act on the assumption that problems must be solved." "As a historian, you have to be conscious of the fact that every civilization that has ever existed has ultimately collapsed." And this chestnut from my pirated *Moby Dick*: "So what if some old hunk of a sea captain tells me to grab a mop and polish the decks? What does that amount to, weighed, I mean, in the scales of the New Testament?"

[D] On to *The Everlasting Man*. Halfway through my first chapter Augustino begged me to fix his head. I strolled forward thinking a mere clogged intake, hoping the outtake would be virgin. It never happens. I've probably fixed a head 2–3 times but never have I pulled out such miscellaneous crap from a one-inch three-foot outtake line. Crap literally, specifically. Whenever he finished a cigarette he must have thrown it in for good measure. Four bars of soap later I'm clean except for my fingernails.

[D] Everything today seems unimportant except that we've kept steady at 8 knots. CTB is busying himself with repairing the main slide track where 4–5 slides came loose and broke. He's in the bo'sun's chair dangling, trying to see and hold on all at the same time.

[C] Yesterday at lunch I bit into a codfish cake and chomped down on a pebble. Or a stainless steel nut. Whatever, a large filling popped out of my lower left front molar. Eating steak is now an adventure, trying (a) to chew on the right side, and (b) not to mangle my food on the ragged tooth, (c) thereby swallowing an unchewed piece of meat and choking to death (even though it would give Aunt Bill a chance to perform a tracheotomy).

I wake up with a headache and a sore throat. Poor Pup. He told me that his watch went well, despite the fact that everything that possibly could have broken, did. He and Aunt Bill, a formidable combination of post-Columbian navigators, despair over the wanderings of the HP–65. Now even it has gone the way of the gremlin, the digits placing us no less than 100 miles west of Horta, Azores. Aunt Bill was momentarily jubilant at the prospect of covering 1,800 miles in three days and arriving tomorrow evening. As I am growing fond of saying, "Don't count your lands before they fall."

[V] We heard that one of our bottles with a message washed up in Fort Lauderdale and was sent to *National Review*. Caused great mirth and pleasure. We hope with more expectation now that the others will arrive.

[V] A Norwegian cargo vessel, the *North Star*, going by on an easterly course, slightly more northerly than ours, swerved over and took a look at us. We raised our ensign and they did the same, not sure what that means but it seemed the friendly thing to do. They would not reply to our VHF, however. Then we saw a sailboat bearing 150 degrees, thought it might be the *Baccarat*, but she disappeared in the west. Why someone would cross that way at this latitude, I don't know; but maybe Europe-Azores-Virgin Islands is Okay, and Lord knows we didn't get much of the prevailing wind.

[C] 0300. WFB told me Mencken wrote a piece on Schubert's *Marche Militaire*. Make note.

[D] I spent some time between lunch and dinner fixing little odds and ends. The starboard shroud light, sunlog light, the sink in the forward stateroom and took down the broken antenna finally. CTB and I cleaned the port deckbox of 2″ of water and separated the deckhouse cushions from their covers to dry. They were huge sponges oozing H_2O whenever you sat on them.

[D] Chris and I had one of our bi-yearly wrestling bouts. Actually it started with some thrown water and wine. I must confess how funny it looked.

There was Chris laughing, thinking I would not dare chuck the full glass of wine while he stood protected behind his aunt. Ah! wish again. Bill F.'s face turned red, partly from shock, the rest from my jettisoned glass of Livian [Chateau Livran, 1966—WFB]. Chris laughed so naturally, so hard, he nearly forgot to reattack.

We mopped Bill F. and the ceiling, chairs, bunks, floor and window, then went at it again. Like two bullhorn sheep we battled, actually having fun, ridding ourselves of any anxieties. J'ai fini. Again I took a catnap, a sound 2-hour slumber. It's 5:30 P.M., and I've just finished off a bowl of Frosted Flakes, two packages of Oreos (each having six) and a Budweiser. I'm starved; thank the heavens that dinner is in 2 hours.

[V] More blackjack last night—I seem to be a minor winner. Am slightly worried Danny has or is about to lose more than he should. Went to bed after getting off watch at 0100 and taking a nightcap with Bill and Bill F., and slept, again, like a dead man until 0730.

[V] Even without the wind it is pleasant in the sun, reading and puttering about, chit-chatting. Enjoying the luxury of reading and not fretting about business. I should call the office but the hell with it.

"Even without the wind it is pleasant."

[V] There is not too much work to do so the routine is very lazy. We read, sleep, eat, chit-chat around mealtimes and on late watches. Days zip by and I can't remember when I was so nonproductive; I don't know if that is good or bad but I suspect I shall benefit and be raring to go in July. I have a theory why time goes quickly—it is in large part due to the fact that we "work at night." I have heard it said by people who work nights that this is the case and indeed I recall this sensation when I worked summers, while in school, at night. One sleeps away part of the day and the day is gone when night falls.

[D] When you give a sport like sailing all you've got then you can enjoy the rewards of fine days, better in fact the harder you work. Crossing the Atlantic sometimes seems a bore but for the most part it's pure pleasure. In order to starve boredom we fix things, hoist and lower sails, adjust them, navigate a bit, write anti-Communist messages in empty wine bottles and toss them into the sea, hoping some will find their way home. Then we all have our own private thoughts.

I've spent a good deal of time evaluating my short life. Thinking about my many experiences (mostly good) and about my future.

When I sail I relax. I enjoy an inner peace that allows my imaginative thought process, otherwise stagnant, to run wild. The excitement of these feelings can't be analyzed to anything, they're mine. Sailing, ah!

[**C**] 0900. I keep getting sidetracked. After an 11-hour sleep (I forsook my watch to get better)—I woke up and for the first time since we left the Queen's Island, I'm rested. My sum nourishment yesterday amounted to one (1) piece of cornbread, and even that sent me to my bunk with a stomach threatening to explode.

A new feeling, a new day: calm, sunny, with only the occasional swell breaking the monotony of stability. The telltale is full, but we're creating our own wind. Today my beard seems a little fuller.

Last night I dreamt I was the last living soul on board, that we had sailed into the Sargasso Sea, and everyone had been pulled off the boat and killed by . . . seaweed men. Yes, things: half-man, half-kelp, menacing monsters. God, it was horrible. I sat by the helm in the dawn's light, .222 magnum across my lap. They climbed aboard from every direction. I was running low on ammunition. I drew the Very pistol, cocked and fired it. A creature clutched its head and fell back . . . and still they came. Then I heard a noise and sat up, eyes wide open. It was Pup, dropping the main. The winch whined in high pitch. I shivered and touched my forehead. It was hot with a low fever.

This trip is doing strange things to my unconscious.

[**C**] 0322. Here's to Cyrano, ad hoc I.T. of the Atlantic. With three G.B.'s aboard, we've almost got a quorum.*

And here's to *cacoethes scribendi*.**

Cyrano's sailing along at eight knots with full sails flying. Danny's asleep. Figure letting him rest was the least I could do, since I slept through our last watch together.*** That makes me pro tem watch captain. After all these years, a promotion.****

---

* The obeisance is to a society at Yale.
** The itch to write.
*** Both acts are illegal and contumacious. Cacoethes habem hittem both on the head.
**** Short-lived.—WFB

Christopher writing in his journal during a night watch.

A most mysterious night. Sitting by the binnacle with my back to the water while Danny fixes coffee below. I imagine a giant tentacle reaching out of the sea. Danny returns on deck.

"Christo?"

Gurgle. And then, like the beast whose slimy embrace dragged Laocoön and his sons into the Aegean, the monster strikes again:

Slurp.

It's that kind of night: the Milky Way so close it looks like a cloudy belt stretching from horizon to horizon; phosphorescence glittering mirrorlike under a sky perforated with thousands of stars; hot coffee, Camels, and the Rolling Stones. Cyrano is motoring into what seems to be a cloudbank. Very dark. Very calm. Let's call it "eerie tranquility."* A good night for the seaweed men.

* A code word at Yale.—WFB

[**D**] Last night CTB and I were on the 1–4. Needless to say we enjoyed our watch. In particular I realized how beautiful the moon shining through the clouds through Cyrano's backstay seemed. It was a picture. I could see, as I looked aft from the rear of the cabin, the helm offset by a moon glow, a faint pink from the binnacle, the Boston whaler, backstays, man-overboard pole and life rings, all lit faintly with a hint of white clouds in the background. I just stared; it was gorgeous.

[**D**] The wind picked up to 25; the trainlike clouds to port moved swiftly SSE while dark ominous cirrostratus formations boxed us in on the remaining quarters. We dropped the fisherman, main, and Genoa just in time to don our foul-weather gear and stand up to nature.

This is what sailing is about. You sail and sail and sail, enjoying the lovely aspect of God's seas and then you wish for a little change, a bit of adverse weather, something to show off your expertise, perhaps just to prove to yourself you're good at playing the chess game of nature and survival.

Danny on watch.

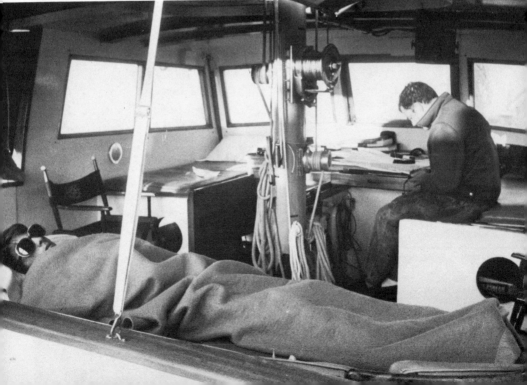

If we were a willow we would have gone the way of willows. Fifty-mph winds have been known to uproot many land creatures but here at sea we play a different game. Chess is a battle of strategy, man v. man, out here with WFB v. wind, waves, competent companion. He's our Bobby Fischer.

Bill F. seemed a permanent fixture in the doghouse like the cleats holding down our halyards. Below, the soft-cushioned chairs, TV, cassettes, Planter's peanut bottle, bounced like a ball in jacks. I was at the helm, Phil to my right, Phil Jr. on my left, Augustino below in the galley, Christo and Company in the saloon when—three or four hours after we started sailing again—it hit. "The Wave," as they refer to it. For 5 full seconds blue water broke across our starboard rail about midship, running steadily aft until it swept the helmsman seat out from under me, knocked Phil Sr. squarely in the chest and set Christo atop the deck box to avoid getting wet.

"What the hell?" remarked Christo. Bill F. found the stateroom a minipool while Van rebounded in the saloon among the chairs. Mr. B. looked about with a relaxed smile knowing it had to be.

Squared away for Bermuda–Azores, 1900 miles. The fuel drums are well lashed down. Visible, left to right: the main staysail, the forward staysail, the Genoa. Not visible: the mainsail, and the fisherman.

Two days later the saloon still shows telltale signs of The Wave. We're here and happy still. We've had a good experience. Cyrano fared well.

[C]   0200 hrs. June 17.

What happened to the 15th and the 16th?

The 16th is easy. I slept through it.

The 15th. Toward late afternoon the winds, which were S.E., increased. More. Then some. Soon they were howling at 50 mph and we hove to.

My first heave to.

As Danny says, "I'm not too sure about this 'heave toing.' "

I'll never forget the sky. At first, a cold, gray bitch of a wind. Then rain, cold and stinging against the face. Waves up to 15 feet. Some of them broke at the helmsman's knees. The radio antennae came loose and swung around from the top of the mast like the Icepick of Damocles. No shit, I was scared. I took the helm for a while, strapped in with the safety harness, eyes darting between binnacle and antennae, my mind on the storm approaching. When WFB said to the skipper "About 50 mph, eh?" and the skipper agreed with him, an icy tingle dripped down my spine like droplets of liquid nitrogen.

"50, huh?" I said.

Oui . . . God.

I remember pulling in the Genoa roller line. My hands were burning. Everything was drenched in salt. A wave half broached us. Down below was chaos. The wave threw Van against the port bulwark. He thought his shoulder was broken. Aunt Bill was resting in her bunk when all of a sudden it was Niagara Falls: gallons of water swooshing through the porthole. The armchairs in the saloon left the floor and crushed against the settee. My dad, who had gone on deck, to windward, to check the telltale as a personal favor to me, came down drenched.

"I chose the single most inappropriate moment of my life to be accommodating," he said, his sweater glistening with beads of Atlantic Ocean.

I was dispatched to the engine room. Being the part of the boat closest to the keel and center of gravity, the engine room was a good

157

place to be at the time. The lurch caught me while I was peering into the bilge with the flashlight. It tossed me against the port water tank. I think it's empty on account of the hollow noise it made when my skull hit.

Earlier, I had had to raise the mainstaysail and I needed a hand with the winch. We winched the sails aback. The lines were as tight as the high E-string on a guitar. We looked to starboard and saw 12-foot rollers moving a 15-foot log our way. Danny was at the helm, and he didn't look any happier about that log than we did. He gave the engine a 2,000-rpm surge. The megaton piece of driftwood passed safely astern.

What keeps me from feeling fear is watching others hiding theirs. The idea is to think of Lucretius' maxim, "It is pleasant . . ." Pretend you're the one who's standing on the shore, watching the struggles of another. When the hurricane struck the *Fernbrook* (as I recall, it was in this same area), it was so damned odd no one seemed to notice.

Waiting for the storm.

Hove to during the storm.

"Well, Buckley," said Arvid, "we haf a hurricane, ya?"
"Uh, is that bad?" I asked.
"Ha! Maybe we sink, ya?"
Other things I remember about yesterday: filming the poopdeck crowd with Reg's movie camera and seeing a Cecil B. DeMille/God production of a rainbow; sitting at the helm slurping hot beef broth, the rim of my hat forming dead air space so the fumes steamed my face; putting a red filter over the camera lens and watching the marriage of nature and optic technology; thinking about Isaac Bashevis Singer's "Life is God's novel; help Him write it"; heaving to and suddenly having the sensation of riding a cork in a turbulent bathtub; popping Marezine and Bayer aspirin with sugar-free 7-Up (Yes, you *can* take civilization with you); saying a "Hail Mary" when the wind hit 60; knowing the fear of falling overboard, the knowing you wouldn't last long; over and over; the Icepick of Damocles slapping the shrouds, feeling a twang through my hand when it bounced off the backstay; lashing the port bladder tank down tight and covering my

159

Shaking off the foul-weather gear.

hands in diesel fuel; and remembering my foolhardy flatulencies in having told everyone in New Haven how I wanted to have at least one storm on the B.O. so there'd be something to write about.

So now there is.

Under way again; the storm recedes.

[**V**] Some of us should have been more tutored in reading the clouds. They can tell you where the fronts are, and the fronts are' where the bad weather is. Admittedly, there isn't much you can do in the middle of the Atlantic to avoid a front—you wouldn't run away, as you would from a hurricane. But it is better to be prepared for squalls or changes in wind direction and velocity. We didn't really know a mackerel sky (the sign of a warm front) from a fish, and Bill is obstinately ignorant about the weather.

[**C**] I long to reach the Azores. Twelve days on Cyrano has left me with a longing for the touch of terra firma. The last three days have been rainy, rough . . . soul-saddening. When I went to retrieve a pair of dungarees I had hung in the engine room to dry, I almost gagged. They reeked of sweat, diesel, and mildew; a foul cocktail of a smell by even the most barbarian standards. These pants would have fit in well in the wardrobe of Attila the Hun.

[**C**] Today, Poseidon blessed us with scores of dolphins and two sea turtles. I think the sea turtles were fucking, 'cause one shell I saw was ridin' mighty high in the water.

[**C**] 1300. I wake up in the saloon, having gone to sleep at four thirty A.M., just as the sun appeared. Augustino, who has a headache, hands me a bowl of Frosted Flakes. Aunt Bill says it's rainy and Danny that it's "shitty."
After a lunch of hot pea soup, fried chicken, and white wine, we sit in the doghouse, chatting about Horta and looking for it. My mood is fresh. I had a good sleep last night. We're all anxious to pull in. WFB raises David Niven on the phone. Dan goes below with his cassette-recorder. It's clearing slightly, and maybe, just maybe, we'll see Horta (Faial) above the clouds. WFB returns from the galley.
"I feel like a Beethoven string quartet," he says.
Several minutes later, a burst of sunlight. WFB sounds General Quarters. Sextant in hand, he bounds to the doghouse roof and shoots the sun. Moments later we have a running fix. But we still can't get a signal on the RDF, just a noise that sounds like Azores rock music. Mick Jaoggeira and the Rolling Piedras.

161

Who will win the landfall pool? All it takes is the stamina to go up the mast with binoculars and sit for a few hours.

Then a burst of wind, giving WFB the enlightening flash that it's time for the gollywobbler. Again, General Quarters. Van and I attach the mainstaysail halyard, where we should have attached the gollywobbler halyard. This understandably creates great confusion. We set the sail, finally, sweating and pulling on lines. Ahead the sky is clearing, but still no sight of our beloved Horta.

[V] We looked and looked and looked but never did see the big mountain on Pico, shrouded by clouds. We finally spotted Faial way to port at about 1630. It was exciting and reassuring. We sailed along the coast for a couple of hours escorted by 100 dolphins. We docked very smartly alongside the quay, and went ashore for dinner at about 8:45.

Shortly after returning from our passage I received a letter from an amateur sailor greatly vexed by the challenge of celestial navigation. He asked where he might find a totally comprehensible essay on the subject that would equip him to navigate celestially. I replied that so far as I knew, no such treatise—absent the full explanatory textbooks—existed; and gave it as my opinion that the principal reason for the failure of those I have read is that they endeavor to explain to the reader *why* celestial navigation works rather than—simply—*how* it works.

Professor Hugh Kenner is one of those rare creatures, endowed at once with a vocabulary so extensive and a facility for using it so resourceful, who can describe—anything ("Nothing is *indescribable*," said Harold Ross of *The New Yorker*). One could, from a paragraph by Kenner, deduce the blueprint of an eggbeater. It is, of course, more than a working vocabulary that equips him to write as he does: It is a gift of mechanical understanding and congruent conceptualization. It is not really surprising that the most lucid exegete of Pound, Yeats, and Eliot should also have written a book explaining the architectonics of Buckminster Fuller.

It is perhaps because all inscrutable matters yield so easily to him that he has for many years patronized the Heath-Kit Company in Chicago, which manufactures the constituent parts from the appropriate assortment and arrangement of which a purchaser can assemble a woman's hair dryer or a color television set (the most satisfactory radio direction finder I ever had was out of Heath-Kit, by Hugh Kenner). Hugh explained to me, enthusiastically, the steps the manufacturer takes before issuing an instruction manual.

Let us suppose the company decides to add to its do-it-yourself line an electric typewriter. The people charged with writing out assembly instructions come up with a first draft. (With luck, they are unrelated to the people who have lately undertaken to explain Christianity.) Then two or three white-collar women are located. It is required of them only that they should be—virgins. They must never ever before have put together anything more complicated than a children's jigsaw.

In the presence of a supervisor, notebook in hand, the selected woman sets out to put together an electric typewriter, starting out with Instruction No. 1. Whenever she hesitates, she is interrogated, and a notation is made, giving the reason for that hesitation. Perhaps the instruction sheet said, "Reach for the needle-point pliers," and she looks worriedly about her. The psychologist is there to ask her what it is that troubles her. . . . "What are needle-point pliers?"

The revised instructions will carry a picture of needle-point pliers. By the time the tribulations of the prototypical assemblers are collated, an instruction sheet evolves which—if you take Hugh Kenner's word for it, and I do—can be followed by anybody who can read simple English.

It is my ambition to do this for celestial navigation—Heath-Kit-wise.

Those curious to know *why* it works can consult the breviaries; though, as a matter of fact, they might, if it happens that their curiosity is of that bent, even deduce why it works. Meanwhile—so help me God—they can set out to sea with *these* pages, and, setting out from anywhere in the world, arrive anywhere in the world they want to.

To begin with, some generalities:

There are several "systems" of celestial navigation. If you learn one, it is easy enough to adapt to others. I like best H.O. 249—because it is the easiest. It makes use of the *Air Almanac* (as opposed to the yearly *Nautical Almanac*), which is issued three times a year, each issue covering a four-month period. The Almanac tells you what is the Geographical Position, at any given second of any day covered by the Almanac, of: the Sun; the constellation Aries; the planets Venus, Jupiter, Saturn; the Moon; and 57 stars.

If you draw a line from a celestial body to the center of the earth, the point at which that line touches the surface of the earth is that body's Geographical Position (GP).

A sextant is an instrument that measures the angle between the horizon and the observed body.

The tables (H.O. 249) are for the purpose of advising you what is the difference between the assumed position of your vessel—on the basis of which you have made your calculations—and the *actual* position of your vessel, based on the angle your sextant has given you.

Let us assume you are sitting in a boat exactly one hundred miles east of the Empire State Building late in the afternoon, without, however, knowing where you are (hecklers are, without any ill will whatever, invited to leave the room, and are invited back for cakes and ale, which resume on page 181). You (mis)estimate that you are 105 miles east of the Empire State Building. When you bring the figures from your Almanac on over to the tables, the Almanac will say to you: It cannot be that you are on a line that runs through a point 105 miles east of the Empire State Building. You are in fact on a line that runs through a point *one hundred* miles east of the Empire State Building.

This, clearly, is the opportune moment to reveal that what you get from a celestial sight isn't a *point*. It is a *line*. They call it a *line of*

The navigator's table, unposed.

position (LOP). You are somewhere on that line. You do not know where. You need a second line to establish that. But, as you would expect, a second line taken immediately after the first would give you a line almost parallel to the first, since there hasn't been much angular movement of the celestial body. You have two alternatives. The first is to take a sight on a different celestial body (let us assume the stars are out, or the planets, or the moon, and that a horizon is still visible, i.e., that it is shortly before dawn or after sunset). Having plotted that second line, you will know that where it intersects the first one is where you are.

The second alternative (let us assume it is only the Sun you are working with, which is more often than not the case) is to wait: an hour, say. Then shoot the Sun again. The LOP, reflecting the movement of the Sun westward, will come in at a substantially revised angle. Again, where the two lines intersect is where you are. If during the interval of that hour you have yourself been moving in your boat—rather than, say, anchoring and fishing—you will calculate how far and in what direction you traveled during that hour. Let us say eight miles due east. You will take the first line of position and draw a line parallel to it eight miles along your course—that is done through the use of parallel rules. Where that line intersects your fresh LOP is—where you are. You have just achieved what they call a Running Fix. Ninety percent of celestial navigation in small boats consists in getting Running Fixes.

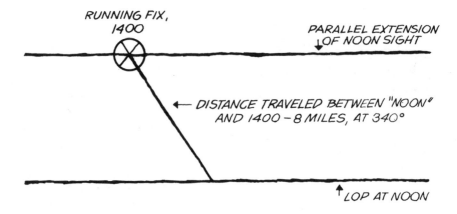

RUNNING FIX,
1400

PARALLEL EXTENSION
↓OF NOON SIGHT

← DISTANCE TRAVELED BETWEEN "NOON"
AND 1400 – 8 MILES, AT 340°

↑LOP AT NOON

Stars are nice, and by all means go on and develop the technique for bringing them down. But they are harder to handle, harder to spot, and you need to work faster. No sweat, in particular; but concentrate on the Sun.

Now, back to the Almanac.

In order to know the Geographical Position of the Sun you must know the exact time of day. In celestial navigation, for conceptual convenience, it is assumed that the earth is motionless, and all the activity is celestial. *The Sun is continuously moving*, and in the course of twenty-four hours travels 360°, right around the globe. This means (figure it out—360° divided by 24 hours) that in one hour it must move 15°. (That is why one moves one's watch forward, or back, by one hour, every fifteen degrees of longitude traversed.)

Now, one degree is equal to sixty "minutes." And a minute is equal to sixty "seconds." We deduce that the Sun moves one degree every four minutes. One 1/60th of one degree is one minute. One 1/60th of four minutes is four seconds.

CONVERSION OF ARC TO TIME

°	h m	°	h m	°	h m	°	h m	°
60	4 00	120	8 00	180	12 00	240	16 00	300
61	4 04	121	8 04	181	12 04	241	16 04	301
62	4 08	122	8 08	182	12 08	242	16 08	302
63	4 12	123	8 12	183	12 12	243	16 12	303
64	4 16	124	8 16	184	12 16	244	16 16	304
65	4 20	125	8 20	185	12 20	245	16 20	305
66	4 24	126	8 24	186	12 24	246	16 24	306
67	4 28	127	8 28	187	12 28	247	16 28	307
68	4 32	128	8 32	188	12 32	248	16 32	308
69	4 36	129	8 36	189	12 36	249	16 36	309
70	4 40	130	8 40	190	12 40	250	16 40	310
71	4 44	131	8 44	191	12 44	251	16 44	311
72	4 48	132	8 48	192	12 48	252	16 48	312
73	4 52	133	8 52	193	12 52	253	16 52	313
74	4 56	134	8 56	194	12 56	254	16 56	314
75	5 00	135	9 00	195	13 00	255	17 00	315

Therefore, for every four seconds that go by on your watch, the Sun has moved by one mile west in the heavens: one nautical mile. One nautical mile (approximately 1.15 of a statute mile) is the distance subtended on the surface of the earth by an angle of one minute at the center of the earth.

It is a pity that the word "minute" is here being used in two senses. There is the degree-minute (one 1/60th of a degree), and the time-minute (one 1/60th of an hour). On the other hand, it is happy that there should be the correspondence: one (degree) minute equals one mile on the earth's surface.

Now all Geographical Positions are given with reference to Greenwich, England, which lies on 0° longitude. The equator is on 0° latitude. The "coordinates" of a vessel's location are given in latitude and longitude. Thus, our boat off the Empire State Building would be located at (say), 44° 18′ 30″ north latitude, 72° 10′ 18″ west longitude. Tip: Drop the seconds from your coordinates. You need seconds when you are talking about Watch Time—remember, an error of four seconds will put you a mile away. But sixty seconds of longitude equals one minute, which equals only one mile—so just take the nearest minute. You aren't plotting the location of an oil rig.

The terminology of coordinates changes, however, when you are dealing with the Geographical Position of a celestial body. Instead of latitude and longitude, you are given it in *Declination*—Dec. (latitude) and *Greenwich Hour Angle*—GHA (longitude).

The Geographical Positions of the heavenly bodies are also given with reference to the time at Greenwich. The time at Greenwich is five hours ahead of Miami (remember the time zones—one hour for every 15°). As a navigator, you have two alternatives. Either set your watch to the time in Greenwich, and always read the time off it. Or simply remember how many hours you have to add to your Watch Time in order to get the time in Greenwich. I prefer to do the latter, counting it no great strain to remember what time zone I am in. (Needless to say, if you are on Eastern Daylight Time, you add only four hours, rather than five, to arrive at the time in Greenwich.)

We set out from Miami at exactly 1919 Local Watch Time. At sea, as in Europe, you use a twenty-four-hour-a-day watch dial. To translate 1919 into the vernacular, subtract 12; and you will see that the time is 7:19 P.M. EDT. But to the figure 1919 we must now add four hours to establish the time in Greenwich. That is, 2319.

The *Air Almanac* gives you the GHA for the Sun for every ten

168

minutes of the day. For 2310 on May 30, 1975, it is 168° 08'.2. (I shall henceforward round off the fraction.) You are given, in the adjacent column, the Declination of the Sun at the same time (North 21° 47). Now the Declination changes gradually, so you need not interpolate it. Just grab it that once, when you take your sight, and make a note of it—it is the latitude of the Sun.

You are left knowing the GHA of the Sun at 23h 10m; but you desire the GHA of 23h 19m—a larger figure—so you need to interpolate. The Almanac does this for you. At the back of the book is a table called "Interpolation of GHA Sun." Under 9 minutes, 0 seconds, you find 2° 15'. You add this increment and establish that the GHA of the Sun at the moment of departure was 170° 23'. We therefore know the exact Geographical Position of the Sun at the moment we sailed out of Miami. (It had just passed Honolulu, directly overhead.) Though I promised not to explain *why* it works, I cannot forbear a hint here, which the reader might find instrumentally helpful. If the Sun is *directly* overhead, it will obviously show up at 90° on your sextant scale. If the Sun is exactly on the horizon, it will be 0° on your sextant scale. We know that one degree is equal to sixty miles. It follows that 90° is equal to 5,400 miles. If you have a sextant angle and you know the Geographical Position of the Sun, you can deduce exactly how far away from a fixed point you are. Where it gets tricky is determining not how far away you are, but in *exactly* what direction.

We'll take now a concrete situation, several hundred miles west of Horta, on June 19, 1975, beginning with the Watch:

1. Your assistant is keeping his eyes on the watch while you ease the Sun down on the horizon as seen through the horizon glass. When it is *just* right, you shout, *"Mark!"*

He instantly writes down the time on his watch which is: 2h 23m 37s. However, radio checks on continuous time signals establish that his watch, which tends to lose 1/3 of a second per day, is at this point 14 seconds slow. Moreover, we are two hours behind Greenwich. And this being afternoon, 2h 23m 37s becomes, on the twenty-four-hour system, 14h 23m 37s.

We therefore add to	14	23	37
a Watch Error of (plus)			14
and a Zone Correction of (plus)	2		
For a Greenwich Mean Time of	16h	23m	51s

We now consult the Almanac.

16h 20m gives us 64° 42′—and a North (the Declination of the Sun is North during spring and summer) Declination of 23° 25′.

340   (DAY 170) GREENWIC.

GMT	⊙ SUN GHA	Dec.	ARIES GHA ♈	VENUS – 3 GHA	L
h m	° ′	° ′	° ′	° ′	
12 00	359 42.7	N23 25.2	87 05.5	311 06	N18
10	2 12.6	25.2	89 36.0	313 36	
20	4 42.6	25.2	92 06.4	316 06	
30	7 12.6 ·	25.2	94 36.8	318 36 ·	
40	9 42.6	25.2	97 07.2	321 06	
50	12 12.5	25.2	99 37.6	323 36	
13 00	14 42.5	N23 25.2	102 08.0	326 06	N18
10	17 12.5	25.2	104 38.4	328 36	
20	19 42.5	25.2	107 08.8	331 06	
30	22 12.5 ·	25.2	109 39.2	333 36 ·	
40	24 42.4	25.2	112 09.7	336 06	
50	27 12.4	25.2	114 40.1	338 36	
14 00	29 42.4	N23 25.2	117 10.5	341 06	N18
10	32 12.4	25.2	119 40.9	343 36	
20	34 42.3	25.3	122 11.3	346 06	
30	37 12.3 ·	25.3	124 41.7	348 36 ·	
40	39 42.3	25.3	127 12.1	351 06	
50	42 12.3	25.3	129 42.5	353 36	
15 00	44 42.3	N23 25.3	132 12.9	356 07	N18
10	47 12.2	25.3	134 43.4	358 37	
20	49 42.2	25.3	137 13.8	1 07	
30	52 12.2 ·	25.3	139 44.2	3 37 ·	
40	54 42.2	25.3	142 14.6	6 07	
50	57 12.1	25.3	144 45.0	8 37	
16 00	59 42.1	N23 25.3	147 15.4	11 07	N18
10	62 12.1 ↑	25.3	149 45.8	13 37	
→20	64 42.1 →	25.3	152 16.2	16 07	
30	67 12.1 ·	25.3	154 46.6	18 37 ·	
40	69 42.0	25.3	157 17.0	21 07	
50	72 12.0	25.4	159 47.5	23 37	
17 00	74 42.0	N23 25.4	162 17.9	26 07	N18
10	77 12.0	25.4	164 48.3	28 37	
20	79 41.9	25.4	167 18.7	31 07	

We need now the interpolation for 3m and 51 seconds. It is 58′.

ˢ	0ᵐ		1ᵐ		2ᵐ		3ᵐ		4ᵐ		5ᵐ		
	°	′	°	′	°	′	°	′	°	′	°	′	°
00	0	00.0	0	15.0	0	30.0	0	45.0	1	00.0	1	15.0	1
01	0	00.3	0	15.3	0	30.3	0	45.3	1	00.3	1	15.3	1
02	0	00.5	0	15.5	0	30.5	0	45.5	1	00.5	1	15.5	1
03	0	00.8	0	15.8	0	30.8	0	45.8	1	00.8	1	15.8	1
04	0	01.0	0	16.0	0	31.0	0	46.0	1	01.0	1	16.0	1
05	0	01.3	0	16.3	0	31.3	0	46.3	1	01.3	1	16.3	1
06	0	01.5	0	16.5	0	31.5	0	46.5	1	01.5	1	16.5	1
					0	31.8			1	01.8	1	16.8	
45	0	11.3	0	26.3	0	41.3	0	56.3	1	11.3	1	26.	
46	0	11.5	0	26.5	0	41.5	0	56.5	1	11.5	1	26.5	
47	0	11.8	0	26.8	0	41.8	0	56.8	1	11.8	1	26.8	1
48	0	12.0	0	27.0	0	42.0	0	57.0	1	12.0	1	27.0	1 42.0
49	0	12.3	0	27.3	0	42.3	0	57.3	1	12.3	1	27.3	1 42.3
50	0	12.5	0	27.5	0	42.5	0	57.5	1	12.5	1	27.5	1 42.5
51	0	12.8	0	27.8	0	42.8 → 0	57.8	1	12.8	1	27.8	1 42.8	
52	0	13.0	0	28.0	0	43.0	0	58.0	1	13.0	1	28.0	1 43.0
53	0	13.3	0	28.3	0	43.3	0	58.3	1	13.3	1	28.3	1 43.3
54	0	13.5	0	28.5	0	43.5	0	58.5	1	13.5	1	28.5	1 43.5
55	0	13.8	0	28.8	0	43.8	0	58.8	1	13.8	1	28.8	1 43.8
56	0	14.0	0	29.0	0	44.0	0	59.0	1	14.0	1	29.0	1 44.0
57	0	14.3	0	29.3	0	44.3	0	59.3	1	14.3	1	29.3	1 44.3
58	0	14.5	0	29.5	0	44.5	0	59.5	1	14.5	1	29.5	1 44.5
59	0	14.8	0	29.8	0	44.8	0	59.8	1	14.8	1	29.8	1 44.8

Adding the two, we get the figure 65° 40′—the GHA of the Sun at that particular moment, its Declination already noted. We know its Geographical Position.

2. We need now to concern ourselves with the sextant angle. At the moment you shouted "Mark!" it read 58° 10′.

When shooting the Sun, it is required that four plus or minus corrections be applied to perfect so crude a finding as the "Hs." "H" is the symbol for Altitude; "s" for sextant.

a. The first of these is the Index Error (IE). By how much is your particular sextant off? Most sextants, like most watches, are slightly discalibrated. It is very easy to establish the extent of your sextant's basic problem. You simply look at the horizon mirror and twirl the fine-tuning index knob until the horizon is exactly continuous on your horizon glass and mirror. Then look at your scale. If it reads 0 00,

171

you have no Index Error. Mine reads *plus* 4 minutes, so I need always to *subtract* 4′.

b. You *think* you are seeing the Sun directly, in a straight line. In fact this is an illusion—unless the Sun is higher than 63° from the horizon there is a Refraction factor (Ref.). In this case, at 58°, you are required to subtract one minute—a datum you take from the inside back cover of the Almanac.

CORRECTIONS TO BE APPLIED TO SEXT/

REFRACTION

To be subtracted from sextant altitude (referred to as observed

R_o	0	5	10	15	20	25	30	35	40	45
				Height above sea level in units of 1 000 ft.						
				Sextant Altitude						
0	90	90	90	90	90	90	90	90	90	
1 →	63	59	55	51	46	41	36	31	26	2
2	33	29	26	22	19	16	14	11	9	
3	21	19	16	14	12	10	8	7	5	
4	16	14	12	10	8	7	6	5	3 10	
5	12	11	9	8	7	5	4 00	3 10	2 10	
6	10	9	7	5 50	4 50	3 50	3 10	2 20	1 30	
7	8 10	6 50	5 50	4 50	4 00	3 00	2 20	1 50		
8	6 50	5 50	5 00	4 00	3 10	2 30	1 50	1 20		
9	6 00	5 10	4 10	3 20	2 40	2 00	1 30			

c. It makes a difference how *high* you are ("Dip") from the water. The higher you are, the larger the sextant angle. At a mere ten feet above the water, which is where I am, you subtract three minutes, a figure you take from a table on the back cover of the Almanac.

CORRECTION FOR DIP OF THE I

To be subtracted from sextant alt

Ht.	Dip	Ht.	Dip	Ht.	Dip	Ht.	I
Ft.	′	Ft.	′	Ft.	′	Ft.	
0	1	114	11	437	21	968	
2	2	137	12	481	22	1 033	
6	3	162	13	527	23	1 099	
12	4	189	14	575	24	1 168	
21	5	218	15	625	25	1 239	
31	6	250	16	677	26	1 311	
43	7	283	17	731	27	1 386	
58	8	318	18	787	28	1 463	
75	9	356	19	845	29	1 543	
93	10	395	20	906	30	1 624	
114		437		968		1 707	

d. When you dangle the Sun in your horizon mirror, you let it down until it *just* glances off the horizon—touching it as lightly as possible. In so doing, you measure an angle from the horizon, to your eye, to—the bottom of the Sun. But the Almanac and tables take their measurements, quite logically, on the center of the Sun. It is therefore necessary to add to your sextant angle one half the diameter of the Sun, which is called the SemiDiameter (SD). It is 16', as seen on the Almanac page you are working on.

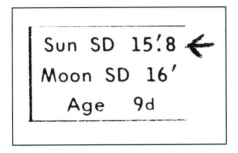

```
Sun  SD  15.'8 ⟵
Moon SD  16'
   Age   9d
```

We are left, then, with:	Hs	58°	10'
	IE		—4'
	Ref		—1'
	Dip		—3'
	SD		+16'
	Ho	58°	18'

What you have now is the true vertical angle of the Sun, the Height observed—Ho.

Your mind is perhaps racing at this point to capture the evolving structure of the argument. If you *know* where the Sun is at a particular moment, and you know how far away you are, then you must be somewhere on a circle from which the Sun is measurable at the angle we have just caught. But, of course, this could be a very large circle (the smaller the angle, the larger the circle) stretching to over seven thousand miles in diameter. There is work left to do, but we are getting there.

3. You must now *estimate* a position for your vessel at the moment you took your sight. *Celestial navigation* (like some forms of logical

argumentation) *functions by proving that you aren't where you say you are*—and doing so so fastidiously as to give you the exact measure of your misjudgment.

Since you don't particularly care what your Estimated Position (EP) is (it having a purely hypothetical function), you select a *convenient* position. A "convenient" position is a position that (a) conforms with the whole numbers around which the tables are constructed, and therefore (b) eliminates unnecessary arithmetic.

You begin by selecting the nearest whole-numbered latitude to where you think you are. In our case, latitude 38°.

For longitude, we select a meridian that ends with *exactly as many minutes as the Sun's GHA at the moment we took the sight.*

The Sun's GHA (longitude) was 65° 40'. Our dead reckoning position puts us slightly west of 32° longitude. So we put the vessel's EP at 32° 40' (West) longitude.

4. We are arranging the "arguments" in such a way as to discover the one remaining datum we need in order to consult the tables. That is the angle formed at the center of the earth by the two lines that rise up, the one to the sun, the other to the vessel. It is known as the Local Hour Angle (LHA). What it does for you is supply the missing trigonometric factor needed to crack the triangle—which is done for you in the tables. The LHA should be thought of as the discrepancy-detector. But never mind, just compute it.

Here you have to remember something. There are other ways of saying this (page A6 of the *Air Almanac* gives you an alternative formulation). But I find it easier to remember how to measure the angle in question by following this procedure:

Plot the position of the Sun on a free-drawn circle at the top of which you put down "G," representing Greenwich. Draw a tiny circle (the Sun) approximately as far west (counterclockwise) from Greenwich as your GHA: in this case (65° 40'), at about ten o'clock. Then draw a little hull (your vessel), approximately as far west from Greenwich as your vessel's longitude: in this case (32° 40') at about eleven o'clock. Your LHA is the angle formed between the vessel and the sun *measured westward only*. In this case the LHA is, simply, 32° 40' subtracted from 65° 40'—33°. But if it happened that your vessel's estimated longitude had been, let us say, 66° 40', then to

174

calculate your LHA you would need to travel *all the way around the circle* (remember: counterclockwise only) until you hit the Sun—for an LHA of 359°. It is instantly apparent that when you selected an estimated position ending in forty minutes you positioned yourself to come up with a clean, minute-free LHA—as is required to enter the tables.

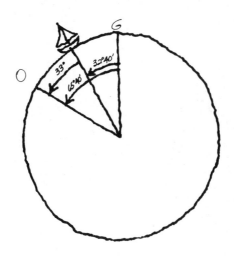

5. You arrive now at the tables, and in order to find the relevant information you must:

a. Turn to the section in the tables volume (H.O. 249) that gives you information for latitude 38°.

b. Turn to the page within that section that gives you figures that relate to your sun sight's Declination, 23°.

c. Turn to the page within that subsection that is headed "DECLINATION SAME NAME AS LATITUDE."

6. "SAME NAME" is the Merrie Olde Englishe way of saying that your vessel and the Sun are in the same hemisphere; in our case, the northern hemisphere. The opposite is "CONTRARY NAME." That would apply in the fall or winter, when the sun sinks below the equator. Needless to say, if you are sailing in the southern hemisphere between September and March, you are SAME-ing it.

Having located the page in the 38°-section, covering the LHA 33° beat, under the SAME NAME rubric, you run your eye across from

LHA 33° until you reach the vertical column that descends from Declination 23°. You write down what appears in the space where these two intersect.

58° 06′ + (34)   109

LHA	15° Hc	d	Z	16° Hc	d	Z	17° Hc	d	Z		22° d	Z	(23) Hc	d	Z	24° Hc	d	Z
	° ′	′	°	° ′	′	°	° ′	′			′	°	° ′	′	°	° ′	′	°
0	67 00	+60	180	68 00	+60	180	69 00	+60			180	75 00	+60	180	76 00	-60	18
1	66 59	60	178	67 59	60	177	68 59				177	74 59	59	176	75 58	60	17
2	66 56	60	175	67 56	60	175	68 56				173	74 54	60	173	75 54	59	17
3	66 51	60	173	67 51	59	172	68 50				170	74 47	59	169	75 46	59	16
4	66 44	59	170	67 43	60	170	68 43				167	74 37	58	166	75 35	59	16
5	66 35	+59	168	67 34	+59	167	68 33				164	74 24	+58	163	75 22	+58	16
6	66 24	58	165	67 22	59	165	68 21				160	74 09	57	159	75 06	56	15
7	66 11	58	163	67 09	58	162	68 07				157	73 51	56	156	74 47	55	1
8	65 56	58	161	66 54	57	160	67 51				155	73 31	55	153	74 26	54	1
9	65 40	57	159	66 37	57	158	67 33				152	73 08	54	150	74 02	53	1
10	65 22	+56	156	66 18	+56	156	67 13				149	72 44	+53	147	73 37	+52	1
11	65 02	56	154	65 58	55	153	66 53				146	72 17	52	145	73 09	51	1
12	64 40	56	152	65 36	55	151	66				144	71 49	51	142	72 40	49	1
13	64 17	55	150	65 12	54	149	66				141	71 19	50	140	72 09	48	1
14	63 53	54	148	64 47	53	147	65				139	70 48	48	137	71 36	48	
15	63 27	+53	146	64 20	+53	145	65				137	70 15	+48	135	71 03	+46	
16	63 00	53	144	63 53	52	143					135	69 41	47	133	70 28	45	13
17	62 32	52	142	63 24	51	141					133	69 06	46	131	69 52	43	12
18	62 02	51	141	62 53	51	139					131	68 30	44	129	69 14	43	12
19	61 32	50	139	62 22	50	138					129	67 53	43	127	68 36	42	1
20	61 00	+49	137	61 49	+49	13					127	67 15	+42	126	67 57	+41	
21	60 27	49	135	61 16	48	13					126	66 36	42	124	67 18	40	1
22	59 54	48	134	60 42	47	1					124	65 56	41	122	66 37	40	1
23	59 19	48	132	60 07	46	1					122	65 16	40	121	65 56	39	
24	58 44	47	131	59 31	46	1					121	64 35	39	119	65 14	38	
25	58 07	+47	129	58 54	+45	12					120	63 54	+38	118	64 32	+37	
26	57 31	45	128	58 16	45	12					118	63 12	37	117	63 49		
27	56 53	45	127	57 38	44	12					117	62 29	37	115	63 06		
28	56 15	44	125	56 59	44	1					116	61 46	37	114	62 23		
29	55 36	44	124	56 20	43	1					114	61 03	36	113	61 39		
30	54 56	+44	123	55 40	+42	12					113	60 19	+36	112	60 55		
31	54 16	43	122	54 59	42	1					112	59 35	35	111	60 10	34	1
32	53 36	42	120	54 18	42	1					111	58 50	35	110	59 25	34	1
33	52 55	42	119	53 37	41	1						58 06	34	109	58 40	33	
34	52 13	42	118	52 55	40	1						57 21	34	108	57 55		
35	51 31	+41	117	52 12	+40							56 35	33	107	57 09		
36	50 49	41	116	51 30													
37	50 06	40	115	50 46													
38	49 23	40	114	50 03													

a. The first of these figures is the Altitude (H) of the Sun *assuming* that its Declination was a flat 23°; which of course it is not—it is, in our case, 23° 25′. Once again we need to interpolate. The center figure, in small type, is the key we take with us to the Interpolation Schedule at the back of the tables. We project the figure 34 over until it hits the line across from 25, isolating the increment to be added. The table yields the figure 14′. You add 14′ to 58° 06′, and you get 58° 20′.

176

d/′	1	2	3	4	5	29	30	31	32	33	34	35	36	37	38
0	0	0	0	0	0	0	0	0	0	0	0	0	0	0	0
1	0	0	0	0	0	0	0	1	1	1	1	1	1	1	1
2	0	0	0	0	0	1	1	1	1	1	1	1	1	1	1
3	0	0	0	0	0	1	2	2	2	2	2	2	2	2	2
4	0	0	0	0	0	2	2	2	2	2	2	2	2	2	3
5	0	0	0	0	0	2	2	3	3	3	3	3	3	3	3
6	0	0	0	0	0	3	3	3	3	3	3	4	4	4	4
7	0	0	0	0	1	3	4	4	4	4	4	4	4	4	4
8	0	0	0	1	1	4	4	4	4	4	5	5	5	5	5
9	0	0	0	1	1	4	4	5	5	5	5	5	5	6	6
10	0	0	0	1	1	5	5	5	5	6	6	6	6	6	6
11	0	0	1	1	1	5	6	6	6	6	6	6	7	7	7
12	0	0	1	1	1	6	6	6	6	7	7	7	7	7	8
13	0	0	1	1	1	6	6	7	7	7	7	8	8	8	8
14	0	0	1	1	1	7	7	7	7	8	8	8	8	9	9
15	0	0	1	1	1	7	8	8	8	8	8	9	9	9	10
16	0	1	1	1	1	8	8	8	9	9	9	9	10	10	10
17	0	1	1	1	1	8	8	9	9	9	10	10	10	10	11
18	0	1	1	1	2	9	9	9	10	10	10	10	11	11	11
19	0	1	1	1	2	9	10	10	10	10	11	11	11	12	12
20	0	1	1	1	2	10	10	10	11	11	11	12	12	12	13
21	0	1	1	1	2	10	10	11	11	12	12	12	13	13	13
22	0	1	1	1	2	11	11	11	12	12	12	13	13	14	14
23	0	1	1	2	2	11	12	12	12	13	13	13	14	14	15
24	0	1	1	2	2	12	12	12	13	13	14	14	14	15	15
→25	0	1	1	2	2	12	12	13	13	14	14	15	15	15	16
26	0	1	1	2	2	13	13	13	14	14	15	15	16	16	16

This is your *Calculated Altitude* (Hc). It is the angle you would have spotted the Sun at, at the moment you shouted "Mark!"—*if the vessel had indeed been located where you hypothetically placed it.*

b. The figure 109 is followed by Z. You must now look up at the top left-hand corner of the page. There you will see the legend: "*LHA greater than 180°, Zn = Z. LHA less than 180°, Zn = 360—Z.*" Since our LHA, at 33°, is less than 180°, we subtract the table's Z of 109° from 360°, and come up with a Zn of 251°.

The Zn is the *Azimuth*—the exact direction ("west by south three-quarters south" was once the vernacular) toward which you are to draw a line originating at your Estimated Position, as now you near the end of the search for the vessel's LOP.

7. But having drawn the line from your Estimated Position of lat. 38°, long. 32° 40′, how far along that line do you travel? And what then do you do?

The LOP is a line drawn perpendicular to the Azimuth line. The distance along the Azimuth you must travel before plotting the perpendicular LOP is called the *Intercept* (yes, "Int.").

a. The Intercept is the difference between your Ho and your Hc. We know that the Ho was not lying to us—that was the *actual* vertical angle of the Sun at the chronicled moment.

The Ho was 58° 18'.

The Hc was 58° 20'.

The difference is: 2'. That is to say, two miles.

Since the Ho is smaller than the Hc, you are *farther* from the Sun than you thought—after all, if you were directly under the Sun, your Ho would be 90°. Therefore, the Intercept is designated as *Away* from (as distinguished from *Towards*) the celestial body.

You take your dividers and measure two miles along the Azimuth line. Put a pencil dot there. Then take a ruler and place it perpendicular to the Azimuth, running across the sacred dot, and draw a line across the ruler's edge. Your vessel is located on that Line of Position.

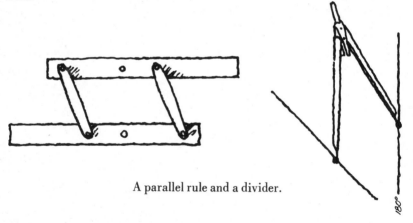

A parallel rule and a divider.

The entire exercise, from the time you shout "Mark!" until the time you draw your LOP, will take you about 3–4 minutes.

Let those who too easily despair submit, for the exercise, to the following drill:

—Measure the distance from the left end to the right end of the piano keyboard, and divide it by two. Then measure the distance

178

from that point to your right until you come to the first black key in the clusters of two black keys (which, you will note, alternate with clusters of three black keys). Having noted that distance, go back and measure from the same starting point but moving this time to the left, until you reach the furthest of the black keys in the nearest two-black-key cluster. Now compare these distances. Move your finger to the closer of the two; and then move your finger left to the adjacent white key. Take a stopwatch, and adopt a rhythmic beat timed by the stroke of every second, except where a different interval is specified.

Begin the exercise: (1) Strike the key already located. (2) Strike the same key again. (3) Strike the fifth white key to the right. (4) Again. (5) Strike the next higher white key. (6) Again. (7) Return to the preceding key—but hold it down for *two* seconds. (8) Strike the next white key to the left. (9) Strike the same key again. (10) Strike the next lower white key. (11) Strike that key again. (12) Move down another white key, and strike it. (13) Again. (14) Down another white key (to the original), strike, and hold it for two seconds.

These are literal instructions, formulated on the assumption of a reader's total unfamiliarity with the piano keyboard, for tapping out the opening bars of *Twinkle, Twinkle, Little Star* (How I wonder/ What you are). And the pedagogic point of the exercise is to demonstrate that it is as easy, having casually familiarized oneself with the sextant and the tables, to transform the apparently forbidding instructions above into an LOP as it is to transform the paragraph above into the simple melody, with only a few minutes' application.

The big enemy (I suppose this is a matter of temperament. More safely: My big enemy) is silly arithmetical errors. I specialize in these, especially in the rusty, early stages of a trip; and I almost always come up, once or twice, with a preposterous LOP. Fortunately, these are exactly that—preposterous. When such a thing happens, you simply go back and check your figures, and inevitably you identify an arithmetical mistake. (That, by the way, takes much more time than working out the sight in the first instance.) The figures are all indelibly set down in your notebook. After a while you develop the kind of operative confidence that permits you quickly to exclude certain hypotheses. If—say—you end up with an LOP that is twenty or thirty miles off your dead-reckoning position, you can usually feel it, even retroactively, in the seat of your pants that your sun sight was a little—blasé; caused, perhaps, by the pitching of the boat. If your figures are okay, and the LOP is bum, *either* the sight was bad *or* the timekeeper was inaccurate. It is *extraordinary* how often the latter is the case. Misreading the minute hand by one minute will put you off fifteen miles. But after a while you start knocking them down, no sweat. *All* the instructions you need are given in these words. Master them, and you have hold of everything you need to go on to the stars and the planets. And, of course, the "noon sight," taken at that glorious moment when the sun squats over your meridian (i.e., the sun is exactly south or north)—it has no other recourse than to do so: for the exploitation of which benefaction you do not even need a sundial, let alone a chronometer. A piece of cake.

Bermuda is a blur, best captured in Christopher's log, and thank God I am old enough to be spared the temptation to the bacchanalian excesses. I think I don't really enjoy what the jet age makes possible: the quickie reunions with one's wife, which are more poignant than exhilarating. A reunion on a transatlantic stop is really defined as a recapitulated departure, because one arrives, really, only for the sake of leaving again. If the schedule were otherwise and you planned to sail to Bermuda in order, say, to spend a week there, only then sailing on, it would be different. At least we'll spend four days in the Azores, but one and one half of these will be spent in traveling along the 350-mile length of the islands. The indomitable Pat and Marvin will not attempt to meet us there, under the circumstances.

Her arrival gave us something of the feeling of the annual visitation of the steamboat in Nome, Alaska, bearing the necessities for the entire winter. She bore the replacement loran unit; the spare propeller (the one that had been blasted off in Miami, pitched now to the desired amplitude); and her own personal little color Sony to remedy the Buckley Home Entertainment Service. To anticipate: the loran did not work, though we gave it another two days' trial. The propeller we did not need. The new barometer failed—Van feels that our imperfect barometer is the saddest commentary on our defective gear, and I try to console him by telling him that I have hardly ever seen a defective barometer before, so simple is the mechanism. It is on the order of having a defective screwdriver. When I *think* of the barometers and altimeters I possess, scattered about, none of which I thought to bring. The television didn't work. My frustration was such that I have suggested to my companions that on arriving at Marbella, we all depart instantly with our cassette-player, television, and tapes to a motel and there watch ten straight hours of "Upstairs, Downstairs," followed by dinner, followed by ten straight hours of "War and Peace." Never mind; it was a cool idea, Danny said, grinning, as he put away the various wires for the very last time.

On the Sunday in Bermuda, two lawyers worked all day long taking down over the telephone from New Orleans endless papers I needed personally to sign in connection with a novation of a corporate bank loan. It always stops me for a moment when lawyers in Bermuda knock formally at your door, dressed in shorts. Like the Bengal Lancers. We chatted as I began signing—and I suddenly recognized one of the lawyers. Ten years ago he had been the assistant counsel in a civil suit I brought against a local scoundrel of great leverage on the Island because he is something of a genius in the boat business— "Mr. Darrell, he's a *mahster*," it was explained to me by a cab-driver. He has a mien like Heathcliff's and a temper like John L. Lewis's, and isn't damaged by the prestige of being regularly selected by Prince Philip as crew when Philip goes to Bermuda to race.

I turned over *The Panic* to him after the awful hurricane trip in 1958, with a list of instructions, work he agreed to do during the winter months. Six months later I had received from him not a word of reply to any of my letters or, finally, my telegrams. I asked Reggie and Peter to fly to Hamilton to see what was up, and they returned three days later with the news that the boat had not been touched since the afternoon in October we turned it over, and was therefore in an advanced stage of dissolution.

I wrote Darrell a letter, recounting the history of our association, and terminating in an explosion of outrage at his unconscionable neglect of my beautiful boat—and filed a lawsuit against him for six thousand dollars, that being a professional estimate of the damage done.

On the eve of our departure on *The Panic* the following June (the trial was set for a year later), Darrell, through an agent, presented me with a bill for the mooring of the boat over the winter, an act under the circumstances of almost magnificent impudence. But he had taken the precaution of lifting our spinnaker pole from the boat and storing it in his loft. Without our spinnaker pole we would be severely handicapped on the return journey. Moreover, being eighteen feet long and weighing about seventy-five pounds, it could not be replaced inexpensively, let alone in time for our scheduled departure the next day. So . . .

Reggie, who went to school in Bermuda, was talking about our plight with one of his classmates, a local merchant, who revealed to him confidentially that Darrell is a man of very regular habits who goes to lunch at exactly noon every day, leaving the key to his loft under the third step of the left-hand of the two entrances to the loft. At exactly 12:05, Firpo and Van slithered into the yard, found the key, located the pole, and in extricating it from the general pile of masts and booms, broke a window—a spinnaker pole is a horribly unwieldy object.

Still, they had it, and carrying it on their shoulders, began jogging down the road to where we waited for them with a makeshift truck; and, from there, we were off to the safety of *The Panic*.

The howl from Bert Darrell was heard through the Colony of Bermuda. He was, it is said, for at least one hour incapable of speech. The second hour he spent with the magistrate. I must imagine that he had some difficulty in explaining how we could "steal" something which was legally ours; but he browbeat the gentleman sufficiently to wrest from him a written order divesting Mr. William F. Buckley, Jr. of "one spinnaker pole, with the identifying lettering, *The Panic*." It was at a vinous cocktail party given for us a few hours later at a small hotel that the bailiff found me.

People are very polite in Bermuda, and the conversation went as follows:

"Sir, are you Mr. William F. Buckley, Junior?"

"Yes," I said.

"Sir, here is an order, duly executed by the Chief Magistrate, requiring that you turn over to me your"—he peered down at the paper to read exactly the description of the article he had been sent to recover—"your spinnaker pole."

"I am very sorry, I do not have a spinnaker pole with me," I said, stalling; the pole was on board, and Peter was instructed to permit no one on the boat without legal authorization.

"I am afraid, sir, that I shall have to search you. Would you please empty your pockets?"

With this the general hilarity overcame the poor bailiff, who must

183

have thought a spinnaker pole a talisman of sorts, suitable for vest-pocket intimacy. At this point our own lawyer, among the guests, took him aside and advised him that the repossession order was defective because no article belonging to a ship could be legally impounded in the absence of a court order approving such impoundment, issuable only after a reasonable length of time during which the shipowner had not paid a bill; and since Darrell's bill had been presented only that morning, there had not yet gone by a sufficient length of time to establish a default.

Late the following summer I arrived for the trial, which was reported garishly on the front pages of the Bermuda paper for a solid week. Emotionally, Hamilton was divided. On the one hand, everyone had a historic complaint against Darrell. On the other hand, it was a foreigner suing a native. It cost me $1,500 in lawyers' fees, and I won a judgment of about $450—the judge ruled that the damage done to the boat from routine, as distinguished from specialized, neglect was the responsibility of a native taxi-driver who had volunteered to moonlight as the boat's caretaker, removed from Darrell's jurisdiction. I have laid eyes on Darrell a half-dozen times since those explosive days, and he still manages to look like Fafner when he sees me. This last time, passing by his yard, I saw him and thought I'd try waving at him. He waved back—until his memory-tumbler clicked. He instantly put on a double scowl—one for me, for old times' sake; the second for himself, for failing, however briefly, to recognize the enemy.

On Monday morning the wind was howling, though, conveniently, from the west. Pat, who had gone out for last-minute provisioning, came in with Van, Christopher, and Danny, all looking rather solemn. I was dispirited. For one thing my cursed disease was back, and Bill had me on antibiotics again. But mostly I was depressed that indeed Reggie's business crisis had matured, and he was leaving this morning for Ohio in a final effort to save his company—promising to meet us in the Azores whether his news was good or bad. This left us seriously shorthanded, and we advertised on the radio for a mate, offering two hundred dollars for two weeks' work, plus return passage to Bermuda. In due course a Cornell junior, a pleasant young man, Jeff

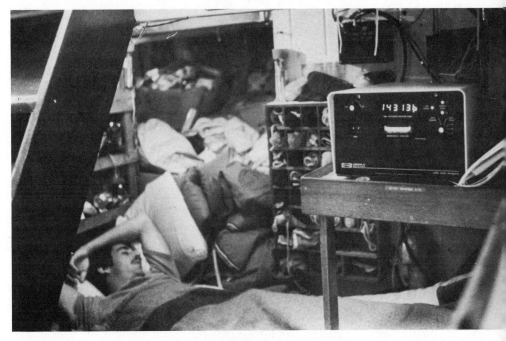

Jeff Gadboys, seasick. Also nonoperational: the loran.

Gadboys, whose American parents were stationed in Bermuda, presented himself, was interviewed by Captain Campagna and found adequate. There is, of course, no way in which you can establish whether an apparently healthy young man of about twenty-two has a stomach for the sea; poor Jeff has been consistently seasick.

The suggestion was that, the winds being as blustery as they were, we should put off our departure by twenty-four hours. Normally I'd have said No; the winds, after all, were not hauling in a dangerous storm front, Van admitted. Meanwhile, a thirty-five-knot wind from the west would catapult us nicely on our way. But the combination of factors was overpowering; so it wasn't until this morning, very early, that we set out. Last night I drove Pat and Marvin to the airport to catch their flight, and our goodbye was a little frozen. Pat suffers so much from her rooted pessimism, and no doubt reasons that since it is not written in the laws of the Republic or of my God that I *must* set out in a small sailboat from Bermuda to Spain with our only son and her only sister, my doing so is at least partly an act of thoughtlessness at her expense. Actually, there isn't any way to answer that argument: it is, in part, just that.

We had, even a day later, plenty of the remains of the strong westerly and, after winding our way out of the harbor and through the tortuous channel on the windward side of the island, past the cut to St. George's, we set the boat on a course of 083° magnetic for the town of Horta on the island of Faial, Azore Islands, a distance of 1,799 nautical miles. We are weighted down by an extra nine hundred gallons of fuel. But these are neatly stowed, lashed down in drums on deck forward, almost out of eyesight from the after section of the boat. That's about six thousand pounds of fuel, and I was anxious to see what it would do to the sailing characteristics of my Cyrano. It did nothing.

My God, what a lovely sailing boat she is! The skies never did clear, and the rollers are steep and decisive. I notice that everyone is tired, very tired. A combination of factors. In the case of the boys, concentrated overindulgence in Bermuda. A little of this too, I suspect, with Augustino and Phil Jr. But even teetotaling Aunty Bill dozes. What there also is, is that faint premonition. We are embarked on the longest ocean passage I've ever been on under sail, and a lot of the gear on board isn't working, including the goddam battery bank which still isn't holding a charge. Reggie's absence is like the absence of a resident benevolence. Even Danny, the most responsive young American since Huckleberry Finn, needs two nickels, instead of the usual one, to get him roused and talkative, amused and amusing. Christopher will be out of action, I expect, for a couple of days. The captain and poor seasick Jeff are on watch now until 4:00 A.M. We are moving at hull speed, and the creaking and groaning of the boat, racing in tandem with the wind off the port quarter, is the sound not of strain, but of exultation; or that, at least, is how I begin to hear it, as my spirits, lying in bed, begin to rise. So what does it matter that the loran doesn't work and the generator doesn't generate and the radio direction finder doesn't find? Is it likely to make a critical difference? Melville is talking to me, words not entirely consoling, but their perspective is useful. "A moment's consideration will teach, that however baby man may brag of his science and skill, and however much, in a flattering future, that science and skill may augment;

186

yet forever and forever, to the crack of doom, the sea will insult and murder him, and pulverize the stateliest, stiffest frigate he can make; nevertheless, by the continual repetition of these very impressions, man has lost that sense of the full awfulness of the sea which aboriginally belongs to it." Fie upon the misimpressions! Now I lay me down to sleep, and pray the Lord my soul to keep.

Saturday. After three days trying to figure out why it doesn't work any more, I gave up on the HP–65 Buckley–Finucane computerized navigational system. During the run to Bermuda it worked flawlessly. I foolishly threw away the notebook in which the computations were made, not anticipating any summons to an inquest. My surmise as to why, on the initial leg, there were no problems is both inchoate and—though I have confidence in it—too uncredentialed to introduce in these parascientific pages.

Suffice to say that a day or two out of Bermuda, on plotting the figures given me by my amanuensis Bill, I remarked a serious discrepancy between the HP's Line of Position and any Line of Position consistent with our dead-reckoning position. So I threw away her figures and worked out an LOP in the traditional way, using the Almanac and the tables. Indeed there was a difference—almost thirty miles.

I assumed (one always does, and one always should) that the operator had made a mechanical error in operating the machine. I was reluctant to float that possibility, since Bill is the kind of person who *does not make errors* when she is burdened with a responsibility of any gravity—particularly in a discipline she does not understand. Living in Mexico, years ago, I marveled at the extraordinary typographical precision of the *Mexico Daily News*, which phenomenon was patiently explained one day by the publisher, who informed me that his linotypists, knowing not a single word of English, approached their duties in the spirit of cryptographers: as, say, I would slow up at the typewriter if I were copying out words in German. Even so, at Bill's merry insistence—which disguised a serene self-confidence—

we did the exercise all over again: and got the same, obstinately incorrect answer.

To compress three days' agony (it was a terrible blow to our pride, having invested hours trying, first, to fathom the HP–65 as navigator, then to validate it), I turned, finally, to the ultimate explanation. Perhaps—I speculated—a piece of magnetic dust, or whatever, had attached to one of the programmed cards, causing distortion. So we took blank cards, and *reprogrammed the entire navigational series.* You may put that down, if you insist, in the category of the Problems of the Idle Rich. But there were seven individual cards involved, each one of them storing a hundred separately labeled transactions, requiring that, without error, Bill should punch a total of seven hundred discrete instructions, dictated by me, reading aloud from the appendixed schematic, into the blank cards.

Having completed this nerve-wracking labor, we came up with—the identical error.

I now wrote carefully in a notebook, exactly describing the discrepancy. And we bade a sad farewell to the HP–65—though we continued to use it gratefully for great circle distances and heading.

By sheer coincidence, three weeks after my return from the B.O. I bumped into—in social circumstances, on the very same afternoon—not only the great Mr. Hewlett, but *also* the great Mr. Packard. Clearly the man I needed was Mr. –65, who guards the secrets so well that he does not readily vouchsafe them to his customers. Mr. Hewlett, perfectly pleasant, was, however, busy playing bridge, and obviously concluded that since I was where I was, rather than shipwrecked on a coral reef off the Azores, his responsibility was academic. David Packard, a dear and diffident old friend, huffed something about getting me a fresh computer.

A few months later (I am skipping ahead), a northeastern representative of HP came to see me, to review my notes. A charming man who, however, could not figure out what I had done wrong, and together we discussed the possibility of regional dead spots. He reached for the telephone to call the omniscient and cheerful Mr. Kenneth Newcomer, who is styled the "Applications Engineer" and is responsible for devising (which he does brilliantly) but not, I hope, for

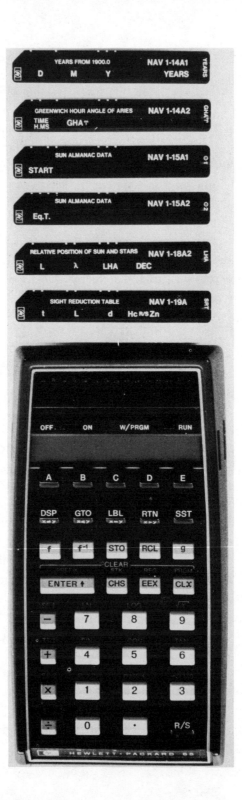

explaining (which *somebody* does miserably) how to use the HP's resources in celestial navigation.

In due course, I having, as my part of the bargain, transcribed the specimen anomaly, he sent me a two-page letter (with an enclosure), the comprehension of which strained every resource of my finite mechanical energies—because dear Mr. Newcomer, for all that he is the world's most obliging man, is clearly used to speaking only to careerists in computer technology.

It is fair to say that it is *not*, repeat *not*, possible to learn, without terminal frustration, how to navigate at sea by computer by reading the publications that accompany the HP–65's NAV-PAC. You need a trot. I attempted, four months before setting out on the B.O., to transcribe from the manual intelligible instructions on the use of the instrument; and I sent copies of my exegesis, like sprays of orchids, to Mr. Newcomer and to a few of his associates. There was no acknowledgment; from anybody. The final paragraph of my presumptuously labeled "Revised Instructions" concluded with a parenthetical note remarking an unexplained discrepancy even in HP's own manuals, which I myself went on to ignore, dismissing it as probably the result of a typo (I had detected others in HP's booklet), but which, I think, should have caused Houston Control, on being alerted, to send out a General Quarters alarm. I concluded the memo in a jargon intelligible only to colleagues in cryptography: "(*Question*: When I feed H. of 1113.16 and depress Hoa, I get −14.3; but then, pushing D, I get Lat. of 40° 25′.75, which is okay; but Longitude of 159° 59′, which is 22 minutes off. What is the problem?)"

There was no acknowledgment of the memorandum, nor any effort made to explain the anomaly. That failure caused us dozens of hours of flailing about in search of an explanation for a failure which proved mystifying, ultimately, even to executives of HP. Moral: If one designs an elaborate machine one of whose uses is the specific performance of a particular, complicated task, it is simply silly to lower one's standards in preparing a manual of instructions. HP needs to hire somebody from the Heath-Kit Company. Meanwhile, I shall do it for nothing. What follows is fascinating, life-saving information for navigators—but of very little interest, I should think, to others, who are invited back, beginning on page 195.

Let me set down, in the most deliberate prose recorded since the Duke of Norfolk staged the coronation of Queen Elizabeth, the procedures by which you can, with an instrument that fits in the palm of your hand, transform the raw data into a Line of Position: after which I shall give an estimate of the usefulness of the system.

We'll use the identical data already used (see pp. 168–177) in explaining celestial navigation by traditional means.

You begin with the following knowledge:

Date: 19 June 1975
Time: 16th 23m 51s
Ho: 58° 18'
EP: 38° Latitude
           32° Longitude

NOTE: Since you will not have to work out a GHA or a LHA, you do not need to add to the longitude of your Estimated Position the increment of minutes that will cause it to correspond with your GHA's leftovers. Accordingly, your Estimated Position (EP) can be rendered in round figures. If you desire, as an EP, to give your Dead Reckoning (DR) position, you may do so; HP doesn't care in the least. I have elected to use round numbers.

Turn on the machine, set to *RUN*.

1. Take the card designated YEARS (Years from 1900—NAV 1–14A1). Having inserted it through the program slot, position it in the dashboard slot. You will see D M Y   YEARS. The D, M, and Y call for the Day, the Month, and the Year. Accordingly, key 19, and then depress (under D) the A button. Then 6 (under M), and depress B. Then 1975 (under Y), and depress C. Now move over to the E button, which appears under the dashboard designation YEARS, and depress it. (Your digital display will read 75.47.)

2. Program GHA (Greenwich Hour Angle of Aries—NAV 1–14A1). It asks first for TIME H.MS, which means that you give the hour, then a decimal point, then the minutes and the seconds. In this case, 16.2351. Now depress A. Then depress B (under GHA). (The display will give you the GHA, expressed as 15314.1—i.e., 153° 14.1'.) (Aries, a constellation, serves the stars as Greenwich serves the Sun and planets—the point from which longitude is measured. The difference is this: Greenwich is geographically fixed and its

navigational satellites are in constant motion. In dealing with the stars, their distance from Aries is fixed—but Aries is in constant motion, as recorded in the Almanac.)

3. You will now program, in succession, the two cards, both called SUN ALMANAC DATA (respectively NAV 1–15A1 and NAV 1–15A2). In each case you depress A (getting, respectively, 272.3 and –0.011 as digital displays).

4. Program now LHA (Relative Position of Sun and Stars—NAV 1–18A2). Here is where you feed in your Estimated Position. (NOTE: If you are in a southern latitude, you must depress CHS after giving the figures; ditto, if you are in an eastern longitude.) These are given without decimal point—in our case (latitude 38°, longitude 32°) 3800 (under L). Then depress A; then 3200 (under λ—the longitude sign) and depress B. After this, depress C (under LHA). (The display will give you the LHA, expressed as 3339.9833, i.e., 33° 39.9833′.) Then depress D (under DEC), to get Declination (2325.3667—23° 25.3667′).

5. Next, program SRT (Sight Reduction Table—NAV 1–19A). You ignore t, L, and d, which perch over keys A, B, and C, and proceed directly to Hc R/S Zn, over D. Depress D and you will get 5750.2—which is your Hc (57° 50.2′). Now depress R/S, and you will get your Azimuth—252.9°.

What you have now is everything the Almanac and the tables would yield you. It is left for you only to do exactly what you would do after closing the covers of the Almanac and the tables.

—Subtract the Hc (57° 50.2′) from the Ho (58° 18′). That yields you (eliminating the fraction) 28′. Since the Ho is larger than the Hc, the vessel is closer to the sun than its hypothetical position. Accordingly, the intercept of 28 miles must be plotted Toward, rather than Away from, the Sun. The Azimuth, pointing to the Sun, is already calculated, so you plot 28 minutes on a course of 253° (rounding out the 252.9°). There you draw your perpendicular. Please notice that it *exactly* duplicates the perpendicular given in the example worked out above (page 178) by the tables, even though the estimated longitude differed by 40 miles.

In assessing the usefulness of the computer for star work, one need say nothing more than that step 3, which calls now for inserting the two Sun Almanac cards, requires instead that you insert the card labeled for the star you are observing (there is a card in the NAV-PAC for every one of the principal navigation stars). Thereafter, the calculations are identical.

If you elect to buy and master the HP–65, what are you left with?

Surprisingly, a great deal. There are, of course, a score of uses for the HP–65 not even noticed here. I have already mentioned the incredible program—a single card—that gives you the great circle distance and the original heading from any point to any other point. There are also programs for (among other concerns): Length Conversions; Speed Time and Distance; Time-Arc Conversion; Distance To or Beyond Horizon; Distance by Horizon Angle and Distance Short of Horizon; Rhumb Line Navigation; Sunrise Sunset and Twilight; Long-Term Star Almanac; and Distance Off an Object by Two Bearings.

As actually experienced at sea—before running into the problem of the card entitled Most Probable Position, which was the cause of all our woe—it is a neat, extremely easy, and totally reliable way of eliminating all the paper work needed in the use of the Almanac and tables. Jot down: the day, the time, the sextant altitude, your sextant corrections, and an estimated position. Then if you like to work with a partner (I like to, especially with Bill Finucane), give her your notepad with that much on it, nothing more. In less than five minutes she will have written, on the same page, under your notations:

The Intercept.

The Azimuth.

The direction ("Toward" or "Away").

You move right to the plotting sheet.

If you are taking a cluster of star sights, you can dictate the information, and by the time you are through taking these sights, your partner can have the calculations all done—without any need for you to touch a sheet of paper. Pretty neat. The time required, as I say, is about five minutes per sight.

Incidental information: the HP runs off its rechargeable battery for about three hours. That's a lot of sights. But if you don't have facilities for recharging 110-volts AC, you can buy extra cadmium batteries, charge them, and take them along.

Thursday. It is easy for some people, looking up at a sail and over to the little wind-direction-indicating telltale, to know if it is maladjusted. (Directions: Take a nylon stocking and slice down, most easily with a razor, a one-inch strip about fourteen inches long; tape this to the upper shroud about two feet above your head. Absolutely no substitute is the equal of this telltale, which shrugs off rain and moisture and responds to the least arousal of wind, becoming instantly tumescent.) Even as some people can tell right away if a note is off-pitch. In both disciplines you *can* improve with practice. But, so far as I can see, it is largely an accident whether the aptitude is congenital; in my case it is—even as I am congenitally incapable of striking, on a piano, the right note, notwithstanding the clarity with which the sought-after tone sounds in my ear. I drive Christopher and Danny nuts sometimes by coming on deck and immediately ordering a wide variety of changes in the set of the sails. Usually my judgment is validated by a corresponding movement in the Kenyon gauge. Sometimes it isn't, and all that this means, usually, is that the wind is capricious; it also gives the boys an opportunity for a wisecrack in their journals about the prodigious athletic demands of serving under me as sailing master. While admitting—indeed, professing—to an effective feel for the right inflection of a sail-set, it is also true that, being bone-lazy, I greatly prefer to be at the wheel when the moment comes for arduous efforts involving the setting of the sails. Since over the years my friends have got used to seeing me at the wheel at such moments, they are good-natured about it; but . . . there, I have confessed it. A usufruct of captaincy at sea. I have never understood the book-captains, who disdain any contact with the wheel, preferring to pace up and down the bridge, like Captain Hornblower, leaving it to a bo'sun to do the steering. It is singularly gratifying to steer a boat, whether out at sea in troubled waters, or gliding into a dock, preferably stopping before you hit it. When it becomes tedious, there is the human replacement, but also the autopilot, the equivalent of an extra hand: moreover, an extra hand who does not keep a journal.

Christopher has by no means revived, and even Van is still sleepy, but the evening was so pleasant, the late afternoon sail so exquisite, the sun sight so perfect, the wind so regular (temperature just right), I played the piano for a bit before dinner. Not easy, because when the boat rocks I need to exert great pressure through my knees on the underside of the keyboard to keep from falling over backward, and the additional challenge to coordination is enough to make the sounds that result a travesty on the Bach partita I am, as usual, struggling with. I left the piano and put on the cassette-player, a late Beethoven piano sonata, as we sat down for a dinner of turkey and stuffing, wine, cheese, fruit, and coffee. I thought I would try—just a flyer—to say something about the difference between the late and the early Bee-

Haircut. A good view of the main winch, concerning the dangers of which, see below.

thoven, a subject concerning which I once got involved in an extensive published controversy. I learned for the one thousandth time that the kind of music that overwhelms me, simply means nothing—nothing at all—to most people; nothing at all to anybody aboard that boat. Occasionally the evangelist in me will push aside the impacted despair of a generation of trying, and I will say, "By *God*, that's beautiful, isn't it!"—and Bill, dear Bill, will agree; and Van will be agreeable, and also Danny and Christopher. But somehow you suspect that the effect is as if you suddenly stopped, between turkey wings, and began hypnotically to recite a sonnet from Shakespeare, thereupon demanding *instant* acclamation on the subject of the joys of poetry.

How did it come to be, for that matter, that we all love the sensation of sailing through the water? I have taken hundreds of people sailing for their first and—it proved—last time: They were bored. John Kenneth Galbraith thinks me quite mad, not only for the usual reasons, but because I will submit to day after day on a *sailboat*. He literally cannot understand anybody's doing such a thing voluntarily; which, come to think of it, makes it odd that he hasn't proposed a law making it compulsory. Besides, he has taught himself to think of sailing as a form of conspicuous consumption made possible by the Ol' Debbil loopholes. I had him and his two attractive, impossibly argumentative sons on "Firing Line" the Sunday of the week that ended with George McGovern's nomination for President— a splendid show: brilliant father and two brilliant sons; alas, no generational gap, all three of them delegates from Massachusetts, all three pledged to McGovern. After it was over, I asked if he would like to come with the family aboard Cyrano and have dinner.

"Kitty and the boys would like to"—Galbraith is always direct in committing himself or those under his effective control; while he was in New Delhi as our ambassador, that amounted to an awesome number of people—"I can't. I have to go to a tax caucus of the Democratic Party. Come to think of it," he looked up with that dour-bright smile of the paternalistic inquisitor, in which the affection is marvelously creased—"if I have my way, this may be the last time you'll be able to invite *anybody* to come aboard your sailboat!"

I think he thinks that all private sailboats are the kind of thing exhibited in cross-section in the Model Room of the New York Yacht

197

Club, those splendid vessels designed for Harold Vanderbilt in our Edwardian age. A few days later, on network TV, he teased me about the end of Republican Yachting with the advent of a McGovern Administration, and I told him there were probably more registered private boats in America than registered Republicans, but that I did not doubt that if McGovern was elected, the fleet of Americans going out to sea would make the evacuation of Dunkirk look like a weekend at Larchmont.

Galbraith, come to think of it, does not understand music either. More accurately said, he does not *need* music. The boys need music, and one night at sea was devoted to a most earnest effort, by me and Van and Bill, to track the lyrics of some of the classics of the Rock and Roll age that engross them. I could tell that there was quality there, but I couldn't tell much else. I am told by Captain Campagna that some of the people who charter Cyrano, although the availability of my huge collection of tapes is brought to their attention, never bother even to plug in the cassette-player. This is the ultimate loneliness—to fail to communicate to others who are close to you the excitement or pleasure you take from certain experiences which are, then, left for you to enjoy alone or in the anonymous company of others who arrive as strangers to the same concert chamber; or, every now and then, with that odd friend who shares your enthusiasm.

I am greatly excited by reading Melville for the first time, and Christopher delights in the delight he has been instrumental in giving me. To my astonishment, with all there is to read on board, I find him reading implacably a biography of Henry Kissinger. Surprised because Christopher's indifference to politics is comparable to his indifference to what it is that distinguishes early from late Beethoven. I'd be astonished if he could be persuaded to read a political biography of his own father, and I confess to liking it that way. I can only imagine that Carl Philip Emmanuel Bach greatly exasperated Johann Sebastian Bach. Van Galbraith, having dutifully read the manuscript of my novel, is reading now the manuscript of David Niven's book, *Bring on the Empty Horses*. All very incestuous, since Christopher is (sort of) a friend of Kissinger's, Niven is a friend of Van's, and I am a friend of everybody's; except, alas, Herman Melville. But I'll have to put off thinking about it if I am to sleep at all before rising

198

for my watch at 3:00 A.M., when I shall with great gusto fine-tune the Genoa, the forward staysail, the main staysail, the main—*and* if Danny is up, I shall, ho ho!, order the fisherman hoisted!

Friday, Saturday. It was the longest stretch yet under straight power, about thirty-six hours, until a northeast wind relieved us, shortly after lunch. Among my preoccupations during that period, other than the conventional ones: Would I *now* get bored? Surely this was the time for it, with no sails to soothe me. We've been gone fifteen days from Miami, and we have eleven hundred miles to go before reaching Horta. It isn't hot, just warm. But somehow the hours pass, and I feel no resistance building within me, not even fired by the relentless soft sound of the motor. I wonder about motors. I was infected via Pat with a most preposterous superstition I have never quite been able to shake, namely that motors should "rest." I have talked the matter over with Reggie, who knows everything, and he once reminded me that the Perkins 150 we have on board is identical to the motor widely used by the little shrimp boats that go out for two or three weeks at a time, without any sail whatever, except perhaps a little steadying sail to use when the winds are very bad. Theoretically, you can use a motor forever if only you will keep it perfectly lubricated. That means (in our case) stopping every twenty-four hours and checking the oil; and changing it every one hundred hours. The filters need to be changed more often. It is they that collect the glop which, after the filters are full, begins to assault the cylinders. Even though you are supposed to get almost perpetual use from a good sturdy diesel, in fact, of course, you don't. Although—I am assured—if you don't get seven thousand hours out of the Perkins, you are neglecting your motor. That's 56,000 miles.

We lost our motor once, on a charter. The circumstances were wonderful. George C. Scott was the charterer, and arrived with his wife Colleen Dewhurst and a friend at the Hudson River on 79th Street where he had directed Cyrano to await him.

"Where would you like to go?" Ned Killeen asked, expecting him to suggest poking about Long Island Sound, perhaps venturing as far east as the Elizabeth Islands or Martha's Vineyard. Rising to attention like George Patton, General Scott said solemnly:

199

"Take us to Bermuda."

It took a little while for Ned to explain that little sailboats, even of Cyrano's adolescent size, don't just set out for Bermuda at the flip of the will, even as (though Ned didn't put it that way) General Patton would not have arrived at the headquarters of the 3rd Army in the spring of 1944 and said: "Take me to Berlin." But Scott was so crestfallen at the prospect of something less than a major blue-ocean passage, Ned agreed finally to cruise down the Atlantic coast to the Chesapeake. Twenty miles from Cape May, Ned turned on the power and in a few minutes the engine burnt out. Oil leak. Mr. Scott limped into Cape May doing about three knots under sail. Now we have installed a bell that clangs if the oil pressure falls below the safety level. A nice idea, with a minor but irritating disadvantage. It requires about five seconds, as in a car, for the oil pressure to rise after you have fired your engine. During that period the bell goes CLANG CLANG CLANG. Super-thoughtful watch-captains, which means Danny, will, if it is after midnight and the engine needs firing, plod silently down into the engine room, turn off the alarm switch, go back to the wheel, turn on the engine, return to the engine room, and turn the alarm mechanism back on. While in Bermuda I went to a carpet store and bought carpet scraps and carpet padding, which Christopher and I bound tightly with shock cord around the base of the mast in the engine room. This has accomplished wonders in keeping the noise below by arresting the sounding-board effect of the aluminum mast. It is now only barely audible in the cockpit area.

Early in the afternoon a cargo vessel passed a mile or so behind us, heading northeast. We made out her name as the *Aizmes*. Captain Campagna "spoke" her. "To speak a ship," a transitive verb happily far gone in desuetude, means "to establish communication with, at sea." The captain routinely asked *Aizmes* where she was headed (Amsterdam) and what was her position (she gave it). This intelligence was relayed to me, and I advised the plebes that the *Aizmes* was, in fact, five to six miles south of the position she mistook herself to be at. This aroused great gales of parricidal laughter, in which Danny joined and finally Van, leaving me only Bill Finucane, who thought it an inescapable deduction that if someone was mistaken in calculating our joint position, it was the *Aizmes'* navigator and not her brother-in-law. I volunteered to rub the noses of any skeptic in the evidence of my sun sight and the dead reckoning of the mere hour and a half that had elapsed but, I told them, since this would require that they exert themselves intellectually, I knew I was safe in making the challenge. Christopher and Danny *love* that sort of thing, and I happen to know that they are, with whoops of surreptitious laughter, planning revenge.

Why do I feel the need to note how beautiful the evening was, sitting at dinner, sliding rhythmically over the water as if drawn by a cable; the cleansing salt in the air; the gray and the blue; our private ocean. Van fusses with the radio and wishes the barometer were more reliable. Premonition? There is nothing in his journal or in his log about it, though it would hit us the next day.

Saturday. Christopher's log tells the story well. I had never hove Cyrano to before. The captain favored running, but I elected not to, and as we strained in the screech and wet to lead the two staysails aback, tight as drums, I remembered prayerfully the representations of the sailmakers, that these sails would stand up against the greatest stress.

We would soon find out, because the wind was fifty knots, gusting well over that, and apparently building, like the seas. The spray came in off the starboard bow, and then one monstrous wave—though not of the size of one that hit us later, after we had resumed sailing—that caught me while I was forward with the sails. It is unsettling to meditate that one wave of that kind weighs many more tons than the thirty the boat weighs. After the storm trysail was up, I took the wheel from Danny to make the adjustments. Cyrano, not being a racing boat, responds less quickly than *The Panic* did, so I felt the necessity for a little rudder control. Otherwise the oscillations, elsewhere described, that make a boat heave to successfully would probably have been a little too widely separated, making for distinct lurches first to leeward, then to windward. I gave the engine 800 rpm, which in a smooth surface would give us about four knots of speed. Then I began turning the wheel to starboard (it requires nine turns to move the rudder hard over from full left to full right). At above six turns, with that much engine, the vessel walked into that magical equilibrium

201

The first star sight.

that is the ecstasy of the boat successfully hove to. It was fine to look about the drenched, wind-blasted, anxious faces of Christopher and Danny, the captain and Van, Augustino, and Phil Jr., and, in the cockpit, Aunty Bill, as, suddenly, Cyrano acted as if we had crossed over the Reversing Falls into a lake. The wind and the noise, the howling and the waves, seemed to mount in resentment at our insulation. The single worrisome threat of the moment was what Christopher has called the Damoclean ice pick. Danny volunteered to go up the ratlines to disconnect it, but the relative serenity of our posture notwithstanding, the delicacy of our stalemated situation, like détente, could not guarantee security over the necessary period; and he would need to use both hands while up there to disengage it.

Three hours later the worst was over, the wind, clearly abating, down now to about forty knots; so we eased off on the windward sheets, picked up the slack to leeward, first the mainstaysail, then the forestaysail, and—remembering the knockdown of fifteen years ago—let them luff as we turned decisively downwind until the air engaged them, and only then made an upwind adjustment toward the heading on which we had been sailing before the storm hit.

We ate dinner buffet-style, silent mostly, but strangely exhilarated, and close to each other after an annealing experience. I halved the watches—two hours of duty seemed enough under the circumstances; and, at 2:00 A.M., rose to take my own, with Van. By then the Genoa could come into service again. Christopher and Danny had experimented with it at my suggestion, then checked with me for the okay to douse it. No telling where we were, so I decided to put the boat on autopilot, and with Van prepared to take notes and clutching the chronometer, I tried to get a Polaris sight, the stars having grumpily come out, giving us a horizon of abnormal clarity. I mounted the top of the cockpit cabin with two safety belts, to make a sort of gimbals out of me: one belt to keep me from lurching sideways into the sea, the other to keep me from lurching forward off the roof. I positioned myself and, for a fleeting moment, got both Polaris and the horizon tentatively in the sextant mirror—when the main staysail boom banged against my head, and a spout of ocean water from a rogue wave, balling the jack on my leeward topside, drowned the sextant in salt. My job became then quickly to clean the sextant (salt water will corrode the mirrors in a few hours). Never mind the navigation: I'll figure out tomorrow where in hell the storm took us. After cleaning the sextant, the boat still under autopilot, making nine knots under sail, I sat for the balance of the hour forward with Van. From the area in front of the cabin you see only a kinetic fleck of red light from the port running light on the stampeding seas, green to starboard, a touch of white in the water, reflecting the forward light. And the sails, snugged in and powerful, working in overdrive, leaving the boat almost erect as it tore through the ocean, and the stars began to assert themselves, while a bottle of wine, secured by the boom vang between us, emptied slowly as we paid mute tribute to Cyrano, her builder and her designer, and the architect of the whole grand situation.

Sunday. I asked Van, after the squall, to make some notes on the weather. He did, and added to them on returning to London after examining the daily weather charts for the month of June.

We made several mistakes—foremost among them, Van reflects, the failure to note the channel and the time of transmission of voice weather reports covering our course. We have two big portable radios on board, and if there had been hurricanes on the prowl, the probability is we'd have spotted them. Moreover, we had a functioning telephone, and the number for the Hurricane Center in Miami was taped onto the set. We'd have reached it easily in the event it became vital exactly to track a hurricane to decide whether to maneuver. This you can do if you spot the hurricane sufficiently in advance. But it isn't an entirely certain business. Hurricanes tend, in the month of June (a good month to sail the Atlantic—there have been only eleven hurricanes in twenty years) to move northeast. But in doing so, they may shuffle-foot about, sometimes wandering aimlessly, like tourists, even executing 360° turns. For technical information, you are wise to keep on board a book on the subject, like *Heavy Weather Sailing*, and to remind yourself early on how to locate the direction of the dangerous sector of the hurricane in order to calculate which way to head (you begin with such fundamental activity as: facing the wind, holding up your right arm perpendicularly, and moving it back about 15°—it is now pointing to the danger sector. Depending on what tack you are on, and in which hemisphere, you do, or you don't, come about).

"On the day we spotted Spain," Van reminds me, "a forty-two-foot cutter with a crew of six set out from Bermuda for Norfolk, Virginia—notwithstanding a provocative low-pressure area sitting off Cape Hatteras and headed north. The next morning, this low had moved two hundred miles NE and reached gale-force winds. These guys had a radio that worked and they could have returned to Bermuda. Instead, they held their course—a collision course with what the next day was officially classified as Hurricane Amy, the first hurricane of the year. Their sailboat was ultimately incapacitated by forty-foot seas and winds in excess of seventy mph, and by a fluke their flares were spotted by a trawler (a Soviet ship, by the way, which probably would have ignored us). Even if it was too late to reach Bermuda, they would have had a better chance of running away from the storm by turning around and heading southeast, the reciprocal of their course."

By the way, those interested in the morphology of death-at-sea can avoid frustration by skipping over the account by Edward Heath of the end of his boat *Morning Cloud*. There surely never was a more disturbingly vague, not to say nonchalant, account of why a seagoing boat went down (drowning two members of the crew). In his final chapter, Mr. Heath contributes surely the most glacial line in the history of seafaring literature. Yes, he begins, sailing *is* a dangerous sport. *"And sometimes there is personal grief at the loss of a fellow sailor, and very rarely, at the loss of a boat."* I am at a loss to parse that sentence emotionally or analytically.

There is always a letdown. After a wedding, as after a funeral. It has to do, I think, with the restoration of natural rhythms, which appear humdrum whether after clearing up the confetti or the seaweed. There was a great deal to do the day after the storm, repairing the damage, minor and menacing. Moreover, the weather was grayish and generally sulky. At lunch, after three or four hours of miscellaneous work, mostly boring, I noticed, again, the barometers on board. Christopher is the most volatile—in part because he finds it hard (like his father) to detach his mood from any physical infirmity, and he is feeling a little sick and achy. Dan, like the ship's barometer, is stuck where it says Sunny and Pleasant. Van, at the least provocation, becomes waggish, and, with a touch of irreverence, brightens the gray. Bill Finucane, if she is truly on her last legs—which happens only when she goes forty-eight hours without sleep, having stayed up to help anybody do anything—simply closes her eyes, while sitting on the cockpit cushion, and goes to sleep, though it is hard to notice.

Bill was married at seventeen, honeymooned on an extensive trip around South America with her lawyer-husband, who was almost instantly sucked into the war, spending December 7, 1941, in a fuel-supply naval vessel at Pearl Harbor. Bill got into the habit of doing volunteer work during John's long absences, and continued to do so after their only child was born. Before long she was for all intents and purposes running the Red Cross in Los Angeles, reaching her

205

office some time before 6:00 A.M., and pumping up hydrants of relief and good cheer all over her vast jurisdiction. Her effectiveness is in one part owing to an icy impatience with red tape, an innocence sheathed in iron, and a fixed determination not to let anyone in trouble pass by her, his burden unlightened. I know her to have acted selfishly only once. She returned from the B.O. to her second home in Vancouver (where her parents lived, and her daughter and brother now live) and was astonished to find husband and daughter and friends utterly uncurious about her forty-four-hundred-mile trip across the Atlantic in a sailboat. "The most they gave me was about two minutes," she later told me indignantly over the phone. "So when I went down for the national meeting of the Red Cross and Frank Stanton called us to order, I went to the door, locked it, put the key in my pocket, and said, *'Nobody's going to leave this room until I tell you about my sail across the Atlantic!'* Everyone was too scared to interrupt, and I talked nonstop for *one hour and five minutes!*" I wish she had written her talk down in the journal she was supposed to keep, and that I had it here.

Lunch of sandwiches, soup, and wine is served, but eaten rather listlessly. I announce that I have a reading to give, to suggest a revised relationship between me and the crew. From now on, the accents of my instructions will be fashioned after those of Stubb, a junior officer on the *Pequod*. I could see an unsmiling look dart at me from Christopher, who knows from years of experience the kind of thing to expect.

This, I said, will be the New Me, and cleared my throat:

Pull, pull, my fine hearts-alive; pull, my children; pull, my little ones [addressing his crew in the longboat]. *Why don't you break your backbones, my boys? What is it you stare at? Those chaps in yonder boat? Tut! They are only five more hands come to help us—never mind from where— the more the merrier. Pull, then, do pull; never mind the brimstone—devils are good fellows enough. So, so; there you are now; that's the stroke for a thousand pounds; that's the stroke to sweep the stakes! Hurrah for the gold cup of sperm oil, my heroes! Three cheers, men—all hearts alive! Easy, easy; don't be in a hurry—don't be in a hurry. Why don't you snap your oars, you rascals? Bite something, you dogs! so, so, so, then;—softly, softly! That's it—that's it! long and strong. Give way there, give way! The devil fetch ye,*

206

ye ragamuffin rapscallions; ye are all asleep. Stop snoring, ye sleepers, and pull. Pull, will ye? pull, can't ye? pull, won't ye? Why in the name of gudgeons and ginger-cakes don't ye pull?—pull and break something! Pull, and start your eyes out! Here! [whipping out the sharp knife from his girdle— I used a table knife] *every mother's son of ye draw his knife, and pull with the blade between his teeth. That's it—that's it. Now ye do something; that looks like it, my steel-bits. Start her—start her, my silver spoons! Start her, marling-spikes!*

Now this did not have the desired effect, but it had the anticipated effect. Christopher groaned audibly and turned his back to me and feigned sleep. Danny thought it entirely uproarious. Van said he preferred my lecture on late Beethoven. Bill asked whether that was Knute Rockne I had quoted from.

By the end of the afternoon the clean-up work was largely done, but the mood was still a little fractious, and later that night I would rebuke Christopher for failing to wear his safety belt. Parents annoy their children; their children, their parents; spouses annoy their spouses over matters that are barely noticed in others. I cannot *understand* why Christopher is not taking a more active interest in learning navigation with the opportunity at hand. Of all times to read a biography of an incumbent Secretary of State! It isn't even escapist literature. Danny, God bless him, reads nothing, when you come down to it. Bill reads the novel she began when she was seventeen and will finish when she is eighty-seven. Van reads everything, on every subject. As I write these words I look up at the wall of my study in Switzerland, where this morning I scotch-taped the report card that came in from Yale University on Christopher, giving his grades for the five subjects he took in the first semester of his senior year: Five A's. My heart beats with pride. . . . On the other hand, goddammit, what is it that kept him from mastering navigation, which would have required *three* days' application? When he was eight (yes, eight), I undertook, for the fun of it, to teach him touch-typing. In twenty minutes he could apply the correct finger to every letter on the typewriter, whose keys I had masked with electrician's tape. When he was fourteen I undertook to teach him every chord there is on the piano. In an incredible half hour, I could say: "Hit F-sharp augmented," and the delay was less than five seconds. But I could not get him to

207

touch-type—until at school he thought to use a typewriter; and perhaps some day he will decide it is pleasant to play the chords to familiar songs. And, of course, by merely reading this book (while on a safari?) he can learn everything about navigation he failed to learn on the B.O. But it would take many times a half hour to teach him not to take shelter in melancholy. I told him years ago what Sir Harold Nicholson wrote in one of his diaries, already cited, that industry is the enemy of melancholy; and Christopher understands this, though he lacks that increment of self-discipline that he needs . . . sufficiently to venerate the advice of his father, who, after all (a) is the captain, (b) is omniscient, and (c) venerates him.

Monday. On taking the morning sight, I didn't like the results. For three weeks I have proceeded on the assumption that Christopher's Pulsar watch (a gift from Howard Hunt) loses ⅓ of a second per day. I decided to check it now with WWV. [That station comes in on five-megahertz bands: 5 7.5 10 15.] Usually you can bring in the signal—they call it the time-tick. The originating transmission station is

Christopher's noon sight.

in the neighborhood of Denver, Colorado (Fort Collins). But today, after twenty minutes' trying, I couldn't get it on any of the bands and I am impatient; so I decide what the hell, I'll call the marine operator in New York on the telephone (we have rigged the emergency antenna to the stern). She not only comes in nicely, but says, I kid you not, "I hope you are having a nice sail, Mr. Buckley." I learn subsequently that these telephone calls, which I assume are gloriously inexpensive inasmuch as you are using *your* power, really, not New York's, are actually charged to your account with some sliding-scale reference to how far away you are, and that the telephone company keeps a vague chart on your movements. Anyway, I said Yes, thanks, we were having a wonderful sail, and—stopwatch in hand—would she please give me the correct time? Of course, she said: "The time is nine-twenty." No, I said—I need the *exact* time. "I told you, the exact time is nine-twenty."

I thought it inappropriate to give her my lecture on how four seconds equals one mile, so I asked her please to ring the number ME 7-1212. That is the number you ring in New York City if you want the *exact* time ("When you hear the signal, the time will be nye-yen tawenty-one and forty seconds. . . ."). She rang the number; I heard the recorded announcement, noted down the time, recorded in the log that Christopher's watch had had an unaccountable loss of thirteen seconds during one twenty-four-hour period and should therefore be checked regularly to establish whether it was shot or whether it was a one-time-only freak—and only then got around to thinking about what had happened. Using my telephone in a small sailboat eighteen hundred miles from New York, I had called a commercial telephone number in New York to find out the correct time. Tomorrow they'll be calling a satellite station for it.

Christopher asked at lunch—he is obviously feeling better— whether I planned to spend "whole hours at Horta"? This is the revival of his and Danny's ten-year-old complaint about how I rush them through places, as in setting out from Antigua years earlier. We banter on the point. The fact of the matter is that I could not have scheduled the B.O. with an open-ended arrival time. We are that completely the slaves of our schedules. But they will have a taste of the Azores. In fact, in Christopher's and Danny's case, perhaps too much of a taste. During dinner we tried to pick up the New York news and were greatly relieved to hear WINS report that the Church Committee had found no evidence that the CIA had intended to assassinate De Gaulle. Granted, such attempts to assassinate him as there concededly were, might have led to the suspicion of CIA patronage. I remember the lead paragraph in *NR* in an issue in the late fifties: "The attempted assassination of Sukarno had all the earmarks of a CIA operation. Everyone in the room was killed except Sukarno."

That night Van and I drew the 0100 to 0400 watch, and checking the log, I saw in Christopher's neat hand: "This has been the best sail of my life." The wind was very strong, south southwest, and the boat was steering close-hauled at 125°. Van and I found the three hours went fast, and turning over the wheel to the captain and Jeff, went down into the saloon and decided to have a nightcap. Bill Finucane, who is awakened by either too little or too much noise, rose to join us. We were all tired, but content, and Van, shaking the moisture from his clothes and balancing a glass, the bottle, and himself with his rump on the piano, finally made it into the couch. He recalled an exchange between Amos and Andy:

"Why do you like to sail, Andy?"

"Well, there, Amos, it's—uh, the sun—uh—and the—uh—air, and the—yo ho ho of the thing!" Van is very precious to his friends.

Wednesday, Thursday. Everyone feels the excitement. We should arrive on Friday. I am, accordingly, taking pains to do some serious star navigation, and I run into the usual frustrations when you tackle stars for the first time. Plus another one. A couple of years ago, a charming young lawyer in Norfolk came to New York to escort me down on a private airplane to address a forum he headed. A specialist in maritime law, he was handling at the moment a gorgeously complicated lawsuit of great strategic importance to a boat owner: namely, who is responsible if a boat carries no insurance and a charterer smashes it up? He got to talking about ocean racing, and his experiences as navigator on a gold-plater in the Bermuda Race, and told me about the *astigmatizer*, about which I had never heard. It is one of those inventions, like the toilet, you simply cannot understand nobody having invented before.

One of the difficulties in star-sight taking is that by the time you bring the sought-after star down to the horizon, any number of things may have happened to cause complications. The lurching of the boat may have resulted in your losing the star altogether; the horizon may have blended into the ocean or into the sky, so as to make it indistinguishable for the purposes of photographing your navigational catch. Moreover, when the time comes to swing your sextant, gently, first right, then left, pendulum-like, to make certain that the star, from its proper elevation, is only just touching the horizon, rather than buried deep within it when the sextant is truly vertical, you run the risk of losing the star altogether. The astigmatizer is a prism you bring down in front of the horizon mirror after discovering the star you are looking for, which elongates it at a perfect right angle. Thus, when you lower it to the horizon you can tell instantly whether your sextant is correctly situated. If so, the silver thread descends flatly onto the horizon, like the sides of a vise coming together. If your sextant is other than vertical, as is probable given the ship's motion, you need only adjust it until the lines, clearly drawn, come together.

I had trotted down to the navigational instrument headquarters of New York City and told the proprietor that my heart had leapt with joy on discovering the news of the astigmatizer, which, he told me with resonant enthusiasm, he would instantly install. I tried it out during Christmas, to find that the relevant prism would not situate itself in sync with the horizon mirror. Defective installation. I took it back. So sorry. Now, three months later, not having retested the reinstallation, I find that *this* time the astigmatizer was put on crooked. I discard it. And reflect briefly that now the list is pretty nearly complete: the radar, the autopilot, the batteries, the motor, the generator, the RDF, the loran, the chronometer, and the sextant. The factual errors in the instruction book for the HP–65 seem almost a diversion. I need now only to discover a mistake in the Almanac. On the other hand, if it is significant, Cyrano will never lay eyes on the Azores.

At lunch, Christopher and Danny put on some Beatles music, and in the general babble, the Beatles were not heard. Christopher suggested that either we turn the music up or turn it off. "Otherwise, we're only wasting batteries." I sympathized—perhaps too noisily, because there was a poetic act of reciprocity that evening, when

211

Alicia de Larrocha was doing Chopin and Christopher suggested we turn up the volume, which we did.

I say "we," I should record, with a degree of self-consciousness, because on board a boat I have found that I do not like to change my seat at mealtimes. I care not where it is, but care that it should be at the same place during a cruise. On Cyrano, I am seated at the center of the half-moon table, and under the circumstances only useful to help pass dishes when they are handed up from the galley through the hatchway. Otherwise, errands need to be undertaken by someone sitting opposite me or at the extreme ends of the table. *"Would you turn up the music?"* means, in practical terms, that one of four people, excluding me and the persons on my right and left, must rise and turn up the music, absent mutiny. It is widely suspected that my querencia at the center of the table was selected with considerable forethought to my derivative unavailability for errand-running. Van turns up Alicia. . . .

Danny told us that, on going up the mast, he noticed that the fastenings attaching the loran antenna to the spreaders were put on with such consummate sloppiness that the screws come through the wood of the spreaders raw, perfectly situated to tear holes in the mainsail when it is strapped in tight, or when we are coming about. . . . Elsewhere on the Bulletin Front: I talked with Pat over the telephone, and she leaves with Marvin for Morocco, for a week's visit, after which she will go to Marbella to be there when we arrive. She sounds excited by the trip, and that gladdens. . . . Two ships passed us, one far, far away, heading roughly in the same direction, the other headed up toward Europe. It exhibited considerable curiosity about us and went well out of her way to sniff, but declined to exchange any civility proffered over the telephone when we attempted to "speak" her. . . . Van, who is perhaps as bad as I am in his compulsions to *move*, I finally approached during the late watch, tactfully suggesting that we should prolong our dalliance in the Azores an additional twenty-four hours. He is, as usual, good-natured about it; besides which—I point out—we can probably make up the time on the last leg to Spain. That afternoon Christopher said to Danny, in a throwaway line clearly designed for me and Van, "Danny, don't *you* think the five hours we plan to spend in Horta is just too . . . long?". . . . Also, over the radio,

212

Danny going up to remove the dangling antenna.

the bad news from Reggie: His deal fell through and the company will file for bankruptcy. This is shattering news; among other things professionally sad for all of us, Van especially, who have been giving him advice for weeks. But, incredibly, before our condolences have a chance even to achieve punctilio, he is talking over the phone excitedly about the *exact* hour of his arrival, Saturday morning, at Horta. First things first. . . . I feel guilty about my private hold of my private cabin, because it gives me so much pleasure. It is four in the morning now, and I am warm and comfortable, and so very pleasantly tired, and don't resent even making these notes in my journal. Tomorrow we'll sleep tied up in Horta, or else I shall have to inform the crew that somebody screwed with the sun and the stars, which are out of sync with the Almanac. I hope there will be sun, and I'll shoot it every hour and try also to bring in, on the RDF, the commercial radio station, with its alleged range of one hundred miles.

Friday. Of course, the radio signal *didn't* stretch to where I insisted we were, and the sun was gone most of the time, though I got a noon sight that was reassuring. The apprehension is palpable. Off the starboard bow is—I allege—the island of Pico, with a huge volcano rising over seven thousand feet. It should be visible for miles—except that it is cloudy today, and we see nothing; not even Danny can see anything from the crow's nest. Never mind, I said, we are, so help me, coming in, and should see the island of Faial in a couple of hours. We did, at 1625, and changed our course less than 5° to head in for the port. The reception a mile out was unforgettable: the conventional honor guard of dolphins, trained as if by the ballet masters at the Biscayne Oceanographic Institute to give us a heroes' welcome. We rounded the dark old fort and slunk in along the great stone wharf that runs the length of the harbor. The customs people materialized, and were thoroughgoing to the point of giving rise to the inevitable question: Are they waiting for—something? Van deftly suggested that he should offer the captain (who was closeted with them) a drink, and then casually ask if they would care to have one too. They declined; and, in due course, authorized us to go onshore. We did,

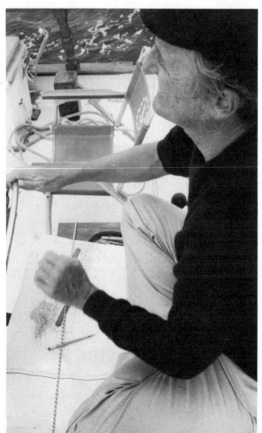

Moving in on Faial.

The harbor, Faial.

wobbly at the knees, eleven days and eight hours from Bermuda, walking shakily around the harbor to the old hotel operated by Raymond Burr, the actor, where we were fed routine stuff and made to listen to a piano player who could not have been employed other than at the Fortaleza Santa Cruz in Horta, Faial, the Azores. The little mariners' guidebook beckoned us to a "famous" bar where they make "the best gin and tonic" in the Atlantic, and there we found three tables of fellow mariners in the little room lit by a naked light bulb. Everyone in our party was by now talking at the same time, flushed, lit, but we paused just long enough to establish the itinerary of two of the tables of fellow-nippers. At one was a husband and wife, aged respectively seventy-two and sixty-eight. They, too, had just come in from Bermuda, and were greatly impressed by the speed of our passage. It had taken them twenty days. Moreover, this was their eighteenth passage from Bermuda on their thirty-two-foot sailboat!

Alone? Van asked.

Oh no! Their dog *always* accompanied them.

215

The other table was larger—five or six happy, scraggly, hairy people in their late twenties, early thirties, from a forty-four-foot ketch. Where were they going? Why, to Ireland. Where were they from? British Columbia. British Columbia! Bill said excitedly. (That's where she and Pat are from.) *Where* in British Columbia? Kelowna. *Kelowna!* (That was where my father-in-law kept a ranch.) Where were they going after Ireland? Well (to compress their itinerary), back to the Azores; then to Grenada; then to Panama; then to Tahiti; then to Hawaii; then back home to Vancouver. When, asked I—the fine-tuner of ocean cruise times-of-departure-and-arrival—did they expect to get back to Vancouver? Oh, said one of the girls, some time in the summer—or fall—of 1978. I suggested to Christopher that he and Danny would have no difficulty adjusting to such a timetable. The boys, as will be seen, Went On. We straggled back to Cyrano, but before boarding her, I just looked at her for a while, pleased, and proud, and grateful.

The Azores. I have wondered whether it is tradition or biological compulsion that requires sailors, on reaching shore, to go berserk. Whatever the answer, Danny and Christopher—accompanied by Phil Jr., Augustino, and Jeff—did not let down the tradition. They seemed to concert perfectly to enact a scene from Henry Miller. . . .

⌒

[**C**] It's late. My skin feels wet with thirteen days of accumulated salt spray. I'm working on my third brandy. The fumes clear out my nasal passages. The wobblies are going away. Outside the gate, Carlos is waiting. It's hot and semitropical. Lizards skim across the pavement where "*Partida Socialista*" (with clenched fist) is stenciled on in white paint. I tell him we'll be ready in a half hour.

Inside, Jeff is talking with the girl receptionist. Half-English, half-sign language.

"I-want-to-go-to-London. LONDON. England. How-do-I-get-there?"

"Oh, you must go to airport."

I tell Jeff the key word: *Phantom Jet.* "Just tell 'em you're Henry Kissinger's representative. America. Big land. Phantom Jet. Many Phantom Jet." But the girl insists he must go to the airport. The plane for London unfortunately does not leave from the hotel lobby.

We order more brandy at the bar. 28 escudos. *Escudos?* "How many escudos for one dollar? *Moit obrigado.* Phantom jet will come. Worth *many* escudos." Phil Jr., whom Augustino has nicknamed "King Kong," locks himself in the bathroom and bangs on the door. Jeff lets him out.

Five of us pile into Carlos' taxi. He says he can only take four. "Police," he says, "much money."

Danny has three glasses of wine and as many brandies in his stomach. The sailor home from the sea. He puffs a cigar and takes charge. The situation is well in hand.

"Carlos, we need one-two-three-four-*five* women," he says. "Fuck the police."

Jeff crouches low in the back seat so the police won't see him and so Carlos won't worry. His spine and the driveshaft casing converge asymptotically.

"Keep humping the floor," I tell him as Carlos turns up a narrow, cobbled road—"Carlos says it is too late to find women 'to make love.' " We are headed for a discotheque. Discotheque? Amidst the painted cries for the "Partida Socialista," a place of night hedonism. Maybe there will be women there.

As we pile out of the car, Danny whispers in Carlos' ear, making intimate overtures.

"*Two* women, Carlos, can you find *two*?"

Carlos says he will try and returns in ten minutes. If this were the Far East, he'd return with his younger sisters. We go inside.

Discotheque? A well-intentioned idea, perhaps, but roughly executed. One room, maybe 20 x 20, lit with red and black lights, a small bar stands to one side. Italian Johnny Cash-type music blasts out of unseen speakers. No one is dancing. Because of the ten or twelve people sitting, I can see only one woman.

Brandies and beer all around. A kind of Azorean boilermaker. It's been thirteen long, lonely days at sea, and tonight we're going to blast our way through Horta. Phantom Jets or no. Danny is just beginning to limber up. Augustino is chaining Kents. Half an hour later, King Kong is bouncing off the wall.

Our talk is choppy, deprecating. Boy-they-call-this-a-discotheque? Waiter, another brandy. *Moit obrigado* and here's to your grandmother. Whaddya mean 330 escudos? To hell with your grandmother. More potato chips.

Danny disappears and comes back in ten minutes. Carlos has failed. But here's another taxi-driver, he says, clutching a little man with a tight scalp and a vacant smile, "and he's getting us five women

218

for five bucks!" His name is Eduardo. We press him for details. He giggles a lot. He doesn't speak English.

"Phantom Jet?"

"Hee hee ah!"

"Shit. You wanna drink?"

"Yes, yes," he nods his head vigorously.

"He understands 'drink' all right," I say.

Eduardo and Augustino lock into pigeon conversation. Neither of them understands the other, but they both understand "drink." Phil makes a stupid joke. No one laughs. More brandies. Yes, it feels . . . good, this loosening up.

Augustino tells me he's unhappy working on the boat. He tries to pay for all the drinks. We tell him he can pay for the *putas* in Marbella and shove handfuls of weathered escudos across the bar-top. The cash register is the most sophisticated piece of technology on the island. It makes a multiwatt ringing noise that congeals with the Italian country-western music.

Danny finds two new friends.

"You speak English? Wunderbar," he cries. More brandies. At this point, we're all getting brandied. After a minute or two, he gestures to me to come over. This is John, and this is his cousin, Victor. John is 17. Eleven years ago there was an earthquake on Faial. A German warship came and took John, his family, and 100 others to Montreal. He's lived in Toronto ever since and is here on vacation. His skin is very brown and his teeth shine phosphorescently under the black light.

"You know," he says, sounding like any North American, "I've been on this island four days and this is the first time I've been to this place. Pretty slow, huh?"

Well, yes, but whatever the discotheque lacks in action we'll make up for in brandy. John translates for Victor, who is a native and has never left the island. Victor's world is a small one, and he tries to keep aloof.

"What does Victor do?" I scream above the music.

"He's a Communist," says John.

"What? Full-time?"

John confers with Victor.

"He's still in school," says John.

"Tell him I spent a month in China last summer," I say. That might prime the pump. I'd like to ask Victor about the sidewalk stencils and see if he has read Marx.

He says he has, but he doesn't want to talk about it.

Phil Jr. comes over and crashes into a chair. He's blind. Blind out of his mind. Reaching across the table, he spills Victor's drink and turns on the light. Bright, angry light-flashes make us feel like vampires caught out past dawn. My hand gropes for the switch.

"Turn that thing off," says Danny.

We talk about women. John says there are more women than men on the island.

"Where are they? In a convent?"

John laughs.

This is killing time. The brandy is racing through my head, killing brain cells and seeping my body in a novocaine trance. Danny disappears again. Phil follows. The blind leading the blind. Cigarette after cigarette has reduced my throat to a dried-up tube. Air's the thing. Augustino, imperturbable, orders another round.

And so the time goes, and uncounted progressions of brandy, beer, cigarettes, of feeling the jukebox-blare vibrating through the chest cavities, of letting your body go and carrying your mind with it.

A half hour later Danny comes racing in. His hair is dripping wet. Phil, also soaked, follows, leaving behind a wake of capsized chairs.

"Christo, we've gotta get outta here quick," Danny says. Although his face is mischievous, his voice is urgent. He had torn off his clothes and jumped into the hotel pool for a swim. Phil followed. They splashed in the unsalty water until three hotel people came out, mad as hell.

"They stood around and tried to get me out. I told 'em I was American." Right. I'm an American. The laws don't apply to me. Phantom Jet. Gerald Ford stands behind me.

"They're calling the police. I think we should leave. Carlos is waiting outside. He's got the engine running."

John says don't worry about the police. Worry about the "local beating." The "local beating" is what befalls ugly Americans, rapists, drunken seamen, and other assorted foreign scum when they disturb Horta's peace. A local posse of brawny law enforcers.

"Hey, Umberto, some Americans are swimming in the pool after hours. Let's go rearrange their faces!"

I am peaceful by nature, and a local beating is not quite what I had in mind. I pass a wad of escudos to the waiter. *Moit obrigado*, baby. Where's the fire escape?

Carlos is waiting, car door open. Danny gets in, head first. On the drive back, his stomach is feeling poorly. He throws up. Carlos leaves us by the front gate of the hotel. Danny kneels in the grass, which is wet with dew, after pounding on the door for five minutes. The night clerk, a young man with sleep-encrusted eyes, opens it. Our room overlooks the harbor. Yellow sodium vapor lights illuminate the wharf. Danny heads for the toilet bowl. When I come in two minutes later, he is naked, hunched over, doing homage to the porcelain deity.

"Leave me alone. I have to do it three times. I'll be okay after I do it three times," he groans.

It took me a while to get to sleep. That night I dreamt President Kennedy was alive, but that he was paralyzed, and a vegetable. Jackie was by his side, but she seemed bored.

〜

So much for Horta. We decided to cruise twenty miles along the coast of Pico, its volcano still hidden by clouds, and spend the night privately under the lee there, somewhere beguiling, before setting out for the 160 miles to Ponta Delgada, at the other end of the island chain, where we will do the serious business of reprovisioning.

〜

[C] We cruise along the north shore of Pico, a magnificent volcanic gesture thrown up from the ocean floor eons ago. Waves splash against proud outcroppings of jagged rock, leaving frothy pools of sea foam. I set two fishing lines and for most of the afternoon repair the mainsail and sharpen knives on a well-oiled whetstone.

Pirate's work.

Letting the steel scrape along the stone makes a scratchy, kissing

221

sound. Rubbing out a circular path, feeling the blade go sharper, watching the magnesium particles mix with the oil and form puddles of dark gray spittle stuff. This is a union: man and his knife: a craft wherein anxieties settle:

> Yes, my hearties, my blade is keen,
> steer thee clear of my sword.
> It's cleft the skulls of countless men
> who dared to board my ship.
> What purpose precise, what aspect grim,
> forged in Hades' furnace.
> So if we meet on the Barbary Coast,
> or on the Spanish Main,
> Look ye! Dare ye debate
> with such a cunning foe?

We're looking to anchor in the Baje de Canas, on the lee shore. Two fishermen in a small boat come up to wave us away from their net. Augustino asks them for langousta, which they don't have. It's a meeting of new and old: Cyrano, the gleaming American, confronting this rusty, rotten heap of a boat. The eyes of the fishermen widen at the sight of so much chrome-plated technology.

We drop anchor in 30 fathoms of cold, blue water.

While Augustino cleaned the fish on the poop and WFB and the captain fiddled with the ship's computer, Van, Dan, and I went ashore. Augustino paused to sharpen his blade; the sound mingled with waves slapping against the hull.

Ancient settlement! Blackened stones painstakingly carved and laid end to end. A town of ghosts, whispering noises, whalebone jaws resting against walls; as though it had been thus for centuries. We climbed past garden walls streaked with flora, lichens dripping dryly. The earth beneath our feet packed, trampled with the weight of arms carrying nets, harpoons, oars, lines, buckets of oil. So many years ago, and yet there—and there!—a windowpane gleaming with a new coat of paint; an oarlock, shining, brassy, dropped and forgotten only a few weeks back; and when we tried to gain entrance to the houses, our way was barred by locks.

We walked on until we came to the church. Deserted like all the rest.

222

Danny drops the dinghy anchor, to explore with Van and Christopher the deserted island at Pico. Cyrano lies at anchor in the background.

Only the solitary cross atop the door linked this place to the rest of the world. That cross! A piece of lava, roughhewn to shape the sign of a divinity whose voice seemed but a whisper as I looked out across, oily waters to the island of São Jorge. *Chingg* . . . the noise of the camera shutter closing at one-sixtieth of a second . . . a technological burp.

Sweet dwelling place of phantoms! How peaceful to walk among the spirits there. Pompeii, Herculaneum, Machu Picchu, Thebes, Luxor, Cornwall, Tombstone, Olduvai Gorge—all ye who speak of man's infant first crawling steps, of cycles of life and death, of gods revered and vilified; rise up, ye stones, and cry.

We are making our way up a path drenched in moss and hanging vines when Cyrano's horn sounded, calling us back to sup. What mysteries might have unfolded had the ship not checked us I cannot say. The light was growing faint, so it was good work finding our way back. We saw things which dirtied the peace we felt on the ascent: a piece of plastic wrapping curled around a root, a large vertebra which Van dubbed a whale's "asshole," and scattered pieces of plastic mass-produced jetsam. Elsewhere these intrusions might have killed the peace, but not here. Still these stones spoke to us as we stepped into the dinghy, slipping over rocks as polished as dinosaur eggs. As the throttle warmed to the flow of gas, I looked back at the village, and I fancied it was glad to see us go.

[**D**] I've never seen anything quite so perfect, old yet perfect. We all read about such things in history in 8th or 9th grade never realizing the time and effort involved nor do we appreciate prior accomplishments with the gravity they deserve. It will be a long while before anything impresses me more than that.

～

Christopher drew the unlucky card, and so was roused by the captain for the first watch at 2:00 A.M., when we weighed anchor—only by leaving that early could we hope to arrive at Ponta, Delgada during the early evening. He woke Danny at five.

～

[**D**] I silently said 2 Hail Mary's and Our Father's this morning at 5 when I got up to go on duty. Please, Lord, give me strength today and tomorrow . . . and I appreciate your lovely world. Thanks. Dan.

[**D**] There were no hotel rooms to be had because of an influx of sailors racing from Falmouth, England, to Ponta Delgada. Chris and I decided at dinner to camp the following day at one of the craters on the west end of the island. We walked home from dinner about 10:30 enjoying the fresh faces, warm friendly faces, who stared at our dungarees and short hair, but mostly perplexed by the alien tongue. While we walked we discussed plans for the camping expedition. We would need a car, tent, beer, wine, sleeping bags, cigarettes, candy,

224

steaks and veg., bread and cheese, the tape recorder, knives and probably 3 people to tote everything. We both looked forward to "our" day.

∽

But first there was work to be done by all hands.

∽

[**D**] Simultaneously we all began our duties on Cyrano. Chris hoisted me atop Cyrano's main to fix the masthead light, port spreader, remount the lower antenna, dismount the broken mounting bracket for the radio antenna and tape up all the sharp extensions whenever I found them. Chris fixed the forecastle hatch and the starboard shroud light while Reg fiddled with the radar and radio.

Bill F., bless her, undertook the provisioning. I honestly doubt anyone else could have done so marvelously what she has. She is always cheery, forever spending dollars for our food and never, never, never have I met a more determined or lovely lady. Bill, you're great.

Danny at the restaurant, anticipating a verbal thrashing.

Van left to rent a car, then returned. We had lunch at a famous restaurant in Furnas. Chris and I arrived at 11:45, about a half an hour early but knowing very well the other would be late. It's historic with WFB that he leaves at the very last second and will be half an hour late. I knew it, Chris knew it. He would have been on time only if we had overslept and were late ourselves. But the verbal thrashing is never worth it. You can't win. WFB went to write 4 columns at the Consulate then later to socialize with some general and talk with him about our atom bombs with Van.

[V] Bill and I dashed to the airport to take a commercial flight to Terceira to have a chat with General Wrigley. We failed at the airport. That night we had drinks at the residence of our lady consul, Miss Linda Pfeifle, who had as a guest General Pinto Magellense, who is the military governor of the Azores and the man around whom the separationists wish to rally. Bill B. and he spoke in French, and the conditions were not otherwise the best; but it gave Bill the basis for a column. Also, the General was opposed to Com's sufficiently to keep open options about separating if the C's take over in Portugal.

∽

Excerpt from *Literaturnaya Gazeta* (Moscow, 6/8/75), by Huriy Y. Artsev:

A HAWK ON THE ISLANDS OF HAWKS

What wind brought William Buckley to the Azores?

They would seem to be merely no more than a dozen bits of dry land lost in the ocean more than 1,000 km from Europe and still farther from America, but he bestirred himself to fly there as a special correspondent for the New York *Times* and Washington *Post* newspaper tandem and sent a report entitled "Freedom and the Azores" via the transatlantic cable.

If Buckley has shown his face there before it has been only at the height of the tourist season in winter in order to bask in the sun; but now, in summer, he is already hot from the burning problems which he has invented himself, such as the "Sovietization" of the Azores and the "tyranny" of Lisbon. He raises the question: Wouldn't the islands' separation from Portugal be an alternative?

The Azores (whose Portuguese name translates as "the islands of hawks") are attractive for NATO in virtue of their strategic position and their bases.

And thank God Buckley is not a politician, strategist, general or admiral.

But although he is merely a journalist and the editor of the archrightwing American weekly *National Review,* he is the kind of person whose characterization fits into a single phrase: "Buckley is Buckley."

July 3, 1975

The Editor
The New York *Times*

Dear Sirs:

Having only just now crawled out of the ocean in Spain, I have begun to catch up on my reading. I note in a recent column by Mr. James Reston the following sentence: "When we arrived [at the Azores] it was reported that a 'foreign vessel' had arrived in the port of Ponta Delgada. We checked this immediately . . . and discovered the 'foreign vessel' was a yacht skippered by Bill Buckley, en route from Long Island Sound to the Mediterranean, with John Kenneth Galbraith, celebrating his retirement from the Harvard faculty, as part of the crew."

Alas, the consequences of congressional parsimony on U. S. Intelligence are already beginning to show: (a) We sailed from Miami, not Long Island; (b) the Galbraith on board was not my friend, the six-foot 11-inch emaciated Menshevik, John Kenneth, but my friend, the chunky, five-foot 11-inch Manchesterist, Evan; and anyway, (c) surely it was Harvard, not Professor Galbraith, that had reason to celebrate?

Yours cordially,
Wm. F. Buckley, Jr.

And published in the New York *Times,* July 5:

To the Editor:

William F. Buckley, Jr. was boasting as usual when he told James Reston [I never saw James Reston—WFB] that I'd sailed to the Azores as a member of his crew.

He is not that brave; nor, may I say, am I.

John Kenneth Galbraith
Cambridge, Mass.

∽

[**D**] We noticed a small dirt road leading around the lake and followed it until no longer possible and relaxed there enjoying the most beautiful little spot on earth. Crater all around, hugging us, mothering us by her lake and woods. Clouds obscured the sun and

227

later the moon and stars, yet the crater lake kept her majesty. The perfect setting brought back fond memories of the Colorado wilderness, its picturesque meadows and unmatched tones of green and browns.

We laughed as our tent took shape, thinking of the Marlboro ads and Camel-filter man among men ads. A bit of wine, four bread buns, some burnt steaks, and potato alongside a roaring fire with such a friend is rare indeed. I enjoyed the night; relaxed conversation flowed like our wine and beer, and I breathed a deep feeling, an inner serenity long forgotten. My memories of sailing are many, but this extension of the transatlantic was, and is, more than my imagination can bear.

Thank you, my friend.

[C] Ponta Delgada! The name rings like a sultry Azorean courtesan. Now, almost a week later, those words conjure up a gauzy daguerreotype. What do I recall now, as the ship passes on into the Bay of Cadiz, with two albacore flopping in sudsy blood on the poop-deck?

Here is Ponta Delgada and the island of São Miguel: the Hotel San Pedro, with whales' teeth to hang one's coat on in the cloakroom, where for lunch they serve *huevos revueltos con churizo* and freshly fried fish; narrow, cobbled streets; people whose blood is half Atlantic and half mainland Europe; a yellow stucco church built in 1791: a story of births, marriages, confessions, burial rites in sacramental, peasant proximity to God; the Terra Nostra Hotel in Furnas, by botanical gardens fed on steamy mineral water gushing from beneath the earth's crust; Tomas Caetan, who left São Miguel 17 years ago with 100 dollars and returned with a million: a no-shit paisan turned capitalist, and such a hearty defender of free enterprise; beer whose taste reminds you that not all beer flows from metallic taps in Milwaukee; hydrangeas—thou hallowed bud, censer of mountain paths—erupting sweetly by the wayside; eating *helados* on the wharf; drinking Martel cognac with a German captain whose hair turned white years ago when he fell off a ship into the icy waters off Murmansk; his first mate, an arrogant Aryan named Tony—"Not to touch the vood; it's varnished, ja"—who came up from the engine room smelling of oil and showed us *de rradio direkktional ffinder*; drinking frothy milk fresh from the udder, intestine warm, offered by a farmer named Carlos who spent four months in Canada; his horse a sleek, fleet-footed beast; his cows robust, complacent, dwelling in that happy harmony between man and land; his son Albert, who had a taste of Oreo cookies and may never be the same; stepping out of a car on the rim of a volcanic crater, peering 2,000 feet down through gusts of cloudy wind and seeing a land redolent of Eden's smells; driving on a dusty road into Lagoa de Sete Cuidades and skidding to a halt before a holy feast day parade; banners, plastic dolls done up as Infantas, bread and wine being blessed and distributed among the people, skyrockets bursting till 2 A.M., children fighting, throwing stones; carts drowning in colored crepe, pulled by brown oxen; pitching a tent (purple) in the crater by the lake; Vivaldi's concerto for guitar and lute mixing with the sound of grunting frogs; tearing up the last remnants of cardboard and knowing this was it, the difference between a cold, black night and a glowing hearth of golden embers; tippling the bottle of Rheingau wine and feeling the throat crud dissolving in a fiery swallow; cooking steaks that ended up charred; peeling the skin off potatoes and biting into steaming, translucent vegetable matter; a taste of Milky Way bars—an intolerable wad of sucrose, dextrose, and stale monosodium glutamate—wonderful to behold; toasting buns by the fire and melting hunks of Gruyère cheese; a cigarette, so good; tearing off our clothes and splashing fresh lake water all over; warming later by the fire; deciding not to put our clothes back on till the last moment; the perfect company of a perfect friend; a sip of beer; another taste of cheese; running through the rain forest looking for another mother log; crickets; hawks circling; a full moon hidden by a Goya sky—leaden tinctures soaking the moist cloth of the clouds—O pagan moon.

And when my eyes could stand no more, the silence of sleep. The purple tent kept off the morning rain.

∾

And Christopher's final impression, set down a few days later, of the Azores, "Inspired by Melville," as noted in his journal. It is a long leap from Henry Miller to Melville; but worth it . . .

229

[C] *1700 hrs.* Avast! I feel poorly; my head aches with the pounding of Vulcan's hammer; my nose brings me olfactory news of diesel fumes spilling from the starboard tank; my eyes droopy with the bouncing of sea and sky; the gyroscope of my brain all askew from those days on land.

—Land! How comes it my logbook is barren? Four days of feet planted on volcanic soil, four days of senses drenched not in salt but in fragrant hydrangea blossoms—those four days spent in a land whose form and color brought me to a drunken, blissful consciousness of Genesis have left me lingering hungrily, the compass needle of my mind fastened, unwaveringly, on the Azores.

Genesis? Could the author of that chapter have visited there, put in ashore and drunk of its beauty? I imagine it so. Did he lay his ground cloth in the crater and listen to the lake's waves speak of creation without beginning? Did he build his fire and watch the smoke drift upward, thousands of feet to where angry rain clouds pass and eagles dare? Did he wonder whose lapidary craft caused such shapes to rise from pumice? The volcano which heaved a million years ago with fiery, pagan passion now sleeps. Where lava boiled and flames leapt up to lick the very stars now harbors hawks, trout, cows, horses, frogs—their voices commingle, quietly rejoicing in that transition from furious creation to benign evolution. God's labor's done.

Azores? What could the name portend? That "punctual spot, wherein all forms did seem divine," the garden Milton spoke of? A strange place; crossroad of mariners; marriage chamber of disparate races; magnet of oceanic clouds; harmonious, inscrutable juxtaposition of land, water, fire, air! Thales of Miletus, Pythagoras, Anaximander—all you who first discerned the base elements in the watershed of Asia Minor—had you laid your minds on these islands then, who could wonder what your legacies might instead have been! There might your sons and grandsons have set up temples and worshiped constellations of hunter gods. There you might have built an acropolis of lava stone and sent your merchant fleet into the west. There might you have made Atlantis!

Four days there was I. And now those islands lie two days to the west. The moon is rising. The sun hastens in prone career to the celestial line dividing sea from sky.

Four days you say, and all you show for them is a weary brow and a chaotic gyroscope? Speak, then, and tell us what went on! Look to the weather bow, hoist the top gallants! Look you well, sailor, and spare us no detail, for four more days shall pass until the dolphins pilot us into strange harbors. Gibraltar, Trafalgar, where Nelson gave his last command and fell bleeding to the deck. Sing, volcanic muses, sweet sirens of cloudswept summits. Sing to me of these symphonies of land and sea, of harbors, hills, ravines, where lingers the fingerprint of God, to give the world assurance of a plan.

I fear I abused Linda Pfeifle, who, at age thirty-three, is our already-experienced diplomatic representative in the Azores, at a time when nobody knows whether the mother country will go Communist or, if it does, what exactly the Azores, where the Communists have only about three percent of the vote, will do. Taking advantage of her hospitality, I wrote a couple of columns on the subject in her offices, commandeered her telephone and, finally, at her urgent request, tiptoed around one or two of the things General Magellense told me at the reception she gave us. She came for drinks on Cyrano and for small out-of-office talk. Then, after a quick dinner at dockside—we took off. Time: 2130. Next stop: Europe.

Strong, strong, wind from the north, ideal for our easterly course. I sat up with Reggie, who explained the dreary disintegration of his company. "It's as if you delivered an airplane someone contracted for, exactly according to specifications, and just before taking it, the buyer says: 'It will, of course, fly at twice the speed of sound, won't it?'" I greatly fear that the gentle Reggie was not born to contend with wolves. But he has a way of retiring, at a moment's notice, any complaint, whereupon his galactic cheerfulness takes over. I told him that while we waited at the airport (his plane was late), Van and I visited the tourist desk to ask for a detailed map of the island. There was consternation. Finally the young lady at the desk opened her purse, and taking out the two remaining cigarettes, handed me an empty package. I pulled it out of my pocket and showed it to Reggie: It had a map of the island on it. About the size of a postage stamp.

Reggie, who arrived with a dozen spare parts in a final effort to repair the loran, the radar, and the closed-circuit television, confessed that science is both imperfect and presumptuous. At just that moment, Bill called me down to the galley. She has become, among other things, the de facto telephone operator, both because of her persistence and because the operators at the other end will do anything for her; most of them by now know her. Pat is on the line—we have reached her at her hotel in Marrakesh. So, forty miles east of Ponta Delgada, the wind keeping us at a 20° heel, I go below in a full moon and chat with my wife by transmitting my voice through an eighteen-foot antenna 2,500 miles west, which in turn is radioed 3,500 miles east, which in turn is radioed 1,000 miles west—to Cyrano. Pat is not enjoying Marrakesh, and will go early to Marbella. I tell her we overstayed at the Azores by one day, but might pick up much of the time, and, who knows, might even arrive on the 30th, as scheduled. I *miss* her. But I am always apprehensive after talking with her, because although I prove by the sound of my voice that I am alive, I remind her by the sound of my voice that I am in the middle of the ocean in

Using the radio telephone beside the navigation table in the crew's quarters.

the same bucket of wood with her only son and only sister. Besides, telephone calls from aboard boats are necessarily stilted: the shore-party's voice booms out over the speaker, heard by everyone in the galley ("How's the cooking?" Pat bellowed halfway to Bermuda, practically knocking the cook overboard with the vibrations and certainly puncturing his popovers). I return to the wheel and tell Reggie we'll have a moment of silence for MIT, which made Cyrano–to–New York–to–Marrakesh–to–Cyrano possible, before resuming hostilities against science.

I worry about Reggie's future, but he tells me, looking out at the sea and the steady furrow we make through it, the sails enjoying the broad reach—a woman in a perfectly-fitted suit, strutting down Park Avenue—that right now his principal regret is the nineteen hundred miles he missed aboard Cyrano. We turn the wheel over to Danny and Christopher, who are tired, but thoroughly content.

Wednesday. The sea is relentlessly cooperative to our course—it is coming now from the southwest, briskly. But also relentlessly, and there are signs of human fatigue. I recall Bill Snaith's warning against setting out at night—always, always start out early in the morning. Christopher is not only tired, he has faint intimations of seasickness and a headache—all of this I discover (a) directly by the simple act of looking at him and observing his mood—if he has a headache or is feeling out of sorts, he is as easy to diagnose as if he had chicken pox; and (b) indirectly he will whisper to Aunty Bill: Does she have a seasick pill? and Bill will tell me, and subtle accommodations are effected at a number of levels (he fears the fish provided by Phil Jr. at lunch will be too emetic, so he orders a . . . grilled cheese sandwich). I have an early evening watch and a late late evening watch, the first with Christopher, the second with Van.

Christopher was coming out of it, feeling better, and he talked about Reggie's future, concerning which neither of us had any useful ideas. This led him to a discussion of Danny. I have been urging Danny for several years to go into insurance-selling after graduating from college, my theory being that no one would refuse to buy anything from Danny because people would instantly realize that the young, open-faced, quick-smiling young man at the door would not

234

Danny makes himself at home.

consider selling anybody anything he didn't truly believe they should
want. Danny has always listened to me with that genuine interest and
animation he feels for those who give him disinterested advice based
on a close knowledge of his strengths. The trouble is, he has told
Christopher, he doesn't really *want* to sell insurance. Then he laughed,
it appears, and Christopher did, recalling the words exactly. "Then
he said: 'Come to think of it, Christo, I don't really *want* to do *anything*!'" The laughter is wholesome because there is nothing lazy
about Dan, provided you do not ask him to learn an irregular French
verb, or for that matter a regular one. Danny, who spent a year in
Geneva and another year in Paris and couldn't order a taxi in French,
could, however, disappear in Paris and return with an armored di-
vision if that is what you asked him to do. Christopher says it is so—
What shall I do after graduating?—with the majority of the members
of his college class, and we agree that the problem is more nearly
related to acedia than to laziness or even indecisiveness. I told him

235

what George Sokolsky, the columnist, told me twenty-five years ago he had told *his* son at age twenty. "Make it a point, by the time you reach twenty-eight, to decide what you will be by the time you are thirty-five." That gives Christopher and Danny plenty of time.

Christopher asked if I would like to hear a passage from his journal. This was my first introduction to it, and I told him Yes I would very much like to, and while I took the wheel, he read with a flashlight from his account of the camping trip at São Jorge and other memories of the Azores. I found his passages striking, and told him so; and added, sarcastically, that after listening to him and Danny on the subject, I had come, however reluctantly, to the conclusion that the B.O. was actually a means of transporting him and Danny to Ponta Delgada so that they could camp out for a night next to a crater. Christopher chortled, and with that instinctive gentility ("Thanks a lot," I said once to J. K. Galbraith, "for being so nice to Christopher when he visited you at Cambridge." "Being nice to Christopher," said Galbraith, "is about the easiest assignment I have ever been handed." I should have added, having heard Christopher's glowing account, "And obviously the least botched"), a gentility that accounts for so much of him that his friends cherish—said he had neglected to put in his journal that although he and Danny had *begun* by putting a Beatles cassette into their portable player, they had found it preferable after a little while to pull it out and to put on a Vivaldi concerto. That would make me feel better. There was only the slightest pause as he pondered, palpably, whether he was being disloyal. He closed that door formalistically: "Not that *that's* any criticism of the Beatles."

It was just after Van and I came on duty at 0100 that I decided that the wind, which had slackened to virtual powerlessness, meanwhile veering directly in our path to the east, no longer justified keeping the mainsail up; so I told Van to bring it down, while I let out the mainsheet to give the boom a little slack. The procedure is to take a few slow counterclockwise turns on the main winch, having first let go the brake; then you apply the brake again, withdraw the winch handle, release the brake, and the sail comes hurtling down. Van miscalculated, neglecting to secure the brake and exerting clockwise pressure on the handle—with the result that it spun about like a propeller at vicious speed and clobbered him by the right eye, causing great consternation, a lot of blood, a totally dazed Van, and a totally galvanized Bill Finucane. Bill was born for such a crisis. She established that the wound was between the bone and the eye, washed and disinfected it, applied a butterfly bandage, and forced him to take a codeine (he'd have swallowed a goldfish, in his delirium, if told to); next she applied an ice pack, which she held in place with an eye mask (Christopher's suggestion); then, while Van went instantly to sleep, Bill sat at the end of the cockpit section, inches away from Van's head, the whole night long, in case he should wake and need extra care. Van will have a splendid shiner tomorrow.

Danny, characteristically, offered to stay up with me a while, given Van's incapacitation, and help with the stars. We sat up on the cabin top. I had pre-isolated the stars (it is one of those rare nights with half the horizon outlined neatly by the moon, allowing the luxury of all-night star-taking). I am exasperated by the inexactitude of my star sights and determined to do something about this in the next few days. By God.

Thursday. Van, though battered, is in good shape. We tape a warning on the mast above the winch, and I suddenly recalled that we did the identical thing six years ago, when Peter suffered an identical accident.

Bill F. stitches Van's face back together. Illumination by Stoops.

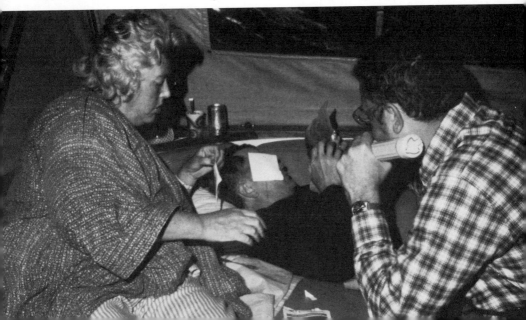

Van back in action.

We swam this morning and felt better for it. We made an incredible 194 miles during twenty-four hours, a tribute to the wind, and a little, I suspect, to a lurking current in the area. Van joked at lunch about his experience, and Bill announced that her principal concern, on returning to Pasadena, will be to remaster the language of civil society after so prolonged an exposure to Van—who thereupon suggests appropriate formulations for the teacup set. "It was a perfect trip, though, of course, every now and then—that sort of thing is inevitable—somebody fucked up." Bill cannot be made to utter a coarse word; it simply will not move past her lips, and there is an amusing extemporary classroom session where the boys and Van solemnly affect to teach her how to move about unnoticed in the modern world—you are noticed only if your vocabulary is continent, is the implicit point.

Van doesn't realize that he is still a little woozy, and the wine at dinner went quickly to his head. Serving as banker during the poker hour, he made a solemn botch of the books, wisecracking his way through his ineptitude in high good humor. At the wheel, as our watch began, he spoke, ever so tentatively, about the crawling intimations he found himself experiencing, for the first time, about transcendent matters, but the difficulties he still had in giving them Christian form. Three years ago Van and Bootsie were to leave with Pat and me in the late afternoon to sail Cyrano in Maine waters, picking her up at Marblehead. At noon Van called and said that Julie (his oldest girl, aged nine) was sick, and perhaps their leaving would be delayed an hour or two until the doctor's diagnosis was confirmed—would the five o'clock shuttle to Boston be all right? The whole family—including Evan (Jr.), six, and Christina, four—had spent the week at Watch Hill, where Julie had fallen in love with, and in awe of, a little boy of her age of high histrionic bent, who every morning during the week on the beach feigned a dreadful incapacitation. On Tuesday he refused to reply to a single word directed to him, having become "mute" overnight. Julie, following him around, would ape the identical malady. Wednesday he bumped into everybody, complaining of the blindness that had robbed him, so young, of his vision; Julie, of course, was dutifully blind, as they jostled their way through the day. On the final day, the little boy woke with a paralyzed leg which he dragged about the beach saying that polio was the very worst of all human afflictions, Julie agreeing wholeheartedly. Somewhat to the relief of, I gather, the entire Watch Hill community, the little boy left the next morning before contracting syphilis; but Julie continued to drag her right leg. Her mother expressed impatience, informing her daughter that after the third act, the play ends; but even so Julie dragged her leg, which was when alarm broke in. They drove right to New York and at noon got a clinical report that it was a harmless bug of some sort, but that it would not be until three that the diagnosis was confirmed. At three the doctor announced that in fact Julie had a malignant and inoperable tumor; and, five terrible months later, she was dead, her parents very nearly destroyed. Little Evan, at the reception after the funeral, was explaining, in his little high-pitched English voice that resonated through the room of mourners, to a grieving great-aunt what had happened. "Julie got *so* sick, Onttie," he said, "she finally went *ker-plonk*!" Van told me the story through moist eyes. And wondered whether Evan and Christina, now nine and seven, resented his going off on so prolonged a pleasure trip. They were stoical about his long business absences—better than that (Van suddenly brightened): "The last time, Christina said tearfully at the staircase I mustn't go. Evan said, 'That's not right, Christina. Let him go. Otherwise we'll be poor!' " He resumed his talk about the divine problematic. I was mostly silent, as I think most people tend to be, lest the wrong note be struck, diverting a journey that might make its way to faith.

I have finished *Moby Dick* in the silence of my cabin, and I prop it up on the nose port, partly in reverence, partly to keep out the light of the sun, which will break out shortly. My mind dwells on some technical matters involving the star sights—tomorrow I'll use my fifteen-year-old sextant, instead of my ten-year-old Plath, and bloody well do without the powerful telescope. I turn off the light and remember during dinner a question Bill put to me: If I had all the money in the world and could build a boat exactly suited to me, how would it be different from Cyrano? I found myself saying—gushily, it must have sounded—In no way different. But it's true.

15.

The last three days were routine, but only in the sense in which that word can be used aboard a sailboat in blue water. Looked at another way, no one was swallowed by a whale; ergo, it was routine. Christopher, having exhausted himself in writing about the Azores, neglected his journal, and wrestled instead with a minor infection of sorts. His journal sprang back to life only on the penultimate day. "It's 1000 hours and I'm sitting at the helm. Aunt Bill is here, and so is Reg. They're talking about Reg's love life. I think they're in love."

Danny's thoughts and reactions burble uninterruptedly on. For him, *everything* is an experience. "The morning is beautiful, the first since leaving the isle of San Miguel three days ago. Just after finishing eight lbs. of pancakes I turned instinctively to gaze around for

"Aunt Bill is here, and so is Reg. I think they're in love."

Augustino, Christopher, Phil Jr.

ships and hell, if one wasn't coming up on our ass 50 yards to starboard. They were so close we could yell over. Van: 'Why the hell don't you get a little closer!' The *American Export* was about 400–450 feet long, throwing a wake four feet. It bounced us like a toy in a tub."

Great excitement over catching first one fish and, after lunch, a second. Danny is unforgiving about the fate of the first. "Reg and Chris caught a fish. Today's lunch is obvious, we all hope the cook won't

Danny and Phil Jr. in the galley.

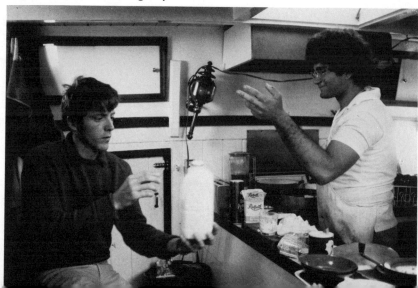

fuck up. Ah! But he did. It was overcooked and dry as a bone." But he paid tribute to Phil Jr.'s handling of the second fish, now that he had learned. And Van notes in his journal that Phil Jr. as a cook was "terrific. Salads were wonderful. Could have used more fresh fruit."

I was appalled, on reading Edward Heath's book about his spectacularly successful racing career, that he had remarked, early in that career, on the eating habits of a guest crew member. It was the fabled Rod Stephens, of Sparkman and Stephens, the great yacht designers (*Suzy* is one of their children). At lunch, while the other crew members ate sandwiches, Stephens ate only an apple. Why? Because, Stephens later explained, when there is an adjustment needed in the sails, a sandwich-in-hand results in a moment's hesitation. You feel compelled to tuck the half-eaten sandwich away somewhere, tidily. An apple, by contrast, can be thrown overboard, or tossed into the cockpit unceremoniously and retrieved later. Mr. Heath takes pride in announcing that thereafter, at lunchtime racing, he served his crew only apples and Mars bars . . . I take consolation in noting that I am not a member of Mr. Heath's crew. On the other hand, there is no

Left to right: autopilot, Christopher, Phil Jr.

doubting that he is the one who has the silver. Who knows, perhaps he emerges, in part as a result of the policies of his government, as the most avid collector of sterling in the world?

After eating the good fish, Dan goes below to the saloon, before turning in. "I'm relaxed, enjoying a peaceful moment alone in the saloon writing postcards to Carol, whom I miss terribly, Mom & Dad, Ricky, Tricia, Cheryl, and Sean. WFB decided to play the piano. Van follows to sing and soon I find myself over there too, enjoying the old ragtime atmosphere. I can't enjoy myself any more than this; it just isn't possible.

"My brandy is warming my innards as well as soaking the Oreos I'm consuming at a horrendous rate."

He and Christopher took a long watch that night, because they wanted time to discuss their camping trip in Morocco, to begin after leaving the boat at Marbella. At the beginning of their watch there

Augustino administers a salt-water shower.

was considerable excitement. "Have sighted what in all seriousness seems to be a periscope light: single light moving on reciprocal course at 30 knots and no running lights. 30 other lights visible at this moment. INCREDIBLE!"

But after the submarine-sighting, it was routine.

༄

[D] I was 400 points down in gin rummy by 5 A.M., getting a little cramped from my cross-legged position which had not been changed in 3 hours except to pee to leeward. Ah! the rough seaman's life. At 6:00 we got rumbunktious [sic], so we cleaned the chart table, washed down the decks, took a saltwater bath, scrubbed our bodies with liquid, rinsed off in the shower, changed clothes; in general made up for otherwise wasted time.

WFB just popped his head up, "Why aren't you asleep?" . . . "I'm not tired yet." . . . "Well, you should be." He asked the usual, which was how did our watch go, and did we get a sight? He always looks groggy until he gets his peanut butter on toast and coffee or has a swim, but he always is the first to say good morning. I'll wager he would even say the same if his toe was stubbed one-eighth of a second earlier. . . Time to sleep, my hearties. I'll be back for lunch, same place, same time, watch and see.

Van writes in his journal that on board a boat one must be excessively courteous and helpful, and that this extends to not quibbling "without strong reasons" with someone else's desire to do something "even though it seems unimportant."

The logbook is useful as something of a lightning rod for fraternal irritations. I note an entry, rather more clearly marked ("1100 hrs.") than usual, indeed written (by me) rather more legibly than is my habit: "Turned off running lights, anchor light, masthead light, and shroud light, in celebration of midday sun." That is the kind of thing that passes for a reproach of the watch that was on duty at dawn and forgot to turn off the navigation lights, now that they have eliminated keel-hauling. For the fun of it, a couple of days ago when the radio was working especially well, I put in a call to my dear friend and semiretired lawyer, C. Dickerman Williams, in New York, and asked him solemnly what was my legal authority over my recalcitrant son. He told me I could put him in irons.

The right of reprimand through the logbook is most democratically distributed. Dan writes, "2200. Why the hell ain't you all making entries in the log? Is this the Polish navy? You too, El Capitan."

The log provides nice and entirely unintended contrasts, it being a constantly recurring phenomenon that one watch captain will enter data without reading back to the previous entry, particularly if the transition is uneventful. I notice, on Sunday morning, Dan, in a belletristic and pious phase:

"0715. Breakfast done; CTB, Augustino, and I enjoying the morning. The sea is calm, sparkling like a billion diamonds in a cone shape with the point toward us. The sky is light blue sparkled with a few clouds on the horizon ahead quickly rising with the sun. We haven't a breath of wind this morning, maybe later.

"I'll take a sun sight at quarter of eight, then get Reg and Van up and crack myself. We had a great watch; I think we all got a good deal out of it. Thanks.

"Let's remember it's Sunday, no bad mouthing."

"0800. Reg feels and sort of looks like shit," is the first entry of the next watch captain.

Our counterrevolutionary psywar against the Communist International was showing, like the USIA's, signs of fatigue. It almost decreased the consumption of wine, it being the explicit responsibility of the person who emptied a bottle to compose the throwaway missive. Van at one point tried to represent his pouring the last drops of a bottle into someone else's glass as nothing more than an extension of his ambition to cultivate chivalry on board; but that got him instant impeachment, and a vote of censure, 6–0. We could forgive him, the day after he was wounded, for sending out to sea in a bottle,

> Some stinking Goddam Red
> Caused a winch handle to hit my head.
> For sweet revenge
> I shall constantly singe
> The beards of all Red heads.

After all, he presumably had a fever. But when he attempted to ideologize a classical limerick by the simple expedient of identifying the principal (Magruder) by means of a footnote (*) as being a Communist, he got a second, if milder, vote of censure:

> There was a young man named Magruder (*)
> Who wooed a stewed nude in Bermuder.
> The nude thought it crude,
> To be wooed in the nude,
> But Magruder was cruder, he screwed 'er.

(*A member of the Bermuder Young Communist League.)

Christopher tried a direct approach to Fidel's material instincts:

> "Fidel: Oiga, viejo
> Te lo tengo
> En Suiza
> Numero F-322"

. . . but he caught the spirit of the thing a few bottles later with,

"Man is born free, but everywhere he is running out of Branc-Cantenac."

My stars were finally behaving, and the last two or three days we had fixes at dawn, instead of just running fixes at noon. I suppose it

247

"Thirty days without tension."

does not matter how long a trip is, the last two or three days will be disproportionately tense—and exhilarating. Danny, through whose membranes no velleity passes unheralded, gave his impatience away with a notation in the log:

"0900. Took sight. Lat 37–10, Long 13–12, which puts us 383 miles from Gibraltar.

> "At 7 knots, 55 hrs.
> "At 7½ knots, 51 hrs.
> "At 8 knots, 48 hrs."

Van's appetites were more explicit. "1535. At sea 28 days and 'looking forward to some leave.' I.e., horny." And on the 29th, Dan again: "Had cake and tea for early breakfast. We're screaming at 8 knots with 1500 rpm. Bilge pumped and all's well. Shit! We're almost there."

After the noon sight on the 29th, I could transfer from the plotting sheet—so anonymous, and infinite in character—to a shore chart that traced the waters off southwestern Portugal. I decided, on impulse, to change course by 25°, so as, at an expense of a mere ten to fifteen

248

miles extra voyaging, to permit us to lay eyes on the tip of Portugal that day, rather than head directly for Gibraltar. The crew approved, and at 1702 on the 29th, we heard Christopher's excited voice from the crow's nest. "LAND HO!"—Cabo San Vicente. Odd, that any other formulation than the traditional one would have seemed, somehow, affected, irreverent.

That night, sailing at hull speed in the Bay of Cadiz, anticipating Gibraltar late the following afternoon and Marbella before midnight,

both Bill and Reggie approached me separately, in whispers, to advise me that the boys had, sua sponte, organized a Captain's Dinner. Bill, musing, added that she could not remember, ever, in all her life, "thirty days without tension." It was our last night seated about the table, with music; the dumpy little low-gravity candles splattered about the chart table, shining through the red, blue, green, and yellow glass; the gas lamp in mid-table; and the gourmet meal, beginning with a can of caviar and champagne bought in Miami by Danny and Christopher (they had, as recorded, proposed smashing the champagne bottle into Cyrano as we left the dock in Miami, but I vetoed that out of instincts frugal and apprehensive, after the dynamite was used to pry loose our propeller). The meal was extensive and imaginative. "I decided to brighten up the dessert," Dan writes in his journal, "with two huge sparklers I bought in Miami for just this occasion."

The sparklers were explosively effective and startling, escorting Phil Jr.'s large cake with "B.O." engraved on it with raisins, and probably there had not been such elation in these waters since the Battle of Trafalgar. But Danny had also committed a poem, a very long poem of nearly a hundred lines, which he now read out to us. It was generous toward all hands, beginning with the strophe,

> I must go down to the sea again
> To the lonely sea and sky
> And all I ask is a tall ship
> And WFB to steer her by.

And ending,

> We bid farewell to Cyrano
> No lovelier ship to know
> We bid farewell to the Captain
> No lovelier man to know.

In his journal Dan remarked, "I wrote this little piece just before signing off to dreamland and in time to enjoy a relaxation long in need. I awoke for dinner and the final moment came. I was feeling good; knowing I meant well, and did well." The poem capped the

250

pleasure of the B.O., and I told him so, clumsily I fear, up to and including this acknowledgment.

∽

[C] *Cyrano is in the Bay of Cadiz about 60 miles SW of Tarifa. Our Marbella ETA is 2200.*

I wonder how strange these entries will seem 10 years from now. What difference will it make how far I was from Tarifa at ten o'clock on this date? And yet, I wonder what difference it makes now where I'll find myself 10 years hence. If, as it was with Ishmael, I find myself in melancholy tempers, brooding meanly and bringing up the rear of funeral processions I chance across, then maybe I'll forsake land and come back to the sea. In that case, then remembering where I was today will be unimportant, only a matter of coordinates.

On the 0100–0400 watch last night, Van and I ruminated on the speed of the voyage. How is it that such a wide stretch of water took such a short time to slip by our hull?

[C] *WFB just came aft and said he wasn't going to take a sun sight. "I got two continents just moving like this," he said, bringing his two hands to a point.*

Not even going to take a sun sight? *Now I know the B.O. is over.*

Last minute observations: at 1330, the northernmost tip of Africa rose through the mist. During the afternoon, a hot, hazy succession of sweltering hours, we saw: Cape Trafalgar, the Strait, a procession of ships and planes, and, at long last, Gibraltar.

Rock of Ages . . .

As we ate dinner, the waters of the Mediterranean seemed oily. To the south, Morocco: high cliffs rising out of the Strait, forming the other Pillar of Hercules. To the west, Spain: desolate mountains and their foothills, a golden sun sinking fast . . . the first time I've seen the sun set over land in 30 days.

30 days! For 30 days of happy sailing, thank you, Pup, from the bottom of my heart.

And even though I've about had it with your logarithmic watch system—(I figure I've been on duty 4/5ths of the time the last three days)—even though the thought of a warm bath and a dry bed at this point is sexually stimulating, even though I couldn't take another Gollywobbler setting or a fisherman dropping, even though the smell of the engine room makes me shudder, even though I'm restless for the touch of land, if you were to set sail tomorrow to cross another ocean, I'd sell my soul to ship out with you. Any day.